MORE THAN OIL

Trappers, Traders & Settlers of Northern Alberta

Frances K. Jean

Published by
City Centre Group Inc
Fort McMurray, Alberta

This book is dedicated to the memory of my husband Bernard Charles Philip Jean, who always told me I could do anything if I really wanted to.

Copyright © 2012
Frances K. Jean
Published by City Centre Group Inc
Fort McMurray, Alberta
Printed in Alberta, Canada

ISBN 978-0-9689339-2-3

Dear Reader:

This book is a collection of short stories about ordinary people, and some extraordinary people who contributed in their own way to make our city what it is today.

I know there will be mistakes in this book, and I know I likely missed stories about interesting people that should have been included. However, I am convinced that it is better to write about the people of our past, even if the telling is not perfect, than to have their stories forgotten forever. I would encourage anyone who criticizes my book to write a better one. You could do it and you should do it.

That said, I want to say thank you to:

- Anne Young and Jean Woodhouse, who for many months have faithfully proofread and encouraged
- Fern Brooks for without her encouragement I never would have started
- Elva Bussieres, for fact checking and corrections
- Kimberly Michelutti, for a final corrective read
- Roger Witmer, our family friend who did the wonderful illustrations
- Grandson Andrew, who suggested the outline
- My children, Mark, Phil, Evelyn and Brian for their encouragement and help with the facts of several of the stories. Phil for plotting the map, and to Brian for taking the time out of his busy Ottawa schedule to put the book in a publishable state once I'd completed the stories
- And, especially, to all the kind people I interviewed, who are so much a part of my McMurray and theirs

I so much enjoyed the research and writing of this book. My first thought, many years ago, was to do a book about the people that Fort McMurray streets are named for. But I couldn't limit it to that; there are too many interesting people that haven't yet been recognized by the city. We have an amazing history in Fort McMurray, I am so proud of our city and its people. I hope in a small way, this book will make you proud too.

Frances Kathaleen Jean

Contents

First Peoples 1
    The Dene (Chipewyan) 4
    The Cree 7
    The Métis 11
Trappers and Traders 15
    Peter Pond, The Renegade Trader 1739 - 1807 17
    Sir Alexander Mackenzie, The River Explorer 1764 – 1820 20
    David Thompson, The Map Maker 1770-1857 23
    The Fraser Factor 26
    Sir John Franklin, The Lost Explorer 1786-1847 29
    William McMurray, The HBC Factor 1820-1877 33
    Henry John Moberly, The Founder 1835 – 1931 35
Settlers & Entrepreneurs 41
    The Gordons, The First Settlers 42
    The Golosky Dynasty 46
    The Biggs Family 51
    The Men Called Sutherland 54
    Which MacDonald Was That? 58
    The Hill Family 62
    The Morimoto Family 66
    The Legendary Loutit Family 70
    The Demers Family, Four Generations 73
    Hugh Stroud, A Working Man 77
    The McCormick Family 79
    Eymundson, The Telephone Man 81
    Jack Fairbairn: Businessman, Councillor & Traveller 84
    Gus Hawker, A Different Sort 88
    Bill Tatum, A Self Made Man 90
    Hawkins, Serving for Three Generations 94
    The Tolens, From Dusty Saskatchewan 98
    The Cross Family, Life Across The River 102
    Elsie Hyska, A Real Lady 106
Transporters 110
    The Amazing Ryan Brothers 113
    The Auger Brothers, A River Tradition 122
    Captain Billy Bird, A Legend In His Time 125
    Julian Mills, Life On The Waters 127
    The Wylies, Riverboat Family 129
    Len Williams, Everyone's Friend 132
    Furbers, The Train Family 138
    We Take To The Air 142
    Punch Dickins 144
    Wop May 146
    Walter & Jeanne Gilbert 149
    Rex Terpening 152

- The Snye, A Northern Base 155
- Bergeron, Bush Pilot Extraordinaire 162
- Ray Ruelling, Last Of The Bush Pilots 168

Newcomers 173
- The Brooks Boys 174
- The Incredible Mrs. Mitchell 181
- Bussieres, Faithful Town Servants 186
- Dim Silin, Our Russian Aristocrat 190
- Caouette, Construction Of The 1960s 193
- The Mysteries Of Eddie Engstrom 197
- D.D. Williams, The Big Eddy 201
- George Deep, The Man From Syria 204
- Haxtons, A McMurray Tradition 206
- Claire Peden, A Man Of Opinion 209
- Bob Duncan, Preserver Of History 213
- Art Hoehne, Came To Build An Airstrip, Stayed To Build A Church 216
- The Chinese Influence 220
- The French Connection 226
- Father Brown, The Priest Remembered 236
- The Robert & Marnie Grant Family 240

Developers 245
- Ewashkos, The Sawmill Family 247
- Bob Lamb, The TV Man 251
- Lawyer-Developers, They Filled A Need 254
- Dr. Karl A. Clark, Oilsands' Pioneer 257
- J. Howard Pew, A Man Of Faith 259
- Frank Spragins, He Had A Dream 262
- Charest & Morton, The Radio Guys: 264

The Others 269
- Doug Schmit, Keyano's Founding President 271
- Jack Shields, MP and Santa Claus 274
- Harry Aime, RCMP To Judge 278
- Darlene Comfort, Recorder Of History 280
- Romance Of The Rumpels 283
- Chuck Knight, Champion Of Recreation 287
- The Hardins, Business, Politics, and Service 290
- Success Of The Sorges 294
- John Wilson, Construction Magnate 296
- A Tale Of Two Avery Families 298
- The Walsh Family, First of the Newfoundlanders 301
- Bert MacKay, Ambassador And Promoter 305
- Norm Weiss, MLA 1979 – 1993 308
- Al Burry, Manager And Developer 311
- The Wolff Family 313
- Men Of Baseball 316
- The Jeans Take Root In McMurray 320
- Postscript 325

First Peoples

Geologists and anthropologists believe the first people to inhabit what we call North America and specifically Canada, came many thousands of years ago, after the last Ice Age. One group believe a series of migrations from Asia to North America crossed what is now the Bering Strait, which became a land bridge as the Ice Age lowered the waters of the oceans. A second theory is that the migration was by boat along the sea coast. All agree the purpose was to follow the large animals that had crossed into the new land.

While this is what the scientists tell us, the native peoples related a story to Alexander Mackenzie that told of a great journey their ancestors had made across a great lake that was shallow and full of islands. Many legends and stories were told of such a migration by the elders; stories which had been passed down through the generations.

We do know that when the white men first came to northern Alberta the land was populated by two distinct peoples: the Chipewyans and the Crees. The name Chipewyan was given to them by the Cree, meaning "pointed skins", as the outer garment of the tribe hung down in the back and front in points. The Chipewyan people referred to themselves as "Dene" which means, "the people, or original people." The Cree on the other hand received their name originally from the French at James Bay. They were called "Kerestinon", soon shortened to Cree. Northern Alberta Cree are of the Plains Cree group.

The Cree language relates to the Algonquian family of languages, while the Chipewyan language is part of the Athapaskan group. Both tribes were nomadic. The Chipewyan followed the caribou migration; the Crees were the first to associate with and aid the white fur traders and explorers.

There was enmity between the two nations and because the Cree first obtained rifles from the fur traders they expanded their area by pushing the Chipewyan out. Intense warfare resulted. A Chipewyan chief named Matonabbee, who also spoke Cree, negotiated a peace treaty between the two tribes in 1765 at Peace Point, in the now Northwest Territories. He later became a guide to Samuel Hearne who was the first explorer to reach the Arctic Ocean by land in 1771.

The story is also told of a young Chipewyan woman, Thah Naltth'er, who was captured by the Crees and taken to Fort York as a slave. She escaped and with the help of the Chief Factor at York Factory, a company trader, and Chief Swan of the Cree, traveled to northwest of Lake Athabasca. She persuaded her people to make peace with the Cree. The two groups smoked the peace pipe, exchanged gifts and hostages and later both traded furs with the Hudson Bay.

Samuel Hearne told of a remarkable young woman found north of Lake Athabasca who had escaped from her captors and survived alone for upwards of seven months in a hut she had built. Her only tools were six inches of an iron hoop, made into a knife and the shank of an iron arrowhead. She had made herself snowshoes, snared rabbits and used their sinews to sew together furs to make her garments. She kept her fire burning all winter as she had lit it with two sulphurous stones. She belonged to the Western Dog-ribbed Indians and had been taken prisoner when her family was killed by the Athabascan tribe. Hearne said she was in good health, and one of the finest women he'd seen in North America.

The white men brought new tools, rifles and different foods to the native people. They also brought diseases that badly depleted the population. Indian tribes had no resistance to the common cold and it could be as dangerous as measles and smallpox proved to be. Tuberculosis became a scourge, and many old and young died from this disease. The traders also brought "firewater".

With no immunity to alcohol this became, and still is in many cases, a dreadful plague.

Many of the traders and explorers took native wives, as indicated by many of the surnames still in use today. This created a new people, the Métis. Written with lower case "m" the word metis was an old French word, meaning mixed blood. Many of the first Métis people were from French voyageur fathers, and the Anglo Métis from Scottish fathers.

Today, we find the Métis, Chipewyans and Crees living side by side in various communities in and around Fort McMurray. They are justly proud of their traditions and heritage, and add enrichment to our municipality.

The Dene (Chipewyan)

"The People" is what Dene means and this is how the Chipewyan people today refer to themselves. The early Dene were nomadic people, following the barren land caribou migration. The Chipewyan had the largest population and territorial area of any northern group in the early 1700s. They mainly populated the Athabasca delta, rich in meat, fur and fish.

The early explorer, Alexander Mackenzie said of the Chipewyans: "they are sober, timorous and vagrant, with a selfish disposition which has created suspicions of their integrity." He said they were tall and fierce warriors, but easy to approach and willing to share their knowledge of the land. Samuel Hearne spoke of them as a "most happy and independent people." Mackenzie said the people were very conscious of their clothing and used great skill and patience in producing both winter and summer apparel. Women with children had a very full top garment and the baby was carried on their back. He wrote "though the women are as much in the power of the men, as any other property, they are always consulted, and possess a very considerable influence in the traffic with Europeans, and other important concerns." Mackenzie stated the Chipewyans were the most peaceable tribe of Indians known in North America.

In Alexander Mackenzie's Journals he says the Chipewyans had a tradition "that they originally came from another country, inhabited by very wicked people, and had traversed a great lake, which was narrow, shallow, and full of islands, where they suffered great misery, it being always winter, with ice and deep snow." They first reached the Coppermine River he said, and indeed early explorers noted the tools made of copper, and this enticed Samuel Hearne to make the first successful journey into the barren lands of northern Canada.

Once the Chipewyans started trading their furs for tools, rifles and food their way of life changed as well. They began using dog teams for winter traveling, supplementing their snowshoes and having their women pull the toboggans, which often weighed two to four hundred pounds. As the fur trade increased the traders started building forts to make their lives more convenient and profitable. The natives visited and often settled nearby and began more and more adapting to the European way of life.

Probably the best-known fort and the oldest continuous settlement in Alberta, took the name of the Chipewyans, and today Fort Chipewyan is home to the Athabasca Chipewyan Band as well as Mikisew Cree Band. Beautifully situated on a rocky cliff overlooking Lake Athabasca, the Slave River flows north from the lake and the Athabasca River flows from the south into the lake. This area was said to be the richest fur trading area in North America and it was here that many expeditions to the Arctic stopped to replenish their supplies.

The Chipewyan Prairie Dene people, living in Janvier, came from Saskatchewan near Garson Lake and many were descendents of Paul Janvier. The tie between the Chipewyan Prairie community and that of the nearby Saskatchewan band is still very strong. George Nokahoo, of Janvier, recalls hearing how his grandfather came to the area from Loon Lake in Saskatchewan. He was only 14 or 15 but had been involved in the Louis Riel uprising and fled because he feared he would be arrested. Jean Marie Janvier, one of the area's foremost trappers, taught his skills to many of his grandchildren and friends. Although he spoke no English, his knowledge of the bush and his stamina at nearly 100 years was unsurpassed.

Today, many of the Dene people are employed in the oil industry but their roots and respect are for the land and they feel an urgency to keep their traditions and language alive.

One of the most interesting historical figures of the Chipewyans is Matanabbee. Samuel Hearne had been tasked with finding the Coppermine River, thought to be a source of riches by the Hudson Bay Company. His first two attempts were unsuccessful and the third proved to be a success because of his relationship with this great Chipewyan. Matanabbee had grown up near the Prince of Wales Fort on Hudson Bay and could speak English as well as Chipewyan and Cree.

On the third expedition Hearne took Matanabbee's advice taking along the native wives of the party. He told Hearne: "When all the men are heavily laden, they can neither hunt nor travel to any considerable distance; and in case they meet with success in hunting, who is to carry the product of their labour? One of the women can carry, or haul, as much as two men can do. They also pitch our tents, make and mend our clothing, and keep us warm at night."

Hearne in his two and half year trip not only found surface copper on the river but went as far as the Arctic Ocean. On the entire trip Matanabbee was his guide and mentor; they lived off the land, made new canoes when needed, and traveled over three thousand miles in all weather.

In Samuel Hearne's book "A Journey to the Northern Ocean" he describes Matanabbee to be scrupulous in truth and honesty, to be courteous and kind and never spoke ill of anyone. Matanabbee was almost six feet tall, well built and of a fine countenance. Hearne wrote: "the nobleness and elegance of his manners might have been admired by the first personages in the world; for to the vivacity of a Frenchman, and the sincerity of an Englishman, he added the gravity and nobleness of a Turk; all so happily blended as to render his company and conversation universally pleasing."

Matanabbee was a successful negotiator between the Crees, the Chipewyans and the English. In 1783 he returned to the Prince of Wales Fort to find the French had captured the settlement, Hearne was gone, and Matanabbee's wife and children were dead. He hung himself. He was said to be the greatest native leader of the century.

The Cree

Long before the white men brought written records, trade, disease and what we today call civilization, the Cree band populated our area. Called by the first Europeans Knisteneaux, they dwelt in lodges of pine boughs and caribou hide, and in summers in pole teepees erected in ideal spots for fishing, hunting and berry picking. Summer was a time for socializing and large groups would gather to pick berries, fish and visit.

The men hunted, fished, made canoes and sledges as well as their tools and weapons. The women's role was to forage for berries and herbs, to snare rabbits, tan hides, cut wood, as well as make snowshoes, fishnets and clothing. The Cree were one of the first nations to trade with the European fur traders and soon adopted some of the European ways. They provided the trading posts with meat and pemmican and traded their furs for coveted tools and rifles. Today we are told there are just over 1000 Cree in our area. Marriages between the Cree and the fur traders and explorers created a new nation, the Métis. They in turn became clerks and traders for the North West Company and the Hudson's Bay Company, as well as guiding the white explorers through the trails and along the river portages.

Alexander Mackenzie in his Journals said the Cree women were the most comely, but he went on to say the life of the women was "uninterrupted succession of toil and pain." Mackenzie said the tribe was generous and hospitable and good-natured except when perverted by the inflammable influence of liquor.

David Thompson told of sharing a tent for a winter with a Cree elder, Saukamappee. This elder described to Thompson events that affected the tribe's lives: the arrival of horses and muskets on the prairies about 1730 and the dreadful smallpox epidemic of the 1780s.

Perhaps the best-known Cree family in Fort McMurray is that of Raphael Cree, son of Chief Paul Cree. He was born in 1893 and died in 2002, just days before his 109th birthday. He spoke Chipewyan and Cree but no English; his wife Louise communicated well in English, as well as speaking Chipewyan, Cree and French. Mrs. Cree, daughter of Paul Fontaine, was born in La Loche in Saskatchewan. Raphael had two brothers: Alex, a local trapper and John who lived in Fort Chipewyan.

In summers the Cree family lived in a tent, complete with their cook stove, on the bank of the Clearwater River. A cousin Julian Cree, born in 1892, and his wife lived in a log cabin on the Clearwater midway between Waterways and the Snye. Mrs. Julian Cree, told a Courier reporter in 1970, that when she first came to McMurray from Fort Chip in 1905 she saw "four log cabins and lots of room under spruce trees to sleep."

In winters Raphael and Louise and children, Louise, Elmer and Jean (Powder) lived on their trapline some 30 miles up the Clearwater River. They had lived for some years during the winters in a former Duck's Unlimited cabin on Gordon Lake. In 1956 son Elmer and his dad built the Clearwater log cabin. Jean said they bought flour, sugar, lard and powdered milk from The Bay and the children snared rabbits to supplement the moose and deer their parents shot. Fur trapping consumed the short winter days; a good catch meant food for summer and winter and purchase of necessary tools and rifles. Jean recalled one year when they trapped many foxes that were traded at the Hudson's Bay in Waterways. In the spring of 1951 Raphael trapped one thousand muskrats in a six-week period. He sold them to Dempson Cross, who had the reputation of being fair, for $2,500. In the summer the father netted fish and Jean recalls playing with the Waterways girls. She worked in Bill Mitchell's Waterways café when she was 15.

Elmer was a remarkable person who taught himself to read and write. His handwriting was precise and neat and he took great pride in it and his excellent spelling. The Cree family had great respect for the King and Queen and always had a picture of them in their cabin.

Raphael was, to his dying day, very fit. When young he was a remarkable runner. The story is told of a day when he left the Clearwater cabin at about six in the morning, ran the 22 miles to town, bought a rifle from Bill Gordon, and ran back arriving home by noon. In his last years, Mr. Cree lived in town, but continued to go up to the Clearwater cabin until he was 106. He loved to cut wood and pick berries; he supplied the cook stove with kindling until he was 105.

Often on a Sunday afternoon Elmer would drop by the author's home and pick up a loaf of fresh bread. One Sunday I had baked brown bread. Elmer said, "My dad likes white best." Fortunately there was a loaf of white in the freezer!

Between the Horse Pasture on the Clearwater and the town of Waterways was an area known in the 1960s and '70s as Cree Crescent. Tents and shanties housed some of the old timers including Victor Cree.

The very first explorers noted that the natives used the bitumous material from the banks of the rivers to patch their canoes. In 1719, Captain Swan, a Cree chief, sent a sample of the tarsands to York Factory. It was deemed to be useless.

One of the most distinguished of the recent Cree tribe was Chief Paul Cree, who lived and governed wisely at the turn of the last century. He would have been one of the signatories of Treaty 8 in 1899. This took place at the Snye and in 1999 Raphael Cree, the Chief's son, told us he remembered the beautiful sunny day with all the canoes beached at the Snye and people from all over coming together while Father Lacombe translated for the government men. Chief Paul Cree died in 1918.

Many changes have come to the area and the Cree nation since that memorable day. With the resilience carried down from their forefathers the Cree descendents have generally adapted to the changes and continue to be good citizens, while revering their traditions and enjoying the bounties and beauty of the land.

The Métis

The Métis Nation, descendants of the first Europeans and the First Nations people, can boast of a fascinating history as the fur trading area became the province of Alberta. They were familiar with the white traders' ways and settlements and made themselves invaluable to the fur traders and explorers.

The Métis acted as guides and river men for the early explorers. Their strength was legendary whether pulling heavy scows through the rapids, or portaging with huge packs on their backs. As trade grew on our northern rivers they worked on the steamboats, as well as cutting and supplying wood for the engines.

One of the distinguished Métis families in our area was the Loutits. Peter Loutit came from Scotland to be employed in Fort Chipewyan by the Hudson's Bay Company and married a local lady. His son Billy, born in 1877, was one of the pilots on the first boat to negotiate the Grand Rapid on the Athabasca River. He was 17 when he began working on the boats for the Hudson's Bay Company and until he left the river at 70 he had worked on every HBC boat freighting on the Athabasca.

As with the majority of the river men, Bill Loutit was strong and swift. In 1904 the town of Athabasca was experiencing a terrible flood. Billy was asked to carry a dispatch to Edmonton. He did so running over flooded roads and rough terrain to arrive in 16 hours, and before the messenger who went by horseback. Another amazing run by this pioneer was when he delivered a Mounted Police dispatch from Fort Chipewyan to Fort Smith, making the journey there and back in three days, pulling a sled. Speed and stamina were qualities of the Métis pioneers.

George, another son of Peter Loutit, once single handedly unloaded nine tons of freight from one scow to another to prevent the merchandise from being damaged by flooding.

When Ernest Thompson Seton, the great naturalist and author, came through our area on a journey to the Arctic, it was Billy Loutit who acted as his chief guide.

Another remarkable man was Captain Shott. Born in Manitoba in 1841. Louis Fosseneuve gained the nickname of "Shot" because of his accurate aim when shooting buffalo. And then his unequalled skill in navigating the tricky waters of the Grand Rapids on the Athabasca, reinforced the name and added Captain. He was able to "shoot" the rapids with a fully loaded scow, thus saving hours of backbreaking portaging or a much longer route.

For almost 100 years goods coming into the area and furs being carried out to eastern markets had used the Meythe Portage, and Portage la Loche. A steep and tough 14-mile portage in Saskatchewan ended at the beautiful Clearwater River that flowed into the Athabasca and thus to northern points. Between Athabasca Landing and Fort McMurray on the Athabasca River there were many rapids requiring portages culminating in the treacherous one called Grand Rapids. Captain Shott successfully shot these rapids in 1867 and in the 1880s proved a loaded scow could navigate them with the right man at the helm. Many other river men lost merchandise when their scows overturned in the tumultuous waters.

A giant of a man, at six foot six, Captain Shott spoke Cree, French, English and Mischif (a Métis language – mixture of French and Cree). His descendants tell the story of once when he transported four nuns down the river, he spoke Cree to his crew and the nuns spoke in French of their fear of this huge man. When they arrived at their destination, Captain Shott courteously helped each nun off the boat, addressing them in perfect French.

The Shott and Loutit families represent the best of the Métis who helped develop our area by their bodily strength and their strength of character. The Métis seem to combine the best traits of the first peoples along with the best of the white newcomers.

A remarkable and much loved Métis woman, Elsie Yanik, is spending her last years in Fort McMurray. Born in Fort Fitzgerald to an employee of the Northwest Mounted Police and a native lady, Elsie was one of ten children. Her mother died when she was eight and she, along with brothers and sister were sent to the Grey Nuns Convent in Fort Resolution. Although it was strange and lonely at first Mrs. Yanik has praise for the Grey Nuns and many fond memories of the school and residence.

At 17, Elsie was reunited with her father, and entered training in Fort Smith as a nursing aide. She soon met her future husband Lawrence Yanik and they eventually settled in Fort Chipewyan where Lawrence started Noralta Air Charters. In later years, Mrs. Yanik often served in the Catholic Church for weddings and funerals. Highly respected, in the community and in the province, she served on the Advisory Board to the Commissioner of Northeastern Alberta as well as various other boards. An expert in many native crafts, Elsie kept up her skills well into her nineties.

For many years Elsie Yanik has said prayers at official and social functions in Fort McMurray, in her native language and in English. Her wisdom and kindness are legendary, and those of us who know her are blessed indeed.

Trappers and Traders

As Upper and Lower Canada became established and Rupert's Land was given to the Hudson's Bay Company, more and more traders pushed westward for the best fur harvests. The HBC began to have competition, first with the XY Company and the North West Company, and increasingly with free traders.

The North West Company traders were the first to venture into our area. Previously natives had journeyed many miles to take their catch to the Bay posts. Now the traders came to the trappers. The great explorers of western Canada were mainly Nor'wester men. These men seem to have been more adventurous and aggressive but even so the HBC had a distinct advantage over the upstart trading company.

When the furs reached the Bay post on Hudson's Bay they were immediately transferred to ships that set sail for London. This meant the Bay fur harvest could reach its market the same year. By contrast, the Nor'westers had to transport their furs all the way to Montreal and then by ship on to London. So it was usually two years before North West furs reached their market.

When the two rival companies amalgamated in 1821 under the Hudson's Bay Company banner the initial exploration into the northwest fur trading areas had been completed. It was now time for a more settled and stable business environment.

In diaries of the explorers and traders who travelled through our area, one thing stands out. They were all impressed by the beauty of the Clearwater River. Dr. John Rae, in 1848 spoke of the Meythe Portage as "the longest, most challenging portage in all of Rupert's Land." The twelve mile portage separates

Churchill and Athabasca River systems and he said the river after the portage was accomplished was the "finest view in all of Rupert's Land.….the like of which I have never seen surpassed."

The years of the 1800s was the time for the explorers, no longer just traders, who wanted to explore the land, chart the rivers and lakes, and look for routes to the east. We are grateful for the detailed diaries many of these men kept so faithfully. It was a time for hardy men who braved storms, rushing rapids and towering mountains to see what lay beyond.

Peter Pond,
The Renegade Trader
1739 - 1807

It was in 1778 that the first white fur trader crossed the Meythe Portage and paddled down the beautiful Swan (Clearwater) River to the junction of the Elk (Athabasca) River. Peter Pond, a maverick American soldier turned trader was said to have a violent temper and was accused of at least two murders in his tumultuous career.

The son of a shoemaker and eldest of eight children, Pond fought in the Seven Years War that resulted in the fall of New France. He also traded for furs along the Mississippi. He established an easy rapport with natives and his semi-literate journal tells of a peace treaty he negotiated between the Chippewa and the Sioux. When the American Revolution broke out Pond abandoned his soldier's uniform for trapper's garb and headed northwest.

With four canoes and 16 men he traveled west seeking the North-West Passage. It took them a week to traverse the Meythe Portage and what a pleasure it must have been to enter the Clearwater River. After portaging Whitemud Falls and four other sets of rapids, they entered calm waters and paddled downstream with the current. It was Pond's ambition, not only to find the sea passage to eastern riches, but also to present a map to the Empress of Russia. Pond's crudely drawn maps, a result of his own excursions and consultations with natives who knew the north country, were accurate enough that Alexander Mackenzie used them when he followed the great river that bears his name to the Arctic. Pond presented his maps to the US congress and also to the Governor of Canada, hoping for interest in further exploration.

Pond and crew spent the winter of 1778-79 in a trading post he established on the Athabasca River about forty miles from the Lake. The site of this fort is not exactly known although it was occupied for about ten years. Alexander Mackenzie noted in his journals "In the fall of the year 1787, when I first arrived at Athabasca Mr. Pond was settled on the banks of the Elk (Athabasca) River, where he remained three years, and had formed as fine a kitchen garden as I ever saw in Canada."

On Pond's first foray into the Athabasca country the natives were delighted to trade with him. The Chipewyan and Cree tribes previously had to carry their furs each year to Churchill enduring many hardships enroute. They were very pleased to have someone come to their country to relieve them of the trip. The first year Pond acquired twice as many furs as his canoes would carry; he left the rest in one of his huts to take to market the next year.

During one his trips, presumed to be in 1778, Pond established a fort at the junction of the Clearwater and Athabasca. In 1791, Philip Turnor, a Hudson Bay Company surveyor noted the post on the north side of the Clearwater. Although they saw no one, Turnor wrote "they have Birch rind, Pimecon, etc. locked up in their warehouse and a Garden planted with potatoes which are in a thriving condition." In 1970, modern day historian-explorers came to McMurray, and with the assistance of our family, located the site of McLeod's House. In 1979 a team from the University of Alberta excavated the site and found beads, a cufflink, a cannon ball and square nails. A double fireplace made of rocks indicated there were two rooms in the house. The excavation was filled in to ensure it would not be disturbed, but, who knows, sometime it may be restored as an historic site.

Peter Pond joined the North West Company in 1785. It was this year that he journeyed to Great Slave Lake and up the Peace River. Alexander Mackenzie spent the winter of 1787-88 with Pond at his post on the Athabasca. Pond left this region and his post closed in 1788. He traveled to Montreal, and then in 1790 returned to his home in Connecticut. He died in 1807 in poverty, having in his lifetime opened up the richest fur trading area in the world and inspired others to follow his dream to locate the Northwest Passage.

Sir Alexander Mackenzie,
The River Explorer
1764 – 1820

The first European to travel the vast land, which is now known as Canada, from Sea to Sea to Sea, was Alexander Mackenzie. Indeed he crossed the continent several years before the famed American Lewis and Clark expedition.

Born in Scotland, Mackenzie immigrated to Montreal with his father and aunts in 1787 from New York. The family moved to Montreal at the start of the American Revolution. He became a partner of the North West Company at 23 and was posted to Ile-a-la-Crosse. In 1787 he was second in command to Peter Pond at "Old Establishment" about 30 miles from the mouth of the Athabasca. Peter Pond shared his maps and his knowledge of the area to the north from his own travels and information from the natives; this helped inspire Alexander Mackenzie to explore north and west.

In his journal Mackenzie spoke of the North West Company post on what is now known as Macdonald Island. He said he saw the finest wheat growing here that he had seen since leaving the States.

In 1789 Mackenzie left his cousin Roderic McKenzie in charge of the operation at the new Hudson's Bay Company post of Fort Chipewyan and set out to find the river route to the Pacific Ocean. They returned just 102 days later having traveled down the Slave River, crossed Great Slave Lake and down the Mackenzie River to the Arctic, a distance Mackenzie estimated at 1540 miles. In actuality the voyage was over 3000 miles. He was so upset that he had not reached the Pacific Ocean that he named the waterway "River of Disappointment." He returned to England to study the latest navigation skills determined to travel to the Pacific.

In 1792, Mackenzie once again set out from Fort Chipewyan and spent the winter at Fort Fork, a post near the junction of the Peace and Smoky Rivers. The group of ten paddled the Parsnip and Finlay Rivers and on to the Fraser. The Indians advised him not to travel the turbulent Fraser but to take an overland route.

They descended the Bella Coola River and reached the Pacific on July 20, 1793, missing Captain George Vancouver by 45 days. Mackenzie was just 29 years old. Inscribed on a rock overlooking the ocean, he wrote with reddish paint and bear grease, these words: "Alexander Mackenzie, from Canada, by land, the twenty-second of July, one thousand seven hundred and ninety-three." Today the rock and inscription can be seen in the Sir Alexander Mackenzie Provincial Park at Bella Coola.

In 1802 Mackenzie was knighted by King George III. He published a book "*Voyages*", and his journals and letters, most to his cousin Roderic, have been collected and published.

Mackenzie was said to be a leader who drove his men relentlessly, but drove himself as well. He was described as "blond, strong and well built, with an amazing stamina." The travelling day began at three or four a.m. and lasted 15 to 16 hours. Two of the French-Canadian voyageurs that he took on his first voyage to the Arctic also accompanied him to the Pacific.

Mackenzie's Journals give a wonderful description of our area. *"This precipice, which rises upwards of a thousand feet above the plain beneath it, commands a most extensive, romantic, and ravishing prospect. From thence the eye looks down on the course of the little river, by some called the Swan river, and by others, the Clear-Water and Pelican river, beautifully meandering for upwards of thirty miles. The valley.....is about three miles in breadth, and is confined by two lofty ridges of equal height, displaying a most delightful inter-mixture of wood and lawn. Some parts are covered with stately forests,...where the elk and buffalo find pasture."*

"The river," Mackenzie continues, *"runs, including its windings, upwards of eighty miles, when it discharges itself in the Elk River,....commonly called by the white people, the Athabasca River." "At the junction or fork, the Elk River is about three quarters of a mile in breadth, and runs in a steady current.....till it discharges itself into the Lake of the Hills."*

Like so many other explorers, Mackenzie took note of the bituminous sands with which the natives for many years had used to patch their canoes, mixing it with spruce gum. He said, *"at about 24 miles from the Fork, are some bituminous fountains, into which a pole of 20 feet long may be inserted without the least resistance."*

In Mackenzie's Journals he composed a dictionary of the Cree and Chipewyan languages for the most common words and sayings, as well as of the tribes he met on his journey to the Pacific.

After his second journey, successfully to the Pacific Ocean, Mackenzie returned to eastern Canada and for a time was a member of the Legislative Assembly of Lower Canada. He spent more and more time in Britain and in 1812 he was married in London to a Miss Geddes Mackenzie, described as "one of the most beautiful women I ever saw". His health was failing and in 1820 he went to Edinburgh to seek medical advice and died on the way home. He died without a will and Lady Mackenzie was not able to settle the estate with the Hudson's Bay Company for many years.

The fortitude, stamina and determination of a young man eager to explore new lands and rivers left us a legacy and record of his travels and times.

David Thompson,
The Map Maker
1770-1857

The man said to be the greatest land geographer who ever lived was born of Welsh parents who had immigrated to England. Thompson's father died when he was two and at seven he was placed in a home for disadvantaged children in Westminster. Here he learned math and navigation skills. At 14 years he was apprenticed to the Hudson's Bay Company for a term of seven years, and he left England, never to return.

Although Thompson's sojourn in our region was brief, his remarkable life had such a great influence upon Canada's geography that he must have a place in this book.

Thompson's first posting was at Fort Churchill where the noted explorer Samuel Hearne was governor. He spent the winter transcribing part of Samuel Hearne's book "A Journey to the Northern Ocean." Perhaps the stories in this epic tale inspired him in his future explorations. At 16 years, he was sent to York Factory, a journey of some two weeks along the coast of the Hudson's Bay. He and the two native packers lived on ducks and geese and avoided polar bears by "the Indian rule of walking past with a steady step without seeming to notice them." In his travels the next year into what is now Saskatchewan and Alberta he learned the Cree and Assiniboine languages.

In 1788 while performing routine duties at Manchester House he slipped down a riverbank and broke his leg. He later said, "by the mercy of God, it was the best thing that ever happened to me." He was left at Cumberland House to recover, it was eight months before he could use crutches, and here he met Philip Turnor, HBCs official surveyor and astronomer. Although Thompson had been educated in the basics of surveying he eagerly learned all the navigational skills Turnor was just as eager to teach him. The surveying that Thompson did more than 100 years ago has been proven accurate by modern technology. During this time he became blind in one eye, and he always walked with a limp from his damaged leg.

David Thompson came into this area in 1792 when he made the first significant survey of the route to Lake Athabasca. In 1796 he, with two Indian packers, explored a route from Lake Winnipeg in the east to Lake Athabasca. On the return trip they lost much of their supplies in rapids and although Thompson's surveying equipment and journals were rescued they were forced to exist on gulls, baby eagles and swans. They tore their tent into three pieces to use as blankets. Meeting with a group of Chipewyan natives they were supplied with shoes for Thompson, a kettle and some ammunition, to be paid for when the natives next went to the trading post.

In 1797 Thompson left the Hudson's Bay Company to join the North West Company, where he continued surveying and mapping. Two years later he married Charlotte Small, a Scottish-Cree girl of 14 who spoke French, English and Cree. She and her children travelled with him on many of his journeys. Their marriage lasted 58 years and they had 13 children. Thompson was a deeply religious man who neither smoked, drank or swore and he refused to give alcohol to the Indians. After a long day's paddling he would sit around the campfire and read to his companions from the Bible in French.

Thompson's employment with the North West Company allowed him to survey for the British government and he mapped the 49th parallel, the border established in 1783 by the United States and British governments. He mapped the country from Lake Superior to the Pacific. His complete map of 1814 was used for more than 100 years as the basis for Canadian government maps. In all he surveyed and recorded maps of 3.9 million square kilometers, one-fifth of the continent of North America. He walked and canoed 55 thousand miles. He filled 77 field notebooks that became the basis for J.B. Tyrell's book "David Thompson's Narrative".

Much of Thompson's explorations took him into the difficult terrain of the Rocky Mountains and the rushing rivers of coastal British Columbia and the western U.S. He was the first white man to travel the Colombia River. He named the Fraser River for Simon Fraser and Simon Fraser named the Thompson River for this extraordinary man. He located the sources of the Mississippi River, mapped the upper Missouri River as well as southeastern B.C. The Quebec eastern townships were mapped by Thompson, as well as the Muskoka area in Ontario.

The natives called David Thompson, the "stargazer", as he was always gazing into the night skies. He was a phenomenal storyteller and many commented on his masterful skill at weaving a great story out of every experience. Here is how one close friend described him: " *he has a very powerful mind, and a singular facility of picture making. Thompson can create a wilderness and people it with warring Indians, or climb the Rocky Mountains with you in a snowstorm, so clearly and palpably that you only have to shut your eyes and you can hear the crack of the rifle or feel the snowflakes melt on your cheeks as he talks…"*

The Thompson family moved to Upper Canada after retirement from the NWC and he worked for the International Boundary Commission as Chief Astronomer. As with so many of our early explorers and heroes he died penniless, but he has left us an incalculable legacy.

The Fraser Factor

The surname Fraser is threaded into the history of our area through records of the earliest fur traders and explorers and today many descendents of these hardy men still make their home here.

Simon Fraser (1776 – 1862) while best known for his explorations of "New Caledonia", (British Columbia), Simon Fraser had as his first assignment with the North West Company, the Athabasca Department.

Simon Fraser was born in the state of New York of Scottish Highlander parents. His father, a Loyalist general died in prison in Albany, NY during the American Revolution. In 1784 his mother moved the family to Upper Canada and an uncle, a judge, undertook Simon's education. At age 14 he moved to Montreal and at 16 he was apprenticed to the North West Company. One of the leading Nor'westers, Simon McTavish was related to the Fraser family.

From 1792 to 1805 Simon Fraser was in charge of the Athabasca district, the richest furbearing area in Canada. Although little is known of his activities in our area, he must have acquitted himself successfully as he was made a full partner of the North West Company in 1801.

At the first part of the 19th century the rush to see who would control the western part of the continent became intense. Not only was the United States interested in the fur economy but also the Spanish were venturing up the west coast. The North West Company chose Simon Fraser to cement the British claim to the land past the Rockies and thus ensure the lucrative fur trade.

The journey across the mountains and down the turbulent river named for him accorded Fraser a distinguished place in Canadian history. Said to be grumpy and forbidding Fraser never established a rapport and a respect for his native guides as David Thompson had. After making his mark in the region he called New Caledonia, for an area in his mother's native Scotland, Fraser returned to the east and in 1820 married and settled near Cornwall. His financial ventures were failures and he died almost penniless. At his death in 1862 he was one of the last partners of the North West Company.

Colin Fraser, a cousin of Simon Fraser became piper to Hudson's Bay Company Governor George Simpson, who ruled the fur trade after the amalgamation of the Bay with the North West Company. Simpson was said to be mean and cheap with his factors and employees, begrudging them pickles, mustard and crockery dishes. But he liked to put on a show and used a piper to announce his arrival and departure from the posts. Colin Fraser was awarded the contract after blowing the bagpipes, in his kilt, for a 22-mile march ahead of the governor. He retained the position from 1821 – 1856.

Fraser's bagpipes were in Fort Chipewyan until sometime in the 1980s. They were presented to the Alberta Provincial Museum by his grandson Horace Wylie.

Colin Fraser II – son of the famous piper, was born in Jasper in 1850, and when growing up lived in many northern HBC posts. In his youth he was a scout for the Hudson Bay Company and a buffalo hunter. He took up a homestead in the small town of Edmonton on what is now Jasper Avenue before returning north to Fort Chipewyan, and establishing his own trading post in 1894. That year his fur sales brought the largest amount of money to date in Edmonton, the sum of $20,000. On his return trip to Fort Chip he loaded his scows with cedar shingles for his warehouse.

Colin Fraser was probably the most prolific independent fur trader in northern Alberta; one year, early in the century, he sold his fur for $35,000.

Fraser carried on his trading business in Fort Chipewyan until he was almost 92. He died in 1941. He was married to Flora Rowland from Saskatchewan.

For almost half a century Colin Fraser was one of the most respected men of the north. There are many descendents of the Frasers in Wood Buffalo today; people with surnames Sutherland, Wylie and Fraser can claim this historic ancestry.

Sir John Franklin,
The Lost Explorer
1786-1847

No name in the 19th century aroused such an interest in the adventurous people of the time than that of John Franklin. Britain was at the height of its glory; every European nation was keen to discover new lands and new riches. The excitement of Franklin's third expedition to locate the elusive North West Passage was followed by years of news of the searches, all made in vain. The mystery of his disappearance with that of the entire crew of two ships diminished the accomplishments of the man himself.

A member of a large family, Franklin joined the Royal Navy at 14, against the wishes of his father. He fought in the famous Battle of Trafalgar in 1805 and the Battle of New Orleans in 1814. With his captain uncle he explored the coast of Australia and studied botany and surveying.

In 1819 the British Admiralty commissioned Franklin to explore the northern coastline of Canada, taking an overland route over the Meythe Portage, down the Clearwater River to the Athabasca and north to the Coppermine River and along the coast. On this expedition he mapped 340 miles along the coast. Ten out of 21 of his men died of starvation; the rest were rescued by friendly Indians. It was on this trip that Franklin earned the nickname of "the man who ate his boots." The men were boiling their leather boots for sustenance.

Franklin was said to have great respect for the Inuit and their igloo homes. In 1820 he wrote of the comfortable buildings, the purity of material, elegance of construction, translucency of walls – in appearance far superior to marble buildings.

The second overland expedition of 1825, again through our area, was planned with care. Franklin had found the boats supplied on the first trip too heavy and not well designed. He had boats built that were light enough to carry on land but were fit for rivers and deep seas. In his book "Narrative of a Second Expedition to the Shores of the Polar Sea", Franklin tells of crossing the Meythe Portage with a three a.m. start in June 1825. The water in the Clearwater was so shallow in spots they had to drag their boats.

Franklin wrote of the bituminous shale he observed at the union of the Clearwater and Elk (Athabasca) Rivers. He noted the fluid bitumen in cavities was in such quantities as to flow in streams from fissures in the rocks. Passing by Fort of the Forks (present site of Fort McMurray) and Fort Chipewyan, the explorers went down the Slave River and then the Mackenzie. Franklin divided the group in two; one party went east and the other west. In his two expeditions Franklin, along with George Back and Dr. John Richardson, mapped nearly 2000 miles of the northern coastline, two-thirds of the entire north coast of North America. It was on this trip that he performed two marriages in Fort Chipewyan.

On his return to England Franklin was knighted and appointed Governor of Van Dieman's Land (Tasmania). A British penal colony with a mix of convicts, Aborigines and free settlers it was a challenge to govern. He established a state educational system, founded the Tasmanian Natural History Society and subsidized the Journal of Natural History.

Franklin's first wife died of tuberculosis after giving birth to their daughter. He married Jane Griffin, a strong minded, intelligent and ambitious lady. In Tasmania she explored the island, crossing from Hobart to Macquarie. Lady Franklin established a botanical garden, a university and a museum. The Franklins were popular with the people and were credited with making Tasmania the intellectual centre of the Australian colonies.

Mapping of the Northwest Passage was of prime interest in Britain and Franklin, at 59 years, was chosen to head the sea expedition with the *Erebus* and *Terror,* two ships outfitted with the new invention of steam engines, 1000 books, and food for three years.

Twenty-four officers and 110 men made up the crew, who left Britain in May 1845. They were last seen by Europeans in Lancaster Sound in July of that year. Five men were discharged and sent home, leaving a crew of 129 men. They were never heard from again.

Thus began the largest search of the century. Forty expeditions over 12 years searched for signs of the men. Some were financed by the British Admiralty, some by Lady Jane and some by public subscription. More men and ships were lost in the search for Franklin than were lost on the expedition. Lady Franklin and her influential friends kept the search ongoing.

It wasn't until 1854 that any clue of the lost expedition was found. Dr. John Rae talked with Inuit hunters who give him artifacts from the surviving men whom they had seen on their trek southward. Rae reported that the ships were stuck in ice and the men died of starvation and exposure after resorting to cannibalism. Because of the reference to cannibalism his report was disdained and he never received in his lifetime, credit for the great explorations he carried out.

Franklin's diaries have never been found but a note found on King William Island told of his death in 1847. Three graves on a slight and windy hill on Beechy Island look out over the frozen sea. They are of sailors who perished from pneumonia, tuberculosis and perhaps lead poisoning from improperly tinned food.

A century and half later interest is still high when any discoveries are made about the ill-fated Franklin expedition. Although Franklin did not find the passage that many had pursued so relentlessly his social connections through Lady

Franklin and the British Admiralty gave him much recognition. What Sir John did do was map 1200 miles of the Arctic coastline and collect information on geology, weather and plants.

Credit for discovery of the Northwest Passage must go to Dr. John Rae, who was given the reward of 20 thousand pounds that he shared amongst his men. Not only did he find the way from the Atlantic to the Pacific in his fourth expedition of 1853, but as well he discovered the fate of Franklin's expedition. Unlike many of his contemporaries, Dr. Rae did not receive a knighthood. When he went back to England with remnants of some of the expedition's tools and told of the native's report of cannibalism amongst the men he was ostracized and disbelieved. Like Samuel Hearne in his quest for the Coppermine River, Dr. Rae was successful because he adapted to the local Indian customs, food, clothing and transportation.

Sir John Franklin was a soldier, sailor, naturalist and explorer and although the discovery was not his, his name will be forever linked to Canada's Northwest Passage. The esteem that he was held in is evidenced in the naming of Fort McMurray's main street for him over half a century later.

William McMurray,
The HBC Factor
1820-1877

The man Fort McMurray is named for was Canadian born, son of Chief Trader Thomas McMurray, of the Hudson's Bay Company. William received his education at the Red River Academy in Manitoba that was established to educate sons of the Bay men. In 1837 he was apprenticed to the Bay as a postmaster and later as a factor.

Unlike many of the great explorers we have no journal of McMurray's. We do know that he was chief factor at the bustling post of Fort Chipewyan in 1869. He was away at Norway House when his old friend H.J. Moberly stopped in on his way from the Peace River, planning to winter down the Mackenzie. Moberly found McMurray's wife sick at the fort and so stayed to care for her. When McMurray returned he persuaded Moberly to stay for the winter.

McMurray's persuasive powers must have been great because he talked Moberly into rejoining the Hudson's Bay Company and establishing a post at The Forks, upstream from Fort Chipewyan at the confluence of the Athabasca and Clearwater Rivers. Moberly wrote, *"I named the new post Fort McMurray after a chief factor, one of my oldest friends."*

McMurray was said to be a quiet but competent person. He was appointed as one of four Inspecting Chief Factors. He wrote, *"The position of Inspecting Chief Factor may by some be considered a great honour, but for me it never* had, and never will have any attraction, unless the grade gives me some discretionary powers and thereby enables one to do some good." He cared about the men who worked under him and whom he was responsible for.

A letter from General Sir J.H. Lefroy written to William McMurray in 1845 encourages him to learn the Chipewyan language. Lefray wrote, *"I hardly know any way in which you could make so valuable and creditable a use of your leisure and advantages as by acquiring a mastery of that language. Remember that Rome was not built in a day – if a dozen years hence you can produce a Chipewyan dictionary and grammar, you will have done much."*

He must have been successful in mastering the language as Chief Factor Roderick MacFarlane later wrote: *"Among other good qualities in his make-up, Mr. Wm. McMurray was probably one of the best speakers – orators perhaps – in the Saulteaux and Chipewyan languages. He was also an excellent shot, and among the best winter travellers of his time."*

Mr. McMurray was married twice; once to a daughter of Chief Factor John Ballenden, and after her death to a sister of Sheriff Inkster, the second marriage taking place in 1868. In 1944 Lefroy writes that Mr. McMurray walked on snowshoes about 200 miles for the New Year's Day festivities in Fort Chipewyan. It was thirty below zero.

William McMurray was appointed chief factor for the HBC, but held the position for just two years. He died in Winnipeg just after his 53rd birthday, in 1877.

Henry John Moberly,
The Founder
1835 – 1931

Since the time of Peter Pond there had been a fort at "The Forks," junction of Athabasca and Clearwater Rivers. Journals of explorers tell of the different sites, from MacLeod House on the bank of the Clearwater to an abandoned North West Company post on MacDonald Island. And when Henry John Moberly built a permanent fort on the bank of the Athabasca in 1870, he too found signs of previous occupation.

Moberly was born in Ontario, the son of a navy captain and a Polish mother. He was a younger son, not interested in studies but keen for adventure. When he was 16 his father obtained a post for him with Lloyds of London in St. Petersburg. He soon tired of the work and headed back to Canada. He met a man who had been on one of the searches for the Franklin Expedition, and was greatly intrigued by the stories of roaming buffalo and the freedom of the prairies.

An application to Sir George Simpson to join the Hudson Bay Company was approved and a date was set for Moberly to meet Simpson's group to travel west. Moberly was impatient and set immediately out with two Indian guides for the west. He finally met the Governor and was assigned duties in the northwest.

By 1869 Moberly had left the employ of the Bay and was intending to travel north on the Mackenzie River. He stopped and wintered in Fort

Chipewyan, finding that the factor was an old friend, William McMurray. Over the course of the winter McMurray persuaded Moberly to head south, not north, and establish a Hudson's Bay Company fort at The Forks.

With two boats and a crew they paddled upstream on the Athabasca to the junction with the Clearwater River. A three-day snowstorm made the trip most unpleasant and on May 2nd they landed in a foot of snow on their desired site. He named the new trading post Fort McMurray, "after a chief factor who is one of my oldest friends."

Moberly was tasked with building a fort and trading with the natives, but also to establish better routes for bringing in supplies. He improved the trail over the Meythe Portage, established the fact that steamboats could traverse the rivers, and discovered salt deposits.

During Moberly's time in the new trading post two drastic things happened. In 1875 an early dramatic spring breakup caused waters to back up and engulf the lower plain. In just two hours the river rose seventy-five feet. Moberly reported that trees three and four feet in diameter were "mown down like grass." Only one house was damaged but of the thirty-seven oxen, all were drowned but one.

The other incident was well described in Irwin Huberman's book "The Place We Call Home", and with the author's permission I am reprinting it here.

Dutch Henry and the Fire: John Moberly and crew were not alone for long. Trappers and explorers had for decades paused at the fork of the Athabasca and Clearwater rivers, and one day in the spring of 1871, a man known as Dutch Henry appeared. Henry was a trapper and labourer who had landed in the Peace Country in 1869 and who had completed some work for the Roman Catholic Mission.

Moberly described Henry as "a short stumpy man with a small pug nose in a round pink face, down the sides of which straggled a thin growth of sandy hair." Henry insisted at one time he had been a head coachman and personal friend of both the King of Bavaria and the Crown Prince.

Henry had come to Fort McMurray due to the spring flooding of the Athabasca and Clearwater rivers. The flood did not affect Moberley's fort, but it did make travel out of the area impossible. Henry agreed to stay until the waters subsided. He stored a small packet of furs under the counter of the Hudson's Bay store and ventured out to find a place to rest.

It was a hot afternoon and according to Moberly's account, the mosquitoes and other insects were ferocious. The Hudson's Bay crew was on its way to Fort Chipewyan to stock up with supplies, so Moberly and Henry were alone. Moberly lit a coal smudge to keep the insects away from the horses and then paddled over to his garden, which was likely located on present day MacDonald Island.

Suddenly, Moberly felt a blast of heat and heard an ear-shattering explosion. Moberly turned to find a column of black smoke rising from the Hudson's Bay post. As he landed back on shore, Moberly saw two things. First, he saw his store in flames. He also noticed the darting figure of Dutch Henry dashing by with his precious packet of furs under his arm. For hours, Henry could not be found. Moberly cursed as he tried on his own to douse the fire.

Parched with thirst, Moberly walked to the shore of the river to fill a pail of water but was distracted by moaning sounds coming from a clump of willows. There was Dutch Henry, his hair, eyebrows and whiskers gone. His singed face was swollen, highlighted only by his bright red nose. Despite Henry's discomfort, Moberly howled with laughter. As Moberly described it, "it would have made a mummy laugh."

It took ten days before Henry could use his eyes or walk. Finally, he disclosed what had happened. When Moberly was gone, a whirlwind had kicked up, tossing hot coals from the nearby smudge on to the Hudson's Bay store roof. This ignited a fire, and Henry dashed to the riverbank, filled a pail with water and climbed up to put out the blaze.

Unbeknownst to Henry, a few days earlier, Moberly had stored a keg of gunpowder in a loft under the roof. The idea was to keep the explosives out of *the way of tobacco smoking trappers and traders. Just as Henry had climbed to the top of the building, one of the coals dropped through the roof into the loft and landed directly on the keg of gunpowder. Henry was sent hurling into space amidst a sea of fire, smoke and wood. When Henry landed, he dashed into the store, rescued his furs and raced to the river to cool his face. That is where Moberly found him.*

Within a few weeks, Henry's face healed and he continued on his journey. Moberly spent the next nine months rebuilding the post.

Although Moberly's tenure at the fort he established was only eight years he accomplished a great deal in that time. In 1878 he was transferred to Fort Vermillion and later was chief factor at Isle-a-la-Crosse. Not only did he make cart roads for the Clearwater portages but he also determined that steamboats could travel the waterways. This eventually resulted in a steamboat traveling the Athabasca River from Athabasca to Grand Rapids and another from Grand Rapids to Fort Fitzgerald, with a third beyond into the Arctic.

The HBC inspector W.J. Christie visited the post in 1872 and reported on the potatoes and excellent vegetables grown on the island. Years before, this was the site of a North West Company post and Alexander Mackenzie said he saw the finest wheat growing there. The naturalist John Macoun visited Moberly's fort and said that enough wheat could be grown here to supply the whole north. None of them predicted the future of our city to be in oil but they all remarked on bitumen being used for roofs and for caulking canoes.

In 1893 J.W. Tyrrell and his brother were engaged by the Canadian Geographical Society to travel the barren lands. In Tyrrell's book he says Fort McMurray had five small log buildings – a store, warehouse, the trader's house and two Indian houses. Natives had come to the fort to trade furs for food, but the food supplies were exhausted and the entire population was starving. The scows, brought down from Grand Rapids by the famed Captain Shott, arrived five days later with the fort's supplies as well as the Tyrrell's.

Huberman states in his book that in 1901 the population of the fort was just 28. In 1907 when Ernest Thompson Seton stopped at Fort McMurray he found a settled small community, with a post office and store run by Christine Gordon, a large garden and active trading.

Moberly, like so many other Canadian explorers and traders, had a spirit of adventure, great fortitude, and I would think a vision for the future. But I'm sure he never dreamt that his little fort would in just 140 years be the economic engine of the nation.

Settlers & Entrepreneurs

What makes a community? What brought these settlers to a little known northern town nestled between two rivers on the edge of an endless forest? We know why the fur traders and explorers passed through this way; they were seeking their fortunes in furs, or had the urge to see what was around the next bend of the river. Each of the early families who came to McMurray and Waterways had a purpose or a reason; some of these reasons we can only guess at.

What we do know is that these early families set standards for the rest of us.

They worked hard, or they couldn't have survived; they took advantage of the opportunities and above all, most enjoyed the bountiful and beautiful outdoors. Each in their own way have made our community a more interesting place, a good place to raise families, a great place to live.

I've touched on only a few of the early families; there are others who deserve to have their stories told. We admire these first families and are grateful to them for paving the way and giving us such an abundant history.

The Gordons,
The First Settlers

William and Christine Gordon left their mark on Fort McMurray. We honour them in the names of rivers, lakes and streets. They came from Scotland, like so many of our earliest northern settlers, settled first at Athabasca Landing where they operated a restaurant, and at the turn of the century they made their way to the tiny Hudson's Bay trading post at the confluence of the Clearwater and Athabasca Rivers.

The Gordons started a trading post in competition to the powerful Bay and soon operated the first post office in the area. They built a house and store and raised a large garden. Among her possessions Christine had brought from Scotland three significant items: a medical book, two panes of glass for windows and an original oil painting which had once hung in the Royal Academy of Arts in London. The medical book was of much value as Christine doctored the various ailments of the natives who also delighted to listen to her "music box". Her family had sent her a phonograph for Christmas one year, along with a record of Beethoven's Moonlight Sonata, and this was played over and over. Miss Gordon was proud of her grandfather who had discovered the cure for scurvy, and of her relative General "Chinese" Gordon, a British military hero.

The Gordons grew a large garden and the jams and preserves from the abundant berries provided food all year. They were generous in supplying food and medicine to poor or sick families.

William Gordon was appointed as the first postmaster to the settlement of about 150 people. In 1910 "Fort" was dropped from the settlement's name and it was many years later that the town once again proudly took on the historic designation. While William was away trading with the natives Christine kept the store and post office. The log building housed the store and post office, and was located by the Athabasca River near the present day bridge. As well as buying furs the Gordons had a lively trade in food, tools and rifles.

The famous naturalist and author, Ernest Thompson Seton writes about the Gordons in his book "The Arctic Prairies", an account of a 2000-mile journey he made in 1907. Miss Gordon was keeping the post office at that time, according to him, although some accounts say it was 1909 before Ottawa made the official appointment.

On Seton's return trip in October of 1907 their canoe capsized in rapids in the "Canyon of the Athabaska", the treacherous Grand Rapids. Much of their supplies were lost; but Seton's paddlers, Billy Loutit and Elzear Robillard were able to save the satchel with Seton's all-important journals.

The next day they met a scow, equipped with canopy and stove, coming downstream. It was William Gordon. Seton's book says, *"Then did that generous man break open boxes, bales, and packages and freely gave without a stint, all the things we needed: kettles, pans, sugar, oatmeal, beans, jam, etc."*

Seton records that on the shore above Boiler Rapids was a pile of flour in sacks, inscribed in Cree**, "Gordon his flour."** *"Here it was,"* he wrote, *"the most prized foreign product in the country, lying unprotected by the highway, and no man seemed to think the owner foolish."*

Perhaps the most important legacy the Gordons left to Fort McMurray is the Golosky family.

In 1903 William Gordon was in Edmonton looking for hired help. He brought back a 12-year old, George, who lived with the Gordons and used their name for some years.

In 1912 William and Christine were on their way back from a visit to Scotland. Coming down the Athabasca River their scow hit a rock in the Grand Rapids and they lost $3500 worth of supplies as well as their scow.

William Gordon was a member of the first Board of Trade started in 1915. It was in that year that he, along with George (Gordon) Golosky and Nick Moore, built a steam-powered sawmill on the Prairie. The mill and accompanying farm were located between Franklin Avenue and the Clearwater River, occupying 27 acres. They produced lumber for scows and shiplap for houses.

Logs, mainly spruce, were cut from stands up the Clearwater River and floated down to the mill. In winter they logged the forests close by and skidded the logs in with horses. The mill employed 15 to 20 men, and as well as being sold to local residents lumber was shipped north on barges.

William died in the early thirties and is buried in the town's first cemetery on what is now Biggs Avenue. By that time they had given up their store and Christine continued to live in their home at the end of Franklin. She and her good friend Miss Ross were members of the Imperial Order of Daughters of the Empire. Elsie Hyska, who as a youngster visited Miss Gordon, recalls that she was tall and thin, loved her garden, and always had a slice of bread and berry jam for her young visitors. Christine Gordon, the first white lady to live in Fort McMurray, died in January 1949. She was 85.

Both Christina Lake and the Christina River were named for Miss Gordon, while Gordon Lake, formerly Swan Lake, on the border of Alberta and Saskatchewan honours their name. Historian J.G. MacGregor states: *"As evidence of the respect in which she was held, her first name, erroneously spelled, was bestowed on the large Christina River and on one of its large headwater lakes....."*

Christine Gordon was honoured by the natives that she befriended and cared for. When Chief Paul Cree lay dying at 96 he was completely blind. He was living in a small tent with an old stove and bed of spruce boughs. Miss Gordon visited him every day, took him food and kept his fire going, always giving him the respect due to a great chief. And Chief Paul Cree on his deathbed asked his tribe to erect a lobstick in her honour. A lobstick is a living totem pole; the tallest tree on a prominent hill overlooking the river would be chosen, all the branches would be lopped off except two at the top, which were left as wings.

Dorothy Dahlgren, an Edmonton historian, said she saw the lobstick in the 1950s. It was not far from the town of Fort McMurray overlooking the Athabasca River, and Miss Gordon's name was carved into the trunk in the Indian language.

One wonders at the spirit of adventure that would bring a brother and sister so many miles across an ocean from their comfortable Scottish home to an unknown land and future. Not only did they carve out a living from the wilderness but also they gave back to the community in kindness and example.

The Golosky Dynasty

When Christine and Bill Gordon hired a young apprentice in 1903 they could never have dreamt what an impact and legacy their decision on that spring day in Edmonton would have for the years to follow on their chosen home.

Eleven-year old George had crossed the ocean, and then the continent, from Romania with his father, step-mother, sister and her husband. They were enticed by the promise of free farmland and a better life. He ran away from his father's homestead where he was worked from dawn to dusk and then spent the winter in Edmonton working in a livery stable. Here he met Christina Gordon and was offered a job at their trading post in far off Fort McMurray.

The trip to Fort McMurray was via Athabasca Landing and this necessitated a four-day trip with their wagonload of goods. Two nights they slept in the open; one night in a halfway house. After arriving at the busy port on the Athabasca River their goods were loaded onto a 50-foot scow with a stove in the middle. It took them 11 days to reach the Grand Rapids. And here they found their crew had disappeared in the night and Bill Gordon had to walk through the bush to Fort McMurray to get more men to move the load from one end of the island at Grand Rapids to the other end. This transfer by-passed the dangerous rapids and the goods were reloaded onto the scow for the balance of the 90-mile river journey to the fort.

In Jack Golosky's story of his father's life *One Man's Journey*, he described his years as the Gordon's apprentice as happy; when he finished his chores he was free to roam and play with his young friends. Miss Gordon tried to teach him to read and write, but he said he would rather be out playing with his friends. George's days were spent helping in the store, which was across the road from the home, carrying water, cutting wood and in winter he often travelled with Bill Gordon to trapper's cabins to trade for furs.

The Gordon home was on the bank of the Athabasca River approximately where the end of Franklin Avenue is now. George, in 1908, cut a trail to the Prairie area and then later to the Hangingstone River. Along with Grant Owens and Roger Hummingbird, he cut the trail that was later to become our main street, Franklin Avenue.

For years the young immigrant was known as George Gordon, but in early years when Miss Gordon was teaching him to write she translated his Romanian name to Golosky.

In 1915 George Golosky made what he said was the best decision of his life. He married Agnes Biggs, the daughter of a Forest Ranger from Saskatchewan who lived near the Hangingstone River. Before they were married George built a house for them on the Prairie. He said Agnes was a very great cook and when he went out on the trail she would send meals for him frozen in tin pie plates that could be heated on the campfire.

George said Bill Gordon was like a father to him; he continued to buy furs for the Gordon trading post and in the early 1920s the two men decided to build a sawmill. It was located along the Clearwater River and during the summer logs were cut up the Clearwater and floated down to the mill. In the winter logging was done closer to the mill. There was a great demand for lumber as more and more new residents settled here. They also shipped lumber north on the boats. The sawmill required a blacksmith shop, barn for the horses and cookhouse for the staff.

In 1921 Mr. Golosky built a two-storey home on the Prairie; it has recently been moved to Heritage Park and contains wonderful museum pieces of the early days, as well as a model of the Gordon-Golosky Sawmill. On the 100th anniversary of his father's arrival in Fort McMurray Jack Golosky published a wonderful book telling of his father's life and displayed the model of the sawmill he had made as well as many artifacts of the early years.

In the great flood of 1936 the mill was completely destroyed and much of the lumber and firewood ended up in the trees. A wall of ice 20 to 30 feet high came down the river sounding like a steam engine. The water in their house came up to George's shoulders and it left six inches of silt on the floors. His book says *"A large cake of ice lodged next to Franklin Avenue in line with our home. When the water began to drop it was about eight feet high by about 15 feet wide and 30 feet long. That chunk took all summer to melt."*

Meanwhile the young family flourished. Although George was away a lot in the winter tending traplines and buying fur the Golosky home was a happy one, even with its share of hardships and tragedy. Eleven children were born; three died in infancy. The children all had their daily chores: hauling water, cutting wood, milking cows, cleaning out the barns and feeding the chickens. A large garden was lots of work in the summer but provided the family with ample vegetables for themselves and guests throughout the winter. The Golosky home was always open to travellers, friends and people in need.

New challenges were presented in 1942 with the arrival of the American army who had their camp near the Golosky home, where Keyano College is located. One of the projects of the Americans was to extend the airport runway and George worked on the road to the airport. He also harvested logs for the shipyard, a busy place with supplies being shipped north for US army projects.

When the American army left river transportation was still at its peak and Mr. Golosky worked for Russ Denholm, the boat builder, and later at the Bitumount oil extraction site. George Golosky was a charter member of the McMurray Board of Trade, established in 1915, that later became the Chamber of Commerce.

In 1965 Mr. & Mrs. Golosky celebrated their 50th anniversary. The next year the family was saddened by Agnes' death from cancer. Mr. Golosky continued to live in the family home until 1980 when he passed away in the McMurray hospital.

George and Agnes Golosky were no strangers to hard work and their children and grandchildren inherited their work ethic and the ability to succeed at whatever career or trade they chose. In Fort McMurray today perhaps the best known businesses of the Golosky family were that of Clearwater Welding and Golosky Trucking.

Doug Golosky said he got tired of working for companies that folded leaving him not only without a job, but also with no pay cheque for the work he'd done. And so he decided to venture out on his own. This was in 1984 when our region was experiencing a dramatic downturn in construction and business. Doug recalled his first welding job, for realtor Frank Garvin, which paid $40. Carol, Doug's wife, worked at Dr. Nicholson's office during the first years they operated Clearwater Welding, and did the family company's books at night and weekends. Each Sunday morning for the first several years Doug and Carol would sit down at the kitchen table to assess whether they could carry the business on another week. As partners, Doug and Carol each had their own role and built the business from the small start into a multi-million dollar operation.

Brothers Grant and Bruce, along with finance manager Carol, started a trucking business. Bruce commented, "It is the second time Goloskys would operate a transport business in town, my father (William) and Grandpa George hauled ice and freight decades ago."

Up to 1000 employees worked at the Golosky enterprises, and many young people took their apprenticeship through Clearwater Welding.

Perhaps the favourite business started by Doug and Carol is their fishing camp on Lake Athabasca. Indian Head Camp, on the Saskatchewan shores of the beautiful lake, is a fly-in fishing camp. As the Goloskys divest themselves of their businesses, much of the summer will probably be spent at this camp.

For more than 100 years the Golosky family have contributed to our community, often in quiet, unassuming ways that most don't know about. We hope they will always call McMurray home, as without their influence over the past many years our town would not have been the same.

The Biggs Family

Just after the turn of the century a young family arrived in Fort McMurray and built a house near the Hangingstone River. An employee of the Hudson's Bay Company, it is presumed that William Biggs came from Scotland. He was posted to Isle Le Crosse in Saskatchewan, and there he met and married a "country wife", Ellen Harper.

In McMurray Mr. Biggs worked as a forest ranger, and covered the area from Lake Athabasca to the Saskatchewan border. Their home, located on the old power plant site near the Hangingstone, was of two storeys and sided with shingles. Their oldest daughter, Agnes, was four years old when they arrived in Fort McMurray. In 1915 she married George Golosky in the little Catholic Church, now located in Heritage Park.

Three other children made up the Biggs family: Kathleen, Christine and James. Mr. Biggs' job took him away from home often; he travelled by canoe in the summers and dog team in the winters. He went into partnership with Jack Lazard of Athabasca Landing to start the first sawmill in the area. In 1913, along with Roy Field, William Biggs started shipping lumber to the north on the river steamers.

About 1912 two of William Biggs' daughters from the Old Country came to visit. Daughter Mamie did not stay long but her sister Cassie remained and married a local businessman, Grant Owen. Cassie loved the outdoors; she had her own dog team and delighted in decorating the dogs with colourful collars, blankets and bells.

William Biggs was a charter member of the Board of Trade, established in 1915. He was listed as owning property in the very first survey done of the "Plan of McMurray Settlement" that was ratified in Ottawa in 1911.

The town's records show that William Biggs died in 1925. Ellen was also known as Helene Kokan and several of her sisters from Saskatchewan settled in Fort McKay.

Tax records of the town show a Mary J. Biggs as owning considerable property. We understand William's first wife came to McMurray from England; some said he went back with her. He did, however, return to Canada, as old timers say he is buried here. His tombstone simply says "Biggs". Old cemetery records show a Mrs. Biggs, who died on the train, and was buried in April 1936. Which wife this was we do not know.

Agnes' sister Christine married Dolphus Norris and they moved to Aklavik in the North West Territories. One of their sons became a Commissioner of the North West Territories and three of their grandsons joined the RCMP.

Kathleen (Katie) the third Biggs daughter married Ray Shanks who came to McMurray to work as a forest ranger. He found an excellent trapline close to the Willows on Lake Athabasca. The young couple spent winters on the trapline and summers back in Fort McMurray.

William and Ellen's only son, Jimmie, was an excellent carpenter and worked on various northern construction projects. He also was an avid trapper and worked for both Northern Transportation and the Hudson's Bay Company, in their shipyards and at Norman Wells. His first wife was Edie Fraser (later Dafoe). His daughter Aleta, lives now in B.C. and recalls moving to McMurray from Fort Chipewyan when she was five. She became great friends with her cousin Merle Golosky (now Rudiak), and has fond memories of her early years in Fort McMurray.

There are some unanswered questions about the Biggs family but we do know of their contribution to the community in the fine children they raised, and the example of honesty and hard work that characterized their lives.

The Men Called Sutherland

Angus Sutherland was Fort McMurray's first druggist. John Sutherland worked with Dr. Karl A. Clark on the experimental plant on the bank of the Clearwater opposite the Marine Park.

Sutherland, the pharmacist, was born in Ontario of Scottish parents, and took his training at the University of Winnipeg. He went to work for the Northern Trading Company's water transportation division headquartered in Athabasca Landing. In the winter of 1918 he was sent to Fort McMurray to look after the company's business.

The local population soon recognized his medical knowledge and he began stocking some drugs. During the terrible flu epidemic of 1918-19 he was credited with saving many lives. And so he started a small chemist business in the Old Franklin Hotel owned by the O'Coffeys. During summers he took employment as a purser on the boats going north and Mrs. O'Coffey kept her eye on his drug supplies.

The drugstore business flourished and Mr. Sutherland built a two-storey frame building next to the hotel. He also operated a river freighting business and soon brought the very first motor vehicle into Fort McMurray. This was a flatbed Ford truck. Mr. Sutherland was a major property owner, when McMurray was incorporated into a village in 1947, a total of 125 lots between Hardin Street and Morrison Street, from the Snye to the hill, were owned by Angus Sutherland. Through his pharmacy he served customers from Fort McMurray to the Arctic Circle.

At forty years of age the druggist developed a severe case of arthritis. He sought a relief pharmacist so he could go out for medical help, and Walter Hill agreed to help for a time; he remained for the rest of his life becoming a community icon. The medical help Mr. Sutherland searched for proved futile; he even journeyed to the Mayo Clinic in Rochester. When he returned to McMurray he was very crippled, yet he persevered in his business. He opened a second store in Waterways and in the late 1930s, with Walter Hill, built a store in Yellowknife.

The great McMurray fire of 1934 destroyed the drugstore as well as most of the buildings on the south side of Franklin Avenue. It was replaced and used for many years. When it was replaced by a more modern three-storey structure the original store was moved to Heritage Park.

Angus Sutherland died in his home in 1951 and his body was taken by train to be buried in the family plot in Ontario. He was 69 years old.

John Sutherland was a name well known among oil exploration circles in the early part of the last century. Born in Nova Scotia, he attended the University of Truro and trained as an engineer, boilermaker and millwright. After graduation he went to Newfoundland to build sawmills and there he met his wife. They moved to Edmonton where he was employed to work in the engineering department of the City. He was involved in the 1922 experiment to use raw tar sands from Fort McMurray on the Edmonton city sidewalks and roads.

In Edmonton Mr. Sutherland met Dr. Karl A. Clark and they had a lifelong association. Dr. Clark would tell Sutherland what he needed and Sutherland would build it. The government had built an experimental tar sand separation plant at Dunvegan; Sutherland and Clark modified it and shipped it by rail to Waterways, then across the Clearwater River next to a quarry that Sidney Ells had opened.

This separation plant was run with Sutherland as superintendent in 1929 and 1930 and barrels of oil shipped back to Edmonton. Throughout his experiments Dr. Clark used John Sutherland as his right hand man for construction and supervision.

John and Ella Sutherland had four children: John, Alex (Mickey), Ella and Christine. Although based in Edmonton, John had little influence on his family as he was so seldom home. Despite opposition from their father both sons became involved in the emerging aviation industry.

Mickey Sutherland was born in 1910 in Edmonton, second son of John and Ella Sutherland. His father was an engineer, and very involved with oil sands experimentation, but Mickey was keen to enter the aviation world. He learned to fly under instruction of "Wop" May and studied for an air engineer's ticket, as his eyesight was not good enough for him to obtain a commercial pilot's license.

In 1931 Mickey Sutherland was sent to Fort McMurray to do repairs on a plane; thus began his bush-flying career. He flew from the Snye in Fort McMurray north with such famed pilots as Punch Dickins, Wop May and Lewis Leigh.

Writing of those days, Mickey Sutherland said: "It was bush flying out of Edmonton and Fort McMurray, starting around 1938 that opened up the Arctic. It made a tremendous difference to northern operations and indeed, to the entire area "down north." Much of what we did then still provides benefits, even today.

"While the pilots got most of the adulation, the air engineers were there too. Bush flying was a team effort; it had to be if you wanted to survive. It was just not possible to operate alone on floats or skis; there were too many things that had to be done, such as mechanical breakdowns to be taken care of en route. We carried tool kits, survival gear, a spare cylinder, spare piston, a set of plugs and sometimes a spare magneto."

In 1937 it was time for Mickey to marry and settle down; he went to work, as did his brother John Jr., with Trans Canada Airlines. He later joined the Boeing Company in California and designed equipment for them.

In the summer of 2003 John Sutherland's grandson Gordon, travelled to Fort McMurray to research his family's connection with our city.

Three men named Sutherland; each had an impact on our community and each one in their own specific field.

Which MacDonald Was That?

Over the years several men with the name of McDonald or MacDonald have left their mark on our city. Who is to say which Mc/MacDonald our streets are named for?

In 1898 when the North West Mounted Police made their first visit to Fort McMurray they noted that a Hudson's Bay employee named **John McDonald** had lived in Fort McMurray for 26 years. That would have meant he came just after H.J. Moberly had established the fort. MacDonald Island is probably named for this John McDonald, for in 1893 when Inspector W. J. Christie came to the small fort he commented on the excellent vegetables and potatoes that were being grown on the island.

A **Charlie MacDonald** was a member of the first Board of Trade in 1921. **Harry MacDonald** worked for the Abasand Oil Company in 1937 and built a road from Waterways to Horse Creek, where the plant was.

Another MacDonald of the early days was **Sgt. Jack MacDonald** who served as a provincial police officer after the North West Mounted Police left McMurray in 1917. He transferred to the RCMP and served in McMurray until 1935, when he was transferred. As befitted his chosen career he kept the peace for the local citizens, but had a hard time keeping it with his neighbour.

Prime Minister R.B. Bennett, the first western leader of the country, had a notorious brother. He was a "remittance man". In those days there were quite a few of these characters; most sent out from England, sons of wealthy families eager to keep the "black sheep" of the family out of sight. Each month these men would receive a cheque. The Bennetts, from Calgary, must have considered Fort McMurray near the end of the world and George Horace Bennett ended up here living next door to the local policeman, Jack MacDonald. The feud between the two men provided entertainment for the locals who often helped keep the pot boiling.

Alex and John MacDonald were brothers who both were registered landowners in the 1911 survey. Alex MacDonald gave the bishop an acre of land to build the first Catholic Church, known as the Old Log Mission. There also was an **Archibald MacDonald** who was here frequently in the 1820s when he accompanied Governor Simpson of the Hudson's Bay Company on his northern trips.

And then there was **John A. MacDonald**, remembered fondly by those who lived in McMurray prior to 1980. We remember him as a cheerful man who walked the streets with a bottle under his arm and a curved pipe in his mouth. He would stop in front of the two-storey RCMP barracks at the corner of Main and Manning, salute the flag, stand at attention and sing God Save the King. If the constable's wife, Yvette Rumpel, was on the street he'd serenade her with *Beautiful, Beautiful Brown Eyes.* He'd stop at Dr. Nicholson's house for a loan and a word of encouragement. Joe Gauthier recalls a fire that destroyed the abandoned Haineault house, with its pagoda-like roof, on Franklin Avenue. John A. was said to have started the fire; when the firemen arrived he was standing on the roof playing his fiddle and singing *Beautiful, Beautiful Brown Eyes.*

John A. MacDonald's descent into alcoholism was blamed on an experience when he was captain of the *Slave*, a riverboat bound for Fort Chipewyan. The ice came early that year and the ship got caught in the early freeze of Lake Athabasca. Captain MacDonald left the ice-logged boat to walk to Fort Chip for help. Before he got back all the passengers had started to walk; one was missing and found dead of exposure. This changed MacDonald's life forever.

Four young boys playing near the Snye one Saturday morning saw boots sticking out of an abandoned well. David and Barry Fleming, Don and Gregory Rumpel rushed to call their fathers, Cpl. Don Rumpel and Don Fleming, head of Social Services. Cpl. Rumpel immediately recognized the boots. He thought MacDonald had sat on the edge of the well and fallen in headfirst.

A McDonald family still represented here is that of **Alex and Enid**; daughter Nadean Meints has lived here all her life. They came to McMurray in 1938; Enid was the daughter of J.W. Mann, the town's main carpenter. Alex first worked at the salt plant, helping Mr. Mann on construction as well. Being the town carpenter meant Mr. Mann made coffins and acted as undertaker. In the town's records of burial plots in the first cemetery the names of J.W. Mann and A. McDonald as undertakers are the most frequent.

Mr. McDonald hauled freight from the Bitumount Oil Plant, using dog teams in the winter for the 40-mile run. When the ice broke on the Athabasca River he used his boat. As so many of the first people to come to the town Alex McDonald was diversified in his efforts to earn a living for his family. They lived next door to the Silin and the Ross families, and all three men had trap lines in the area that is now Thickwood Heights.

Mrs. McDonald had a large well-tended garden. Many of the raspberry bushes in the gardens downtown originated in her yard; she was happy to help newcomers develop their gardens. As well as a large garden, Mrs. McDonald took in boarders and nursed both her mother and her mother-in-law. They raised three children.

When Alex McDonald took over most of the undertaking duties from J.W. Mann, Mrs. McDonald made the linings of the wooden coffins. Funerals were rare in Waterways and McMurray, even in the '60s and '70s and the McDonalds carried out this responsibility with respect and dignity until they sold the business to Robert Anderson.

Alex died in 1978 and Enid lived for a further 24 years. She was a very active member of the Golden Years Society and loved to play cards and visit with her old friends.

Many Scottish families settled in northern Canada in the early years and Fort McMurray had its fair share. Hard working, honest and true pioneers, they helped build our north and left us a legacy to be proud of.

The Hill Family

The Hill family name is foremost amongst the leaders of the community from the 1920s to the end of the century. Walter Hill, a pharmacist, arrived in Fort McMurray in 1922 to assist the town's first resident druggist, Angus Sutherland. He became, over the years, the local historian, knowing everyone in town and greeting strangers and residents in a jovial manner when they stopped into the Drug Store on Franklin Avenue.

Walter served overseas during the First World War and it was there he visited old family friends and renewed friendship with Gladys. In 1923 she journeyed to Canada and they married in July. What a challenge and adventure it must have been for the young English bride-to-be to leave London, cross the ocean, embark on a long train journey across a vast continent and after her wedding in Edmonton to take a two day train journey across miles of muskeg to a small, isolated northern community. Such contrasts to her ordered life in what was then the greatest city in the world.

Walter Hill, in 1921, was one of the first graduates of the pharmacy program at the University of Alberta; his son Kenneth followed in his footsteps as did grandson David. Walter was offered two jobs: one in the growing town of Hollywood, California and the other in northern Alberta. His commitment to Angus Sutherland in McMurray also saw him spending some time in the drug store even farther north in Yellowknife, from 1938 to 1951.

The Hills had two sons, David and Kenneth, called Billy in early years. Ken's birth was a dramatic time for the family. In August 1932 the float plane, piloted by Lewis Leigh, was taking Mrs. Hill to hospital in Edmonton, and because of weather had to land at the seaplane base at South Cooking Lake. Mr. and Mrs. Hill were rushed to the nearby Leigh home and several minutes later a healthy son was born. Mother and son eventually got to hospital in Edmonton.

The young family of four lived in an apartment above the store. In July 1934 a disastrous fire burned all the buildings on the south side of Franklin Ave. Mrs. Hill escaped with the children and account books. The store was rebuilt and a new home built on Manning Avenue, in which Walter and Gladys lived until they died. The new store was the first building in town to have electricity and also the first to burn coal. As well as normal drug store items, the Hills sought to supply many needs to the growing community.

In 1945 tragedy struck the family when they received word that son David, the captain of a Lancaster Bomber with the Royal Canadian Air Force, had been shot down over Germany. Charlie Somers, the local telegraph officer, delivered the news to Walter in the drugstore. Within two years Mr. Somers had delivered five tragic telegrams to local families of the small community.

Both Walter and Gladys were active in the town. Gladys, in 1950, was the first woman ever elected to public office when she ran for municipal council. In the 1940s when the Girl Guides were first started in town she was one of the organizers. Perhaps, one of the least noted, but most important roles that Mrs. Hill undertook was to teach many of the local children to swim. They swam in the Snye, just a few blocks from the Hill's home and it was here too that the floatplanes landed and took off.

Walter was a charter member of the Royal Canadian Legion, the Masonic Lodge and a member of the Chamber of Commerce for over 50 years. His fame as the local storyteller and his stellar memory became a reference point for many interested in the local history. He maintained a guest book in the store and many are the names of government and industry officials recorded there.

When son Ken graduated from the University of Alberta he worked in the McMurray store as well as the one in Yellowknife. Gradually he took over the reins of the business but right into the 1980s Walter enjoyed his daily trip to the bank. Both Ken and his wife Diane involved themselves in the community. Diane was on the board that built the first women's shelter in town, served nine years on the Citizens' Appeal Committee and the Legal Aid Society. Ken served on the Town Council, School Board, Hospital Board and Keyano College board. Both were keenly interested in the history of the community and it was through their efforts that both the original Hill Drugs building and the Hill home from Manning Avenue were relocated to Heritage Park, along with many of the artifacts of the store and home.

As Fort McMurray grew with expanding oil sands operations the Hills saw the need for a bigger store and wider range of product. They constructed a new store in 1965 and then in 1972 a two-storey building was erected, housing the Hill store on the main floor. On the second floor CJOK, the new radio station had its offices, and Judge Mike Horrocks began his law career here. The spacious basement housed a variety of stores and offices. The larger store made room for many departments, including gifts, dinnerware and cosmetics. In 1988 the store was closed after being under Hill guidance for 66 years. Many loyal customers felt the loss; most of all the visiting and story telling they had enjoyed on many occasions.

Like most others in the small community both Hill families raised large gardens. There was no television, few telephones and intermittent radio reception in the first half of the century. In summer a Sunday afternoon trip up the Clearwater River for a picnic gave a break to the six and half days the store was open.

Walter Hill often recalled how his partnership with Angus Sutherland was done by a handshake and this partnership lasted until Sutherland's death in 1951. Years later, son Ken and Diane sold valuable property on the basis of a handshake. Trust and confidence in fellow residents and pride in the community they served characterized this remarkable McMurray family.

The Morimoto Family

The first Japanese family to come to Fort McMurray had an impact on our history, but also contributed through their children to their adopted country. Katsuhei (Tommy) arrived in Canada in 1906 and in 1917 his bride, Mitome came to Canada as a "picture bride". They spent their first years in Edmonton running a rooming house and barbershop. They left Edmonton because of high rents and the persuasiveness of Jim Cornwall, who arranged for him to buy two lots in McMurray. They arrived in 1920, and had Sven Swanson build them a two-storey house on their lots at the west end of Franklin Avenue.

The intent was to have a boarding house, when that was not financially successful the Morimotos turned to trapping and then to farming. He trapped muskrats on the Athabasca Delta, and attempted to muskrat farm on Kinosis Lake about 30 miles south of Fort McMurray. The marshy lake was ideal for muskrats; the only drawback was that the natives kept trapping his animals so there weren't enough left for a prosperous harvest. Bill Gregoire and Mr. Morimoto had built a log cabin on the site and the Morimoto family spent a memorable summer there while the father stayed in town to work on the farm. Eleven-year old Tommy and seven-year old Harry walked once a week three miles to the train track to pick up groceries that their father had sent on the train and the obliging NAR men dropped off on the side of the track.

The farming venture was successful with ten acres, leased from the Hudson's Bay Company, near the present day bridges, planted to vegetables. They shipped vegetables north on the steamboats and near the end of the season would invite the entire community for a corn roast.

Mr. Morimoto was a tiny man, just four foot ten, and weighed 92 pounds, but it was said he could easily carry a 200-pound sack of potatoes on his back. During the depression years, governments allowed people to "work off their taxes." And so during the summer Mr. Morimoto shoveled gravel on the roads, and he could outwork any of the strongest-looking and most burley men on the job.

Mr. & Mrs. Morimoto had seven sons, all who helped their father in the market garden. Young Tom recalled having to hoe a certain amount of rows of potatoes each day before being able to join his friends in a baseball game. In the winter they cut ice on the Clearwater River and sold it to residents for ten cents a block. In the days before electricity and refrigeration ice was kept in icehouses between layers of sawdust and in the hot days of summer would be brought out to keep foods cool and make refreshing drinks.

In the summer of 1938 tragedy struck the family with the death of Mrs. Morimoto and an infant son. They were buried in the McMurray cemetery.

All the Morimoto boys went on to make their mark in their chosen fields. In 2001 when the book society launched Irwin Huberman's bestseller *The Place We Call Home,* thirteen members of the Morimoto family came to the Homecoming. It was that weekend that the city put up the signs on Morimoto Drive along the Snye.

The oldest Morimoto boy, Tommy to his friends, loved playing baseball and softball with the local teams; Waterways and McMurray competed each week on the Prairie. Because Tommy was small, just four inches taller than his father, he was picked on and teased at school. He sent away for a book on boxing, and soon became proficient at this sport. Years later, in the army, he was to take the silver medal in the Canadian Forces in Britain.

At age 14, in 1932, Tommy went to high school in Edmonton and completed grades 11 and 12. With high school completed in the midst of the depression, and at 16, the only job Tommy could get was work on his dad's vegetable garden and a spring trip down the Athabasca on a scow with Alex McIvor trading goods for fur.

He started doing odd jobs around the Canadian Airways radio station and learned Morse code. He was offered a job at the trial oilsands plant at Bitumount by Robert Fitzsimmons and spent some months operating the radio and working in many aspects of the plant. None of the men were paid and they walked to McMurray, a distance of about 55 miles, in December. His next venture took him to Yellowknife where he joined his brother Bob and got jobs in cafes, cooking and washing dishes, and then in a mine.

Although too short and too light for Army standards, Tom Morimoto was accepted in the Royal Canadian Corps of Signals because of his radio experience. He was sent overseas and has the distinction of being the only Japanese-Canadian to land on the beaches of Normandy on June 6, 1944. He was with the Third Canadian Division and they fought their way into Germany, and then crossed into Belgium and Holland.

As a returning veteran Tommy was able to go to the University of Alberta and graduated as a chemical engineer. During this time he met his wife, Kim, a daughter of friends of his father. He worked at the Research Council in Edmonton and studied for his Masters.

Tom Morimoto's skills and knowledge of his field took him to many places in the world, including Texas, Latin America, Russia, North Africa and the Middle East. He, and his wife Kim, spent some years in Dubai where he was in charge of getting a gas plant on stream and then engineering and building a second plant. The Morimotos now live in Kelowna, and spend winters in Arizona.

What an amazing life, from Fort McMurray in the north, to wartime experiences and then to be one of the foremost men in the emerging oil and gas industries of Canada, and of the world. And in 2007 Tom Morimoto wrote a wonderful book, *Breaking Trail,* the story of the life of a man of humble beginnings who created his own success and contributed not only to his country but also to the world.

In *Breaking Trail* Tom wrote: "Looking back I am proud of having had a part in conserving some of the earth's resources by recovering propane, butane, condensate, and natural gas – resources that oil companies had previously wasted. I think this was the crowning achievement of my professional career." His book is a must read for anyone interested in the north, World War II, and a Canadian's involvement in the oil and gas industry throughout the world. He is truly a remarkable man.

The Legendary
Loutit Family

In 2004 I was privileged to meet two amazing, gracious ladies who told me the story of their family who lived in Fort McMurray in the first part of the last century. Their nephew, Doug Demers also gave me information on the family's history.

More than 80 years ago Ellen Loutit was born in a log cabin on MacDonald Avenue. Her sister Sarah was born at Poplar Point, north on the Athabasca River, a few years later. Lola, who married Hector Demers and lived in McMurray all her life, was one of the 12 children born to Billy and Agatha Loutit.

The Loutit family has a long and distinguished history in the north. Originally from Scotland, brought to Canada by the Hudson's Bay Company, one branch of the family settled in Fort Chipewyan. Billy was born there in 1877, the son of Peter Loutit, one of the first white settlers at the fort. Peter arrived in the northern fort in 1865 and married an aboriginal woman.

Billy was 17 when he started working as a deckhand for the Hudson's Bay Company. He worked on every HBC boat carrying freight on the Athabasca River until he retired in 1947.

In 1914 the sternwheeler S.S. *Athabasca River* was brought to Fort McMurray over the Grand Rapids and Billy was chosen as one of the pilots on the very first boat to negotiate the dangerous rapids. Just a year previously, while working in Athabasca, Billy met and married Agatha Ladouceur, the daughter of David and Marie Rose Ladouceur. This family name was prominent in Lac La Biche, Plamondon and Athabasca.

Billy was employed by the Hudson's Bay Company on the *Echo*. During the winters the family moved to Poplar Point, some 90 miles down the Athabasca River. Here he ran the HBC trading post. The Loutit daughters, in 2004, recalled their mother's wonderful cooking which was enjoyed by legendary pilots such as Punch Dickins and Wop May when they stopped at the trading post on their way north. Mrs. Loutit was a great seamstress and made all the family's clothing.

Mrs. Loutit could not read but was fluent in Cree, English and French and she played both the violin and the accordion. Billy was born in Fort Chipewyan and spoke Cree and Chipewyan as well as English and was a great communicator for many of the natives as they came to sell their wares.

Although the young family spent the winters almost in isolation at Poplar Point on the Athabasca River, after spring breakup they returned to McMurray where schooling was available. For some years they lived near the river where Boston Pizza is now located and they grew a large garden. Berry picking was a must each summer. In October Mother Loutit started the winter task of knitting socks and mittens for her family. She was also the family doctor, using medicines made from the wild. One winter Billy cut the end off his finger while cutting wood. She bound it up with a substance taken from a tree and it healed.

As well as his duties at the trading post Billy Loutit cut wood every winter for the steamboats that plied the river. He was a hard worker and very honest, and his daughters recalled he loved music and dancing and often acted as caller for square dances. In addition to the records Billy kept for The Bay, Billy kept a personal diary, writing in it daily.

Tommy Loutit, one of Billy's brothers, ran the HBC trading post at Fort McKay for a number of years and then moved west to the Chip Lakes area to operate The Bay post there. Billy took over the Fort McKay outlet for a couple of years after Tommy's departure and it was there that Agatha was mid-wife to numerous children, according to long time elder Fred MacDonald. Some of the Grandjambes of the area are descendants of Tony Loutit.

The two wonderful Loutit daughters that I interviewed in 2004 had come back to visit from their homes on Vancouver Island and Seattle. Ellen raised her six children in Fort McMurray, and worked at St. Gabriel Hospital for some years. Sarah married a US sailor in 1944 and eventually moved to Seattle where she worked at Boeing for 39 years.

The Loutit men had a reputation for hard work, stamina and speed. Athabasca Landing experienced a terrible flood in 1904. Billy Loutit was chosen to carry a dispatch to Edmonton to report the emergency. He ran over flooded roads, rough terrain, crossed overflowing creeks and arrived in 16 hours, before the messenger that had been dispatched on horseback. Each summer the town of Athabasca remembers this feat with the Billy Loutit Triathlon.

Another amazing run by Billy saw him take a Mounted Police dispatch, pulling a hand-sled from Fort Chipewyan to Fort Smith. He accomplished this trip, there and back, in three days.

The president of the Fort McMurray Métis Local #1395 for some years was Billy Loutit, a grandson of Billy and Agatha, and relatives say he is the "spitting image" of his grandfather.

A few years ago, Canadians were justly proud of another member of the Loutit family. Sean Loutit of Fort Smith was the pilot on two daring and successful rescue missions to the South Pole.

The Loutit family played an important part in the development of the northern frontier. Their navigational abilities and their community contributions are the stuff legends are made of.

The Demers Family, Four Generations

As a young man Louis Demers had a keen desire for travel and adventure. He left his birthplace of Minot, ND at a young age and decided that riding the rails would provide him with those experiences. He worked randomly at various towns along the way and became a professional gambler making substantial money. In 1905 Louis found himself in the fledgling city of Edmonton and heard of abundant work in the north at Athabasca Landing.

Athabasca Landing was the transportation gateway to the north, having replaced the Saskatchewan-Meythe Portage-Clearwater route. Louis worked on the docks, helping to load the river scows that took freight to Fort McMurray. He was also one of the first persons to successfully drive a team of horses over the old House River trail to the northern community. He and his partner lost one of their two teams on this first effort.

Louis Demers settled in Waterways and began a water delivery service to residents. He stabled his horses at a cousin's farm, along with the horses of other teamsters. The cousin, Bob Labarge owned the property beside the Clearwater River that is now a municipal park and is known by the locals as the Horse Pasture. It had earlier been called Cree flats. One of Louis other profitable ventures was bootlegging. This was a sideline to his taxi business; he was the first to operate a taxi between Waterways and Fort McMurray.

Louis met and married a young Norwegian lady, Bessie, who was cooking at one of the local restaurants. They lived in a home on Railway Avenue in Waterways until their deaths in 1954 and 1962.

A nephew, Ernie Demers, arrived from Manitoba in 1929 and went to work for his uncle driving taxi. He worked for the McInnes Fish Company for a time, but was laid off during the Great Depression of the 1930s. McInnes could not sell all the fish that their boats caught in Lake Athabasca, and when they had a surplus they would give them to employees and ex-employees rather than throw them away. Barb Mungall, one of Ernie's daughters, recalls that her father would trade fish for other commodities the family needed during these hard times.

Ernie also worked for the Ryan Brothers, who operated a successful transportation business. He later worked at the Abasand Oil Plant.

Nearly all Canadians experienced hard times during the depression of the 1930s, but farmers on the prairies were especially hard hit because they had also had years of drought. And so Ernie's younger brother, Hector, made his way from Manitoba to Fort McMurray in 1937 to make his start driving taxi for his uncle. Hector spoke only French when he arrived and was pleasantly surprised to find so many here who could understand him and speak French as well.

Soon Hector went further north to work in the gold mines in Yellowknife. He staked claims around Uranium City, which was a booming centre in those days. He determined that to do this efficiently he needed a float plane, and partnered with Joe Durocher of Lac La Biche, who owned the power plant in McMurray. Brother Ernie also had a floatplane.

At about this time Ernie decided to start a new business, calling it Demers Lumber. One of his first employees was Edward "Muskwa" Cooper, who started work at the age of 13.

The claims staked by brothers Ernie and Hector were rich but transportation and financial concerns were prohibitive, so Hector came back to McMurray and started his business, Demers Transfer. The railway had been continued from Draper to Waterways, but freight still had to be hauled from the railhead to Northern Transportation yards to be loaded onto barges. One of Hector's first dedicated employees was Elmer Marlowe.

Hector brought in coal from southern Alberta and sold and delivered it to customers in Waterways and McMurray. This is how he met his wife, Lola Loutit, daughter of Captain Billy and Agatha. Lola was cooking at the Oilsands Café, and later at the Abasand Oil Plant. An excellent cook, she enjoyed her vocation for many years; after Hector died she cooked on the dredges of the Department of Public Works and the snag boat, *Athabasca*.

The brothers formed a partnership of Demers Lumber Company, with a mill where the Syncrude towers were built at the end of Franklin Ave. In 1957 Ernie and Hilda sold their share to Hector and moved to Edmonton. Nephew Doug recalls that his uncle said some of his fondest McMurray memories were of the generosity and closeness of its residents. He particularly told how Ed Hansen of Hansen's Store and the managers of the Hudson's Bay extended credit when times were tough. Roy Hawkins, who was CP Airlines manager in those days, told Doug Demers that he had once allowed Ernie to collect a COD package before paying. Ernie's reputation was such that Roy was not worried about collecting.

Hector Demers started the Demers Contracting Company Ltd. in 1956. Albert Lacombe was a fifty percent partner for the new company that had graders, bulldozers, winch trucks and bunkhouses. They provided the oil exploration companies with equipment and expertise in working in muskeg bush country. The company did road building and site preparation in the town as well as maintaining the airport, Stoney Mountain and Fort McKay roads. Along with an out of town construction company, they jointly built the wooden bridge over the Hangingstone.

Hector was influential in the town and well known throughout northern Alberta. He was a cheerful and humorous man, well known for his generosity. He would often keep people on the payroll when there was little work to be had. He would give anyone a chance. Art Hoehne, a young Baptist minister, who came to town in the '60s told Hector's son Doug that everyone he approached for a job at first gave him the cold shoulder, except for Hector who put him to work regardless of his religious calling.

Hector worked at his business until the time of his death in 1975. His wife, Lola, much loved by all who knew her, died in 1986. Their four children all live in Fort McMurray. As Doug says, "We cannot envision calling any other place home; the Demers/Loutit connection goes back almost a century and half, and the aboriginal ancestry even further. This place still provides us the opportunities that our early ancestors recognized so long ago."

Hugh Stroud,
A Working Man

He was born the year the Great War started and served with distinction in the Second World War. Hugh Stroud's father was killed in that first war, and in 1921 Hugh moved to Fort McMurray with his mother and stepfather. Their home and barn were located at the corner of Franklin Avenue and Father Mercredi Street and the cows roamed freely during the day. It was young Hugh's job to bring the cows in for evening milking and the next morning to deliver milk to their customers. He used his two dogs for this chore; they pulled a sleigh in the winter and wagon in the summer.

As a young man Hugh Stroud delivered wood and water to the town's residents. In 1937 he built a rock cairn to commemorate the first explorer and fur trader, Peter Pond. He used his horses to haul the rocks and gravel. It was placed in front of the new Peter Pond School and as well as an historical monument it was used for years as a survey coordinate. After the school was torn down the cairn was moved to the Public School Board office on Franklin Avenue. A few years later the Downtown Business Revitalization Zone had the cairn relocated to the Snye as part of their historical projects.

In 1942 Mr. Stroud joined the Royal Canadian Air Force and was sent to Britain on loan to the RAF. He was a tail gunner and flew in 40 operations. When he returned from the war he brought a bride, Joan, back to McMurray with him.

Always a diligent worker Hugh Stroud built and operated a sawmill on the Athabasca River near the Snye and logged near Mountain Rapids on the Athabasca.

At this time he was a member of the school board and never missed a meeting. He would walk the seven miles from his logging camp on the Athabasca and after the meeting walk the seven miles back to the camp. He served on the school board for ten years and was on the town council for ten years.

In 1966 Hugh was hired by Great Canadian Oil Sands. He worked at that plant, later named Suncor, until he retired in 1978.

Always interested in the community Hugh was a founding member of the Royal Canadian Legion and served as president for some years. He was an active participant and volunteer for Heritage Park and also a member and contributor of the society that published *The Place We Call Home*, a history of Fort McMurray.

From the days when Hugh, as a young boy, delivered milk before school in all types of weather to his later years as a dedicated volunteer, his was the type that made our community a great place to live.

The McCormick Family

Henry Alexander "Mac" McCormick arrived in Fort McMurray in 1936 and his bride, Marion joined him in 1940, Marion, a nurse at the Royal Alexandria Hospital in Edmonton, went on a "blind date" and met the man with whom she would share her life for the next 40 years.

Mac McCormick came from a wealthy Ontario family who owned Lake of the Woods milling company that produced Red Rose flour. The youngest in the family, Mac rebelled against following the family tradition and scorned a career in banking and rode the rails to the west. In those days of little employment he made his living as a pool shark. In fact he was so good at the game that pool halls barred him from playing, as he was unbeatable.

When he arrived in McMurray, Mac went to work for Jack Fairburn who had the flour concession for the village. He also worked for the Hudson's Bay Transportation Company as a foreman, traveling into the north.

In 1953 the McCormicks, with the help of Marion's father, a pharmacist in Edmonton, purchased the Imperial Oil Bulk plant on the Prairie. This was sold in the 1970s to Orest Bodnarchuk. During the years the McCormicks ran the plant they sold oil and gas to all communities in the north, shipping it by barge in the summer months. He also delivered heating oil to homes in Waterways and McMurray.

A reserved, quiet, intelligent man, Mr. McCormick was said to work around the clock. He may have left the family business behind in Ontario but he brought with him the skills and ambition that made his local ventures prosper. He was able to add columns of figures, without error, at a speed that made customers marvel.

Marion McCormick, on the hand, was an independent outgoing woman who liked to entertain the couples' friends. Just like her husband she was involved in many aspects of community life. At times she assisted Dr. McDonald, the local physician. She was president of the Anglican Women's Group and played the organ for St. Aidan's Church in Waterways. She was an excellent singer and also led the choir.

The McCormicks adopted two children, Stuart and Elizabeth. Stuart was a teacher and moved to Edmonton. Elizabeth married a former schoolmate, Bruce Golosky.

The Fairbairns had their son-in-law, Tommy Fraser, build for them a beautiful log home overlooking the Clearwater River in Waterways. When the McCormicks bought the bulk agency from Mr. Fairbairn they also bought this house. For some years residents went to this home for marriage licenses or to register births, as the McCormicks looked after the vital statistics for the province. Mr. McCormick was Town Board chairman from 1965-1968, and served as board member for several terms. He was active with the Chamber of Commerce and also was acting magistrate for a time.

Like his friends Claire Peden and Bob Duncan, Mac McCormick was vocal in opposition to blocking off the Snye. He predicted this important waterway would become a stagnant pool. Mac commented that the engineers from the city might be book smart, but they knew nothing about rivers and bush country.

Mr. McCormick died of cancer in January 1974. Mrs. McCormick battled cancer for many years and died in 1996 in Edmonton. They were a remarkable couple that through their business and community involvement left our home a better place.

Eymundson,
The Telephone Man

Telephone installation between Waterways and McMurray was just one of the enterprises the ambitious Charles Eymundson undertook. At various times he operated a trading post down the Athabasca, ran a store near Draper and one in Waterways. He opened a pool hall, and later converted it to a bunkhouse for the fish plant workers. In his pre-McMurray days he worked for a detective agency, as well as being a cook, a sawyer and lumberjack. His motto was: "Efficiency, Economy and Endurance. Apply these three Es now, they lead to ease later."

Mr. Eymundson was a prodigious writer and his granddaughters have shared some of his newspaper clippings with me. These excerpts tell the story of this amazing man. He subscribed to the London Times (bound into monthly segments), the Chicago Herald and National Geographic. He had a collection of Shakespeare as well as many other books.

Charlie Eymundson was born in Iceland in 1872 and immigrated to North Dakota with his parents at age nine. Charlie's father, Sigurdur, died just four years later and his mother, Johanna, and her children immigrated to Canada.

A newspaper article he wrote in 1941 says: "In 1910 I became tired of roaming around and took unto myself a wife, and in order to get away from all the deviltries of civilization moved that year into the wilds of the north, Fort McMurray." His wife Sophia, was also of Icelandic origin, and in 1897 had immigrated to Manitoba, walking behind a Red River cart from North Dakota.

After a trip down the Athabasca River by scow, when Sophia's trunk of precious possessions was lost in the Grand Rapids, the couple took up squatter's rights on the river. They built a log house, chinked with moss and with a sod roof. Charlie trapped and sold furs to the Hudson's Bay Company. Then he began trading with the native trappers himself and one time took his own furs to Chicago where he received top prices for his prime furs. He bought the Franklin Hotel, and rumour has it he lost it in an all night poker game.

The Eymundson's first son Romeo was born in July 1911 and he had the distinction of being the first white baby born in this northern community. The next year Charlie Eymundson, in a community meeting, made a motion that a public school be established in Fort McMurray. William Gordon seconded the motion. Appointed to the school committee were: William Biggs, Mr. McKenzie and Alex MacDonald.

Also in 1912 Mr. Eymundson wrote of traveling to Edmonton for supplies with his wife and infant son and meeting many travellers coming north ill-prepared for the weather and hardships of the journey. "Oil fever" had struck, he said, and it would cause a rush similar to that of the Klondike.

When the railroad came the family built a large home and trading post at Cheecham. Later when the railroad reached Waterways they moved to that community and built a "General Merchants Store" which operated in competition to the Hudson's Bay Store until the 1940s.

In 1929 Dr. Karl Clark hired Charlie and son Romeo to take him up the Clearwater River to view a site where Von Weimarn had set up a drilling rig on an island about 50 miles from Waterways. Dr. Clark was impressed with the Clearwater River, calling it "one of the beauty spots of the north." It was a few miles lower on the river that Romeo for many years had a trapline and built a log cabin across from a wooded island. Romeo worked at the McInnes Fish Plant, loaded barges and helped his father maintain the telephone lines, and trapped in the winters.

In 1942 Romeo, along with brother Darrow, joined the Royal Canadian Air Force. With two of his sons away, Mr. Eymundson sold his store to the HBC for $2000.

In 1944 Romeo met his wife Agnes Olson, a member of the Canadian Women's Army Core, at a service function and they were married in Calgary. After they were discharged they settled in Waterways near the Hangingstone River and Romeo built a log house. Romeo's father lived with the family for a time and then went to a home in Edmonton. He died in 1966 at the age of 94.

The Eymundson family spent winters on the trapline up the Clearwater. In 1960 the family, now with eight children, moved to a home on Bulyea Avenue, directly opposite the Legion.

Romeo was well respected at any job he held. Art Hoehne, whose job it was to pick up men to work on the construction of the airport in 1955, wrote: "I was very impressed with Romeo as he was always ready and waiting when I would arrive – which is more than I could say for many of the other men who had partied most of the night." Romeo was an expert in navigating the ever-changing Clearwater River channels, and said his river experience was gained while traveling on the Athabasca River with his dad when trading for furs.

Always an early riser, in the winter Romeo could often be seen shoveling his sidewalk at four or five a.m. The Eymundson home on Bulyea Avenue was torn down a few years ago, but the shed that Romeo built of logs from the Hawker Store still stands on the back lane. He converted his wood cook stove to gas, and when he bought a new one gave the old one to his neighbour. It was reconstituted as a wood stove and now serves to warm a trapper's cabin on the shores of Gordon Lake. Romeo died in 1990, having seen the tiny village of Waterways amalgamate with its neighbour three miles away to become the booming City of Fort McMurray.

Jack Fairbairn:
Businessman, Councillor & Traveller

One of Waterways earliest entrepreneurs is remembered fondly and with respect today. Elmer Cree remembers him as a real gentleman that liked to help the native people; as long as you were honest and paid him back he would give credit when you needed it. Elmer recalls Mr. Fairbairn spearheading the construction of a bridge each spring to cross the Hangingstone River. He would either supply or scrounge the boards and help with the building, thus enabling native families who camped in the bush along the Clearwater to cross to Waterways.

Elsie Hyska said Mr. and Mrs. Fairbairn were always there when a family had needs. Because he kept a warehouse with Robin Hood flour, oatmeal, dog food and other staples there were often times when local families turned to him for help.

John Richardson Fairbairn came to Calgary from Scotland as a young bank apprentice. He had begun his apprenticeship at the mature age of 13 in Scotland. He worked for a time in Calgary, but hearing that there was more money to be made in the north he and a friend headed for Athabasca. They got jobs with Lands and Forests cruising timber.

The summer that Jack turned 17 they were working in the Horse River area and had to survey a specified amount of bush each day. Their groceries were supplied, along with their regular "grub" they brought along a case of Carnation condensed milk and a case of Pabulum. With a length of cable 13 feet long, frazzled on one end, they pushed it down a foxhole. When it came to a stop they turned it and then withdrew the cable to inspect the fur. If it was a silver fox they immediately started to dig and claim a kit for themselves. These kits were fed on the condensed milk and pabulum, and transported to their next camp in a gunnysack.

When winter arrived they headed for Athabasca and were able to sell the live kits for $1000 each. Their summer catch was nine baby foxes; their trapping hobby paid more than their day job.

When Jack arrived in Athabasca he was to learn war had begun in Europe. He lied about his age, enlisted, went overseas, and the first day on the front his leg was shot off below the knee. He was angry and miserable and felt his life was over. He was moved to a ward where all the soldiers had missing limbs; one had lost not only both legs but his arms as well. And yet the men in the ward were cheerful; when he arrived they struck up "For he's a Jolly Good Fellow." His attitude changed and he determined to make something of his life.

A few years later he married Edna and they moved to "old Waterways", just above Draper at the end of the rail. He acquired the Imperial Oil Agency and delivered fuel by loading five-gallon square tins of kerosene and oil into his canoe and delivering to McMurray customers. When the railway was finished to Waterways he set up his oil depot next to the Hudson's Bay warehouse on the river.

When World War II broke out there was a boom in Waterways. Before the Fairborn's son Roy enlisted in the navy he bought a truck to haul freight to the Northern Transportation docks. He made enough money the first month to pay for the truck and give him wages for five years.

Jack was hired by the American army to expedite their freight that came in on the train. He shipped Imperial Oil products to the U.S. project at Norman Wells, in the Territories. He was able to provide valuable expertise and advice for barge loading and he could always find equipment and supplies. His enterprises and hard work made him a wealthy man.

A few years later Mr. Fairbairn sold the Imperial Oil agency to his daughter and son-in-law, Jean and Tommy Fraser. They built a beautiful log house overlooking the river on Cliff Avenue and later sold the home and agency to Mac McCormick.

As well as starting the Imperial Oil agency Jack Fairbairn had the franchise for Robin Hood flour. His warehouse was on the bank of the Clearwater just behind the Northern Alberta Railway station. He shipped flour, rolled oats and dog food north on the barges, often as far as the Arctic Ocean.

In 1959 Edna Fairbairn died suddenly. For several winters Jack travelled on ocean freighters seeing different parts of the world. He would return in the spring to attend to his flour business and go fishing at the mouth of the Hangingstone River. The bridge he initiated each spring gave access to a great fishing spot and he'd often present Art Hoehne, then Swanson Lumber manager, a catch of walleye first thing in the morning.

Mr. Fairbairn's Scottish ancestry and his banker's training were evident in his business practices. One winter, Art Hoehne recalled, he was asked to look after the flour business while Mr. Fairbairn was off on a freighter. When spring arrived and Jack came back to Waterways, Art handed him the sheet of accounts that were off by a penny. "Find it," said Jack, "if you are out a penny, you might be out $1,000. It has to balance." Hours of checking the accounts passed and Art found he'd written a figure down wrong. When he returned the balanced sheet, Mr. Fairbairn didn't even look at it, but remarked, "Now that is proper bookkeeping!"

Jack Fairbairn's generosity and kindness were known throughout the community but he was no pushover. One time he noticed his woodpile was going down quicker than it should be. He hid behind it during the noon hour break and saw one of his workers helping himself. A resounding whack with a board across the worker's backside caused him to drop the wood and go on his way. Jack said he never lost any more wood, but kept good relations as well with his workers.

When the Fairbairns first moved to "new" Waterways they lived behind the Imperial Oil warehouses between the main railway tracks and the spur line. Later they moved to a house next door to the Anglican Church, where they had a beautiful yard with fruit trees and a large bed of peonies.

Mr. Fairbairn served on the McMurray town council from 1955 to 1958. He died in 1967, at the age of 77, and is buried next to his wife in the downtown cemetery. He overcame his personal tragedy, was a contributing citizen and businessperson, and I would think enjoyed his travelling years.

Gus Hawker,
A Different Sort

Among our Fort McMurray characters, Gus Hawker must be counted in the top ten. He was born in the Cotswolds in England and educated in Bath, where he was more interested in trapping moles for pocket money and fun. There were twelve children in the Hawker family, and by age 20 Gus decided to leave home and as well left a fiancée behind. He landed in Montreal with just ten cents in his pocket and made his way to Winnipeg.

Gus tried farming in Saskatchewan and then decided to homestead in the Peace River area, leaving another sweetheart behind. His crops failed in the Peace Country so he set off for Fort McMurray to trap squirrels. He said he made $80 the first season and lost it all when his boat sank in the Athabasca River and he had to walk seventy miles into town.

For twelve years Gus Hawker lived in Waterways and had a store stocked to the rafters with groceries and supplies. He amazed his customers by seeming to know where everything was in the most untidy clutter. For Gus, far away fields always looked greener or for him golden and in the early fifties he left for Goldfields in Saskatchewan. When Uranium City started to boom he was one of the first to erect a tent and start selling supplies.

Hawker's Store did a brisk business in groceries as well as buying furs and selling trapping supplies. He had orders for furs from Italy and other parts of Europe. Although he claimed to have no faith in uranium he staked some of the prospectors and took shares in their claims. In 1952 he said he had sales of over $200,000.

The Hawker children were all named for the months they were born in: April, May, June, August and October. Gus had been back to visit his brothers on their farms several times and in 1952 he decided to take his children to witness the festivities around the Queen's coronation. They got as far as Toronto and found there was no available seat on any plane. This did not stop Mr. Hawker who chartered a plane and crew for a cost of about $17,000 and flew across the ocean.

While in England he caused quite a stir with his tales of the wild north and the uranium. He was dubbed "Mr. Uranium" by several British newspapers and spoke on the BBC radio. He returned and started several uranium companies, including one in New York and Britain, none of which were successful.

Gus Hawker died in July 1979; his Uranium City store was torn down in 1981. And what happened to his buildings in Waterways? Art Hoehne, the Baptist Church pastor bought the property for just over $300 in 1958; it was going to be put up for tax sale. There were four well-built buildings on the site; Mr. Hoehne gave them away. Gary Wilson, who lived directly across the street from the store, took the garage and shed; Romeo Eymundson took the log house. He took it apart log by log and used part of it to construct a shed. In 2011 this sturdy shed is still standing facing the lane behind Bulyea Avenue on Eymundson's lot.

Joe Dixon, former policeman and later a Waterways market gardener, attempted to move the store but the skids went to pieces at the junction of the old airport road and the main road to Fort McMurray so it was pushed off to the side road. Joe carefully dismantled the well-constructed building bit by bit and then built it again.

Gus Hawker wrote a book of about one hundred pages but could not find a publisher because of the libel content. He was critical of authority, of the police, the church, and the banks. He was always up for a new challenge and I'm sure those who knew him would not soon forget him.

Bill Tatum,
A Self Made Man

Many extraordinary people have populated the Wood Buffalo region, as well as many ordinary citizens, and each one in one way or another has left their mark on their families, friends and community. This story is of such a man; a character and individual that sadly we do not see too often in this modern conformist era. I wrote this story for the Fort McMurray Express in January 1985 just after Bill Tatum died. My sons, Mark and Phil were having coffee with their dad and I on a cold winter morning and reminisced about this extraordinary man.

Bill Tatum, a man who lived life to the fullest, was a man well known to old timers in Lac La Biche, Chard and Fort McMurray. Standing six foot three inches in his sock feet, and weighing in at 275 pounds in his prime, Mr. Tatum was a big man, with a voice to match, and everything he did, he did in a big way. He died at age 67 in Edmonton of a heart condition.

Bill Tatum was born in the Lac la Biche area, into a family that had emigrated from Kansas. His father was a farmer who owned an island in the lake at Lac La Biche and had a fantastic market garden. Young Bill and his only sister Lucille attended school in Lac La Biche. Then Bill was sent to school in Edmonton for two or three years and in later life said it took ten years of pure living in the bush to get the pollution out of his lungs from the coal-smoke-filled air of the city.

For some years Bill fished commercially on the lake at Lac La Biche and when he died he still had the old fishing nets from those days. He made his living trapping for a time. From all reports he was an excellent trapper, as hard work was the thing he did best.

Bill and his wife Alvina moved to Christina Crossing in 1959. They were so poor they lived in a tent made of flour sacks. They began a trading post to service the communities of Christina Crossing, Garson Lake, Chipewyan Prairie and Cheecham. He built roads into the areas and constructed bridges as well as clearing considerable farm land, thus opening up the area for natives who lived there.

At that time there were almost a dozen families at Christina Crossing; now there are none. Garson Lake boasted 20 to 30 houses. The trappers came for miles with their toboggans laden with furs to trade at Tatum's. One year Tatum's Trading Post shipped more fur than any other independent buyer in the north. The trappers came from all over northeastern Alberta and nearby Saskatchewan.

In 1961 the Tatum family moved to Janvier (Chard). Here they leased one-quarter section of land for a ranch and operated a store and trading post. Hard work and paying one's own way were cardinal rules in the Tatum household; Bill, Alvina and their ten children worked together to develop the ranch and store.

Bill ran 100 head of cattle right up till his death. He raised them on the ranch and trucked the ones for market over a winter road to Edmonton.

Bill loved horses and always kept some. Most of his road building and land clearing was done totally with a team of horses. He hayed his quarter section of land with horses until 1969 when he bought his first tractor.

The Tatum family kept three acres of garden and grew fantastic vegetables. Some potatoes were sold but most of the vegetables were used by the family throughout the winter. They were stored in a well-built root house that withstood the minus-fifty degree days. Mrs. Tatum canned and pickled hundreds of jars as well.

Bill was too independent to believe in a lot of our modern ways. He never did apply for his Old Age Pension – he didn't believe in getting something for nothing. For years he refused to pay Alberta Health Care premiums. But he didn't quibble when presented with a hospital bill; he simply paid it with $100 bills, quantities of which he always carried. For Bill did not believe in writing cheques. He always carried cash, and lots of it. It was not unusual for him to have $30 to $50 thousand dollars on him in cash.

School held too many distractions to hard work, Bill believed. Consequently he refused to send his youngsters to school and Mrs. Tatum helped them with correspondence at home.

Someone as independent as Bill was sure to skirt the edge of the law at times in his life. Although in court several times, he was never convicted of an infraction. A day in court when Bill Tatum appeared was even better than a Holywood movie. His courtroom manner was both boisterous and witty; his booming voice could be heard throughout the building.

As well as being strong-minded Bill was exceptionally strong physically. On his 66th birthday he was moving hay bales with a forklift. A dog chasing mice in the hay distracted him for a moment and he was not in time to get out of the way of a bale falling directly toward him. He saw the 1000-pound bale coming at him and bent over the steering wheel to minimize the effect. The bale hit him full in the back. Soon after his two-week stay in the hospital he was back to his usual working day.

Under his bold and brash exterior Bill had a kindly heart. While the Tatums lived at Christina Crossing, Bill and his team were the official taxi. One winter a grandmother, thought to be at death's door, was to be sent to hospital in Edmonton by the twice-weekly train. The grandma, believing herself ready to die, begged to go to Chard to see the priest. Although this was a 40-mile trip out of the way, and the weather was at 40 below zero, Bill took her. He built a tent on the back of the sleigh and put a firebox into it to keep grandma comfortable. Bill and his horses safely saw her through the trip and met the train to

Edmonton. Add to this the facts that Bill was not a Catholic and that he refused payment for the trip.

Bill was said to treat his customers fairly and kindly. He was well liked and respected in the community of Janvier. He was a real leader. One who knew him well described him as a Howard Hughes type. Another said, "If everyone looked after their self and their family in the independent way he did we wouldn't need all the social programs he so despised."

Bill was a self made man. When he died he was considered a prosperous man with considerable assets, all acquired by hard work and a natural aptitude for success.

However Bill Tatum is remembered: as a kindly neighbour, as a bold entrepreneur, or as a self-driven man; one thing is sure, he will be remembered. His inclusion in this book is a tribute to the man himself.

Hawkins,
Serving for Three Generations

When Syd Hawkins was transferred by the RCMP to Fort McMurray in 1926, he couldn't have known what an influence his family would have on this community. Born in Scotland, Mr. Hawkins came to Canada and joined the North West Mounted Police. When the Great War broke out in 1914 he went back to England and joined the Black Watch. He was a prisoner of war for two years.

When the war ended he returned to Canada and rejoined the national police force that had been renamed Royal Canadian Mounted Police in 1920. In Edmonton he met his wife, who was from Scotland also and had come to Canada to follow her nursing profession. In 1921 the Hawkins family saw McMurray for the first time as they came by train to Waterways and took a steamboat north to an RCMP post in Fort Simpson, NWT.

When the transfer from isolated Fort Simpson came it must have seemed like a step towards civilization when they arrived at the new posting at Fort McMurray. His son, Roy, five at the time, recalls walking from the steamboat that had brought them out of the north to the RCMP station. After a further two years with the police force Syd Hawkins decided to venture into business and left the force. He bought a wagon and team of horses and hauled salt from the plant at Abasand to the railway in Waterways. In 1947 the RCMP told town council policing would be their responsibility from then on. The town went through several policemen and finally persuaded Syd Hawkins to serve and this he did for a year.

Son Roy was a much loved and respected McMurray citizen. As a youth he attended a two-room school on Franklin Avenue and remembers some days when it was so cold the ink would freeze in the inkwells. He was a keen sportsman, playing ball and hockey on fields and rinks the players often developed themselves. He vividly recalled the fire that destroyed much of Franklin Avenue in 1934.

When World War II broke out Roy had just completed grade eleven and despite objections from his father, along with four of his friends, rode the train to enlist in Edmonton. As none of them had the train fare, Patrick O'Coffey, Alphonse Dusseault, Johnny Webb, Real Martin, along with Roy jumped into a boxcar to make the two-day trip. In December they were sent to England.

Roy joined the Canadian Army security section, working under the British MI-5. He was given a motorbike to use. One of Roy's missions was on the ill-fated Dieppe raid. The intent of the raid was to determine the strength and knowledge of the German radar operations. One of Britain's foremost radar experts, Jack Nissenthall, volunteered to investigate. With him went eleven soldiers who were to guard and protect him. Because of Nissenthall's knowledge of top-secret information, the book written about him and the raid says the soldier's orders were to shoot him if there was any danger of him being captured alive. Roy disputed this claim, saying Canadian soldiers would never have been ordered to shoot an ally.

Sgt. Roy Hawkins was one of these soldiers; he later described the day as the wildest in his life. He was wounded but managed to swim to an Allied ship, as did Nissenthall. Years later Jack Nissenthall visited Roy in Fort McMurray. The Dieppe Raid, thought for years to be a disaster, actually is said to have changed the course of the war. The gripping story of the raid is told in a now out of print book, *Green Beach*. Long time McMurray history buff Bert MacKay located and purchased old books and presented several to the Roy Hawkins Fire Hall. Roy Hawkins was honoured and received medals from

Canada, Great Britain, France and the United States for his role in the Dieppe raid.

One night while in England Roy summoned up the courage to speak to a pretty young lady outside a movie theatre. Rowena would become his wife and move to Waterways in 1945. Roy and Rowena had three children, Rick, Pat and Bev and after they were grown Rowena worked for many years at Hill Drugs. She died of cancer in 1987.

Roy's great boyhood friend Pat O'Coffey was killed in Sicily in 1943; he single handily attempted to take out a German gun nest. Mrs. O'Coffey welcomed the young men who returned from the war and along with other members of the International Order of Daughters of the Empire, was instrumental in starting the branch of the Royal Canadian Legion.

Roy joined the volunteer fire department. There were no fire hydrants but barrels of sand were located throughout the community and water was hauled to the scene of a fire. McMurray's first fire truck was so heavy when full of water, that only burly Mike Kolewaski, owner of the Oilsand's Hotel, could drive it. On its very first trip down Franklin Avenue the back wheels had fallen off the axel and were proceeding down the street ahead of the fire truck that then ground to a halt. The tank was shortened and the truck served McMurray from 1956 to the early '60s.

After 19 years as a volunteer Roy was hired as a full time fire chief in 1974. Archie Goodwin, Joe Gauthier and Tom Weber, also staunch volunteers, along with chief Hawkins made up the town's first fire department.

As the city grew fire halls became a necessity and Roy oversaw the building of three fire halls in two years. Number One Hall at the corner of the highway and Tolen Drive was named for our first fire chief. Besides building fire halls, Chief Hawkins instigated the amalgamation of the ambulance with fire protection, McMurray becoming one of the first communities in Alberta to do so.

Roy retired in 1981 and remained very active in the community until his death in 2007.

Son Rick served in the Fire Department, first as a volunteer, then as a paid fire fighter, and then headed up the fire prevention division. Now Rick is retired and a Heritage Park director and active community supporter. Seldom has a community seen three generations as dedicated to their hometown as the Hawkins have been.

The Tolens,
From Dusty Saskatchewan

Ma and Pops Tolen first came to Waterways in 1926. They rented a house for a few years and then returned to Saskatchewan but came back in the early 1930s and Ma declared she would never again move back to the dirty, dusty, windy prairie.

Peder Tolen had gone to Saskatchewan from the Dakotas where his parents had settled after emigrating from Sweden. Lavina, of Welsh ancestry, came from Manitoba. A brother Nels also came to Alberta and had a farm in Anzac. He was an accomplished chef and worked for a time on the riverboats.

Pops worked at the Hudson's Bay Company warehouse, and during the busy summer months Ma took in boarders. They had three sons: Lawrence, Russell (Herc) and Roy. Ma Tolen wanted a girl desperately and kept Russell's golden locks long for a few years. One of his cousins looked at him and said, "He looks just like Hercules in the funnies." From that time on the second son was always called Herc.

In the winter of 1938 Peder, his brother Nels and son Herc cut down trees on the present site of the Legion. They skidded the logs across the street and built a log home. Total cost of $120 included land, doors, shingles, flooring and nails. In 1972 the house was jacked up and the bottom logs replaced. This was also the year they celebrated 60 years of marriage. The home, with a cottage roof, still stands on Bulyea Avenue but the logs have now been covered with siding. Ma Tolen planted spruce trees in front of the home.

The Tolens bought the first wringer washer, powered by gas into town, purchased from the T. Eaton catalogue. Pops built a shelter for it in the side yard. Ma invited the other Waterways ladies to come and use it and washdays became a social occasion. She bought a 1950 Austin from the Yellowknife HBC manager; delighted to drive her friends in summer, but never drove it in the winter. During the war she cooked on the boats; in winter she had knitting bees in her home and sent the socks and mittens to the soldiers.

Pops Tolen always had a project and was very organized. He had a jar for straight nails, one for crooked nails, one for rubber bands, and a place for string. Nothing was wasted and his policy was: measure twice, cut once. He built a root house that was always stocked with vegetables from their abundant garden.

Both Herc and Roy joined up during World War II. Herc was an MP in the Airforce and with the Canadian forces that liberated Holland. He also helped liberate the extermination camps and worked in Germany during the trials at Nuremberg. A friend said he was a changed man after the war. He had been top of his class in university in Latin and physics. During his university years he worked on the boats for Mackenzie River Transport.

It was after the war while working in construction building Highway 16 that Herc met Alwyn. They were married in 1954 and lived in Edmonton until 1957 when Lawrence persuaded Herc to move back to Waterways. They sold all they had and joined Lawrence, who was married to Jessie, in the business of Tolen's Cartage. They hauled water to homes, delivered freight throughout Waterways and McMurray and Lawrence had the Robin Hood Flour and McGavins Bread concessions.

Later on Herc worked for Alberta Power; Bob Duncan who headed the electric company here was his great friend. When he retired he maintained the grounds at the Legion and at St. Aidan's Anglican Church.

Alwyn worked at the Northern Alberta Railway station just across the street from their home on Railway Avenue. She volunteered as Secretary-

Treasurer of the Public School District, and when the boom came and McMurray expanded rapidly this became a full time paid position. Alwyn loved to read and belonged to the Waterways Community Club that started the first public library. She was a most outspoken lady and was not afraid to speak her mind to anyone. If she believed an injustice was being done she would do what she could do fix it, and not quietly. Her daughter Rhonda recalls her mother taking a phone call in the kitchen one Sunday morning from a corporation discussing why they should pay school taxes. Rhonda says her mother won that argument. Her motto was: "If you don't fight city hall, you get what you deserve."

A little known aspect of Alwyn's role in the community, according to daughter Rhonda, was that of taking in children who needed temporary shelter. Rhonda said it was not unusual for her and her brothers to awaken to find little ones asleep in the living room. It might only be for a night or two, but neighbouring children knew there was a safe haven at the Tolen house on Railway Ave.

Ma and Pops Tolen remained active in the community until they moved to Barrhead in 1977 to join Lawrence and Jessie who had moved the year previously.

Her granddaughter remembers Ma's Hallowe'en tradition of special homemade fudge, caramel popcorn balls, and the little ghosts and goblins at her door having to speak before they could take a bag with the goodies. Ma hated litter and would make kids pick up anything they dropped, or if it were a broken bottle she'd be out with a broom and dustpan and see they swept it up. Already getting her old age pension, she could still outrace the youngsters at the July 1st field day.

Lawrence and Jessie had no children; Herc and Alwyn had a daughter Rhonda and sons Richard, Mark and Alun. (No that isn't a typo, it is the Welsh spelling.)

Three generations of the Tolen family have made their mark on Waterways and when you venture to that little community you will travel on Tolen Drive.

The Cross Family, Life Across The River

Roots of the Cross family go back to one of the town's first magistrates who also operated a meat market at the present site of the A & W. Arnold Skelton's daughter Patricia was born in Fort McMurray. Patricia was married to Howard Mein who joined the Royal Canadian Air Force and was killed overseas during World War II. He left a one-year old son, Jack, who became one of McMurray's premier entrepreneurs in the latter part of the last century. Patricia Mein later married Dempson Cross and Jack took his name.

Dempson was also a successful Fort McMurray businessman. He too had lost his father at an early age, and enjoyed a good relationship with his stepfather, Alex McIvor. Mr. McIvor had a general store in Waterways and in later years lived on Franklin Avenue near the two schools. Many of the homes that were moved from Uranium City to McMurray were transported by Mr. McIvor. He loved prospecting and staked claims in our northern area. He also loved barging houses and materials across Lake Athabasca, which is why so many of the Uranium City homes came into our town.

In 1952 scrap metal was in demand. Dempson Cross arranged to transport and salvage metal from an abandoned well site, 50 miles up the Clearwater River. Remnants of the equipment still remain on what locals call Oilwell Island, a beautiful spot heavily treed with birch opposite a sulphur spring. Weyman Petroleums drilled the well in 1928 using steam powered cable reel rig to pound the drill into the ground. Workers lived in a camp on the riverside. The site was abandoned December 31, 1931 and left untouched until the middle of the '50s.

Hector Demers made a winter road with his Cats, and hauled the heavy pieces of metal out on his trucks. Also involved in the project were Alex Lacombe and Raymond Couture. The four men stopped at Raphael Cree's cabin mid-way between the island and Waterways and enjoyed a lunch of squirrel stew.

Son Jack really wanted to be a helicopter pilot but his mother had her heart set on her son becoming a teacher. And so Jack went to university for his teaching degree.

In 2004 Anne Young, of FOCUS magazine, interviewed Jack and the following is part of her story.

Jack recalls his first teaching assignment as a 30-day contract in Fort McMurray. That coincided with the 30 days a local teacher had been suspended while serving in the local cell for the misdeed of serving alcohol to minors. It so happened, says Jack, the he was one of those minors and at the age of 19 had been enjoying one of the infamous local bush parties when the police raided. Judge Franchuck handed down a 30-day jail sentence and Jack's teaching career was launched with a 30-day subbing job. "I drank his beer and got his job," says Jack who fully appreciates the irony of it all now.

He soon got his own job teaching at Fort McKay. In his first class, which was K to Grade three, Jack recalls a bright, young kindergarten student raise his hand and ask, "Teacher what comes after 99?" Jack told him 100. The boy raised his hand again and wanted to know what came next. Jack said the young student excelled in other subjects as well, as he absorbed lessons of the four grades. Today that young student is still in the community of Fort McKay as its leader – Chief Jim Boucher.

Jack continued teaching for three years before he admitted to himself and others, that teaching was not really his calling.

It's not surprising that Jack had an entrepreneurial spirit and at the age of 22 and with the urging and support of his father and grandfather – plus a loan of $2,000 – and Jack was in business. Jack paid his dad's and grandfather's loans back in six months. The family owned a gravel pit where the Sawridge is now located. In 1965 Jack bought a truck and started a construction business. His first truck was delivered by the NAR to Waterways, but they had sent the gravel box on the rail line to Peace River.

There were many tough years for Cross Construction, just like all other McMurray businesses in the 1980s and '90s, but Jack and wife Roberta managed to always pay their employees and suppliers and weathered the recession. When Anne Young interviewed Jack in 2004 they had 60 employees and a fleet of heavy equipment.

The Cross family built a home on the bank of the Clearwater about 20 minutes from Waterways by jet boat. Along with the Weber families they crossed the river by boat in summer and truck in winter and drove to town past Draper.

While some people collect stamps, others hockey memorabilia, Jack Cross collects tanks. He began purchasing his first tank from Britain in 1996 and between the negotiations and transportation scheduling it was three years before it landed in McMurray. He has several armoured vehicles and tanks and they often can be seen on the grounds of the Royal Canadian Legion in Waterways.

In 2006 Jack and Roberta sold their construction business and now divide their time between homes in Salmon Arm, Arizona and McMurray. They particularly enjoy their home on the beautiful Clearwater River.

The FOCUS article describes a hunting episode with Jack's good friend Torchy Peden.

Jack recalls a nice evening with a few beers around the campfire, followed by a four a.m. wakeup call and a "bone-crushing" dune buggy ride 10 miles up the river. It was only then that Jack realized that he was expected to portage the boat the last mile. Jack said he'd been looking forward to a long, leisurely float down river where he could soothe his head from the previous evening's beverages.

Darned if Torchy's friend didn't shoot a moose and of course it fell into the river. Jack said he had to wade in and drag it to shore and help load it on the boat. When the other passenger got in, the boat sank to a level that ensured there would only be one passenger. Jack started the walk down the river – his only reward, would be another campfire and spirits. It occurred to him only later that the moose would have to be hauled up the embankment. This was all done with his good friend Torchy urging him on - from the top. To his utter disgust Jack found the camp "dry" and that was the end of his hunting pursuits.

The story doesn't mention the good steaks and roasts produced from the morning's hunt, which would have been shared amongst them all.

The Cross home on the Clearwater River overlooks a little set of rapids and is surrounded by poplar, birch and spruce. Wherever Jack and Roberta live or travel, their home on the bank of the river must always have a special place in their hearts.

Elsie Hyska,
A Real Lady

Written for FOCUS magazine by Anne Young in August 2001.

"It's always been home," says Elsie Hyska who was born in Fort McMurray in 1925. She married in Fort McMurray; gave birth to five daughters and one son and raised them all here.

The fourth of nine children, upon the completion of Grade 8 at age 15, Elsie left school to contribute to the family finances, as was the custom of the day. She worked as a waitress at the café in Waterways for a period, and later at the salt plant.

"There were few opportunities at that time," says Elsie. "I wish there could have been some of the work opportunities then that there are now." She fully appreciates what the ensuing growth of the community offered her children. Opportunities, as experienced by one daughter who recently celebrated 20 years with Syncrude Canada Ltd., which has afforded her a lifestyle of home ownership, recreational vehicles, and a car, all as a single person. "It's wonderful," says the proud mom.

Employment at the Waterways salt plant did however provide the backdrop for meeting Bill. He had arrived in the community in 1942 to work at the pilot oil sands plant and later found himself at the salt plant. The two were married in 1945.

As a young girl, Elsie recalls the train as the mode of transportation. One highlight in particular was a school trip to Edmonton via the train to see the

King and Queen in 1939. It would be the first of many train trips throughout the years.

As a young Waterways resident, Elsie and her siblings made the trek to McMurray every day. It took about an hour, recalls Elsie. "In the winter you walked faster."

During the winter months, the trip to and from school was conducted mainly in the dark, as school didn't let out until four p.m. She adds that the northern lights hold little mystique for her, as she routinely saw them "dancing" during her return home from school.

Elsie experienced her first airplane ride the year following her marriage. Bill was taking his bride of a year to meet his parents. Of her initial flight, Elsie recalls, "at first I was scared to death, then I loved it."

The passenger boats were a sight to behold on the river and Elsie regrets their demise.

A big development in the community was the construction of the bridge across the Athabasca, says Elsie. "I had never gone across the river, except by winter road to McKay, before the bridge was built."

A welcome addition to the growing and developing Fort McMurray was public transit, as Elsie never mastered driving a vehicle. "Bill tried to teach me. But I didn't even know how to blink the lights. With the radio on, and Bill holding on to the door ready to jump, I just found the runway wasn't wide enough." You see, Elsie explains, in earlier days they made their home at the airport where Bill was employed. He was instructing her on the empty runway. She adds, that by now, they'd probably want her license back anyway.

Elsie enjoys a lot of the shopping amenities these days, although she sometimes finds the big stores a challenge to get around. Catalogue shopping from Simpson Sears and the T. Eaton Company supplemented the general stores of the day. Elsie remembers when they were doing a survey on the street to see if local residents wanted a Safeway store here. With the introduction of Safeway to the community, shopping changed from telling the clerk in the store what you wanted, and who then brought it to you, to the big store where you had to get your own.

Through the years Elsie's family has continued to grow and now numbers six grandchildren and a new generation of two great-grandchildren.

Today, Elsie continues the practice of canning. She admits to not really enjoying the process, but liking the results. She also attends the weekly luncheons at the Golden Years and takes advantage of its library, as well as the Municipality's great library. Reading and crocheting are favourite pastimes.

Since this story was written, Bill and Elsie moved to Edmonton for health reasons. I remember Elsie as a gracious, wonderful person, good sense of humour and lots of common sense. Above all, she was a lady.

Transporters

For many years Fort McMurray was the hub of transportation to the north. But this distinction was not achieved easily. When H.J. Moberly first established the new post at the Forks, he was tasked to improve the route from the Mythe Portage. He built a cart road and brought in oxen to do the hauling, thus relieving the traders from carrying the heavy load of furs or supplies over the steep 13 mile portage. From the Mythe a portage around Whitemud Falls was followed by five more sets of rapids, and then the rivermen had smooth paddling on the Clearwater to the new fort.

Moberly was also asked to determine whether the rivers had enough water for steamboats to navigate them. He reported that it was possible and by the turn of the century steamboats and river scows carried the freight thus making the long difficult portaging trip from the east obsolete.

The first ship, the *Grahame,* named for the Commissioner of the Hudson's Bay Company was actually built in Fort Chipewyan. In 1882 three large scows were built in Athabasca to carry the supplies needed for construction, including a two and half ton boiler. Not entirely trusting the river route the Bay had more construction material sent over the Mythe Portage route; both arrived in Fort Chipewyan safely.

The *Grahame* was to ply the waters of the Athabasca from Fort Chipewyan to Fort Fitzgerald, where a 14-mile portage would take goods to another vessel for the trip down the Mackenzie River. Returning from Fitzgerald the *Grahame* went upstream to Fort McMurray. The first year it made two trips 60 miles up the Clearwater as far as the first set of rapids.

River transportation was established; 1,854 miles to the Arctic Ocean. From Athabasca a steamer brought goods as far as the Grand Rapids, and then by scows to Fort McMurray. In 1887 the HBC built two warehouses on the island at the Grand Rapids; two years later they built a tramway to transport the goods.

Fort McMurray as a transportation link was never more important than during the Second World War. The United States was anxious to build a pipeline from Norman Wells to Alaska and the Yukon to carry the all-important oil. By this time the railroad had been built and supplies for the Canol (Canadian Oil) road building project were brought in by rail and loaded onto barges for shipment to the north. To expedite this, 5,000 American troops descended on the community of less than 1000 people. Fascinating tales of this time in our history can be perused in Huberman's book *The Place We Call Home.*

The building of the railway, first to Draper, then to Waterways, and by the US army to the Prairie where the Marine Park is situated, was an immense undertaking. Construction of the Alberta & Great Waterways Railway was scheduled to start in 1909 but a political scandal halted the building until 1914. Deaths of three trainmen on unstable tracks further hindered the already difficult processes of building on muskeg. In 1922 the rails finally reached Draper and in 1925 they snaked into Waterways.

The terminus and resulting small settlement needed a name, and so the name Waterways was chosen. Main street, Bulyea Avenue was in honour of Alberta's first Lieutenant Governor.

The twice-weekly *Muskeg Special* carried passengers and freight, which in the long days of summer was quickly loaded onto barges for the journey north. The motto of the town was "*Where steel meets keel.*" A new breed of rivermen carried the freight to the north on tugboats, barges and steamers, braving storms, sandbars and ice. The captains, pilots and crews of these riverboats were a special type of men. Their names are in the memories of old timers;

there is not a lot of recorded history. I will endeavour to tell some of their stories, as told to me by others.

For years mail had been carried from Fort McMurray to northern points by dog team. The energetic Ryan brothers used horses to bring the mail from Athabasca Landing. All this changed in the late 1920s with the arrival of bush pilots and their planes. These men, most returning from World War I, had lived amazing lives and added much to the history of our community. Daring, adventurous men they pioneered the north through the skies. The Snye was their base, winter and summer; what an historic spot this is.

Fort McMurray was an integral part of northern transportation for many years. The transporters, whether in the air, on the river, or by train through muskeg, in many cases were real heroes, and created such an amazing part of our history.

The Amazing Ryan Brothers

Mickey Ryan was, without doubt one of the most energetic, ambitious and controversial entrepreneurs to invest in Fort McMurray in the first part of the century. Elmer Cree told me that Jack Fairbairn, Town Councillor in the 1950s, said "Everything the Ryan brothers did turned to gold. If they'd fallen in a sewer, they'd have come out the other side covered with diamonds."

Mickey came north, with his brother Pat, to work on the Hudson's Bay boat, the *McMurray*, that was transporting supplies north and bringing a cargo of furs back. Of Irish descent Mickey and Pat came from Indiana, where they'd both made a name for themselves as boxers. Loading wood for the guzzling steam engine from the cut piles stacked along the river, hauling on ropes and loading and unloading freight didn't appeal to the brothers and on their return to McMurray Mickey bought a team of horses and started hauling freight. Soon they had a blacksmith shop going.

On his first major trip, taking furs from McMurray to the railway, Mickey lost a horse in the muskeg, encountered a major storm, had to raft across creeks and chop fallen timber, but he got the fur out, dry and intact. When the trader offered him more money because of the hardships of the trip, Mickey refused and accepted only the contract price.

Soon Mickey bought the mail contract from Captain Smalley with 20 additional horses, a boat, and packing equipment. The men of Fort McMurray said he'd be broke in six months, which made him all the more determined to make a success of his venture. Brother Pat, who was almost stone deaf, went to Willow Lake (now called Gregoire) to make hay to feed the horses. Except for occasional trips to McMurray to attend to the blacksmith shop he stayed there all winter. Mickey used dogs for the mail run from Athabasca.

Until freeze-up came, the mail was carried by boat from Athabasca Landing to House River and then was packed onto horses for the trip to Fort McMurray. Letters, although packed in waterproof sacks, sometimes arrived water-stained due to the horses having to swim across creeks with the packs on their backs. This sometimes brought complaints from the locals, who sent lengthy petitions to the Post Master.

When winter arrived a dog team was the only way to get the mail delivered. Though he had never run dogs before Mickey soon learned what type of dog pulled best; he made the dogs moose hide moccasins for running over the rough ice and crusted snow. Twenty tiny moccasins to be tied and untied; and then placed on small sticks before the fire to dry.

The Ryan contract allowed twelve days for mail delivery from Athabasca to Fort McMurray. Mickey usually arrived a few days early. On one occasion Mickey and the dogs limped in two days later than expected. Members of the Board of Trade met him and demanded an explanation. But the McMurray residents admitted their thermometers had registered 73 below all week.

Mickey exploded and told them they had no idea how hard it was to get dogs working at that temperature, and no idea how much the dogs needed to eat in order to work. Even though it had been a grueling trip, he'd still made it in under contract time. But this didn't stop the members of the Board of Trade from writing and complaining to the post office department.

Meanwhile the great link to the "outside", the Alberta and Great Waterways Railway was inching closer to McMurray. When the ground was frozen the trains could take freight to the end of steel, eight miles from McMurray. Rails floating on muskeg in summer months were not solid enough for trains.

By 1917 Mickey persuaded the government to allow him to carry the mail along the railroad tracks north of Lac La Biche. Soon he fitted a Hudson Six auto with flange wheels, which held seven passengers and pulled a trailer to carry baggage and express goods. One of his teams met them at the end of steel, took the passengers to the river where a boat trip completed the journey to McMurray. Fresh fruits and vegetables, eggs and candy, now came in weekly. Cost of the local leg of the journey was $18.

During the great flu epidemic of 1918, Mickey combined his mail run with a stop at each cabin, to restock wood boxes and water pails and leave a box of aspirins.

The Ryans provided service to the townspeople in many ways. But were the locals grateful? They looked on the "Yankees" as upstarts who shouldn't be allowed to get ahead so fast. They sent letter after letter to the Post Office in Ottawa, to the railroad and to the Alberta government.

When the Ryan brothers were called in to see the Premier and shown a stack of letters and petitions from the McMurray Board of Trade, Mickey's response was: "The winters are pretty long up there. We don't get much excitement. We haven't had a murder in quite a while, or an epidemic, so I've taken the place of all of them". Mickey finally sued the members of the Board of Trade for libel. The court was in Edmonton and the defendants rode his speeder in and out. Mickey won the case, was awarded court costs and also collected their fares for the trip.

McMurrayites predicted disaster every time Mickey started a new adventure, and when it was successful they complained that he was reaping the profits. Not only did they complain locally but also did their best to have his contracts taken away. Through it all, the Ryans looked for further expansion and adventure.

Ryan and Bryan – Mickey and Pat Ryan had established a successful hauling business and a blacksmith shop in McMurray by about 1916. Their ambition and hard work came to the attention of J.H. Bryan, a free trader. They met at the Franklin Hotel and Mr. Bryan asked Mickey to take his furs, which he'd brought out of the north, out to the end of steel.

It was a proud day for Mickey when he pulled out from McMurray with his seven horses loaded with fur. But only one day out a violent storm hit. To proceed to the railhead they had to chop their way through dead falls and raft across raging creeks. The muskeg sucked the horses into the bog; one floundered and died. Their food ran out; they caught partridge and rabbits to survive, but no one suggested leaving the heavy load of furs. When they reached the railway with the fur dry and intact, Mr. Bryan offered to pay Mickey more money because of the hardships caused by the storm; Mickey refused, he said a contract was a contract.

Free traders, of which Mr. Bryan was one, were unpopular with the Hudson's Bay Company. Mr. Bryan was the first to pay the natives cash for their furs. There was a hue and cry from McMurray businesses that said he was ruining them; they thought the natives should only trade for their catch. Bryan contended they would have to learn to handle money sometime.

After a call to Edmonton Mickey met with Mr. Bryan who had just obtained a partnership with the Lambson-Hubbard Company, who were going into the north "strong."

There was to be lots of freight to haul, in and out of the north, and Mr. Bryan claimed he wouldn't have gone into the partnership without counting on the Ryans to haul the freight. He backed Mickey at the bank, and told him, "Mickey, I am going to make a fortune in the north, and you are going to make one with me."

The first shipments for the north were late getting to the end of steel, so Mickey wired Mr. Bryan that the freight should be hauled instead three miles from rail to the mouth of the Christina River on the Clearwater River, and put into an abandoned warehouse. The telegraph operator apprised the NT manager of Mickey's plans and it was a race to see who got to the warehouse first. Mickey did, and load after load of freight was stored in the reconditioned warehouse.

Charges were brought against Mickey by the NT Company for unlawful use of the warehouse. The court fined Ryan $4.50 in costs but were unable to give him change for his $50 bill. Just after court adjourned Mr. Bryan came riding in on a big chestnut horse and advised them that he had purchased the warehouse at the Christina River. He had wired Mickey previously that it was his, but the message was never delivered by the telegraph office.

Before Ryan and Bryan could decide what to do about the deceitfulness of the telegraph operator, men rushed into the hotel to say the river was flooding. It carried the Northern Trading Company's boats back into the woods, wrecked their warehouse and damaged all the freight in it. The Hangingstone Bridge was torn out.

Mickey went up to the Christina to see how their warehouse was faring. He took a canoe for the creeks, but lost it in the madly rushing Hangingstone so his horse was forced to swim the rest of the creeks with Mickey clinging to his back. Soaking wet, Mickey forced himself to run ahead of the horse through slush and snow in order to keep warm. Then he would ride until he became too cold, and then once again would lead the horse for another few miles.

When he arrived at the Christina warehouse his men were dismayed to hear all the NT freight was gone. One said, "That'll mean bad times in the North again. And if the food situation gets too bad, there may be scurvy. "

Mickey quickly put his men to work, rolled all the gas and coal oil barrels to one end of the warehouse and piled the sacks of flour, sugar and meal on top; then the cartons, cases and boxes on the very top.

The river rose and then dropped and all the Ryan freight was saved. Because the Northern Transportation freight was lost Bryan and Ryan helped save the north from starvation that year.

At the end of May the Ryan Brothers were to take the first big load over the Fort Fitzgerald-Fort Smith Portage. This 16-mile portage skirted the rushing *Rapids of the Drowned* in the Slave River. There was no real road; wagons and horses got stuck in the mud and muskeg. They built a Halfway Camp with tents and a cook shack so the trip could be broken up and heavier loads could be hauled.

The summer of 1920 came in with rain, and more rain. Even with four horses to a wagon they could only pull a thousand pounds and make only two trips a day from the end of steel where the Christina met the Clearwater and the warehouse was located. With his usual enterprise Mickey built a stone boat that the horses could drag over the mud with a heavy load.

The Lambson-Hibbard Company brought prosperity to the North for a short while. They introduced "fancy" goods to the residents – high heeled shoes, low-necked dresses, silk stocking and cosmetics, all on sale at their new trading posts. And then the price of fur dropped; "just plummeted to the ground" Mickey said. With Mr. Bryan's company pulling out of Canada, the Ryans turned to hauling freight for the Hudson's Bay Company.

For a few years Bryan and Ryan were the wonder of the north. The year of the great flood their supplies carried northerners over; they brought fresh fruit and vegetables to northern tables, and they introduced luxuries to the northern homes. The two men, one huge and strapping, the other small and wiry, went through weather hardships together that we can just imagine. Ryan and Bryan were builders of the north.

The Ryan Road – the first trip Mickey Ryan took north, on the steamboat *McMurray,* gave him a dream he would carry with him for years until he had fulfilled it. The boats stopped at Fort Fitzgerald and the freight had to be hauled on a 16-mile portage to Bell Rock at Fort Smith to be loaded onto barges for the rest of the trip north. An ox could haul five or six hundred pounds, just as long as it didn't rain and box the ox-carts down in the mud. Some years there were 300 tons of freight to haul, and no road, just a trail, which would be used until rutted and boggy, and then they'd move over a few feet and start a new trail.

On the first trip Mickey walked to Halfway Point, gazed at the magnificent, turbulent rapids, and dreamed of one day building a road to cross the portage.

A road over muskeg with the nearest gravel 300 miles away, to most, seemed impossible. The Ryans started the road in 1920, building up the worst spots with logs, doing more every year until it became quite passable. By this time he had the mail contract for Fort Smith, using horses to haul it, along with freight for the HBC.

The first trip the Ryan Brothers made for Mr. Bryan of the Lambson-Hibbard Company, they used horses rather than oxen. Soon they established a tent camp at Halfway Point, so loads could be left out all night and larger loads carried. It also meant a cook could give the men a hot meal and lunch for the next day. Soon a house, barn, granary and bunkhouse were erected. Mickey married Katie Poitras and her homemade desserts were famous.

By 1925 the Ryan Brothers had four taxis running between Fort Smith and Fort Fitzgerald, and then that summer they added an 18-passenger bus. When the bottom fell out of the fur market and the Lambson-Hubbard Company went broke, Imperial Oil needed to have freight carried across the portage and Mickey contracted with them and the Hudson's Bay Company. He also subcontracted to other teamsters in McMurray and the north.

The next venture for Mickey was a ranch at Halfway where he grew hay and fattened cattle to feed his crew. On the ranch he had a two-storey house and a garden with vegetables and flowers. Every building had electricity on the ranch; Fort Smith still used oil lamps and candles. His family and crew enjoyed the ranch life until one year when the hay fields and pastures were flooded; calves drowned, and soon after the ranch was abandoned.

When Mickey's wife Katie died in 1934 he decided to make Edmonton his headquarters, as it was better for his children.

In 1929 Mickey had gone to Winnipeg and bought two trucks and a tractor to maintain the road and haul heavier freight. He had his first plane ride that year, flying to Edmonton to hire teamsters and buy more horses. It was that year that he lost the mail contract as it was now flown north by plane. That winter he went back to Muncie, Indiana to see his parents. It was the first time in 25 years.

Mickey Ryan, who already had a franchise on 200 miles of railway track, was said to be the only man in the British Empire to hold dominion over an empire of railway. And so there were once again complaints and petitions against the Ryans getting the Bay contract and shipping in 750 tons of machinery and supplies for Imperial Oil. He was called to Edmonton to face an enquiry into the running of the road. He produced his accounts, explained how with no gravel, every time it rained they had to reinstall the corduroy foundation and sand it over. He kept the franchise and the dislike of the people who petitioned against him. Because of the hard feelings, Mickey asked the government to take the road over. The government refused saying they didn't have the money to maintain it.

One of Mickey's most ambitious trips across the portage was taking a 125-ton boat, *Pelly Lake*, across the portage. It was done after the frost came, hauled up onto a specially built sleigh, pulled by a big tractor and in six hours it reached Fort Smith.

The Governor General, Lord Tweedsmuir took a trip across the portage on his way to see the mining ventures in the Northwest Territories. He rode in Mickey's car, stopped for dinner at Halfway, and told the formal gathering at Fort Smith that he'd ridden over one of the finest highways in Alberta.

In 1938 twelve thousand tons of freight crossed the Ryan Portage. When the U.S. army was building the Canol Project during World War II, they asked Mickey's advice about getting the freight across the portage. They were aghast when he told them frost went down to 90 feet. He advised them to get dog teams with native drivers to take their engineers and surveyors to the job. He told them they needed extra teams on hand in case a plane went down or they had to do a rescue. They asked Mickey to keep the dogs at his acreage in St. Albert. To keep them in shape he gave rides to the neighbours and then soon to American Air Force boys, soldiers from around the Empire, the Alaska Highway workers, and soldiers on leave. The extra teams were never needed but gave pleasure to many.

When the war was over Mickey Ryan retired to Quebec. But first he heard the march of many soldiers' feet as they returned from the war and headed to the North Country. "I built the road for them," he said in proud-humility, as the feet that had tramped through the mud of the battlefields marched up his trail to the north.

The Auger Brothers, A River Tradition

Three Auger brothers, William, Edward and Gilbert, carried on the family tradition of rivermen. Their father, Eli, had worked on the early scows hauling barges through the rapids with long lines. In 1926, parents Eli and Virginia Auger, with their 10 young children traveled on the Athabasca River from their home in Lac la Biche to make a new home in Fort McMurray.

Winters were spent on the trapline at Celine Lake and the boys learned trapping skills from their father, as well as being home schooled by their mother. When they returned to McMurray in the spring it was a return to school to take the exams for their grade, and every child passed. The family lived on the Prairie and had a large garden, kept four cows, and picked an abundance of berries every summer. Each one of the boys became skilled in the bush on their trapline. In a 2003 interview, Edward recalled in 1941 catching 150 foxes, which sold for about $5.00 each. Gilbert's line was 50 miles long, and with no skidoo he walked every mile.

Some winters the men of the family cut wood along the banks of the Athabasca and stacked it for the steamboats to use in the summer. The ships required refueling every 30 miles, and stacks of cordwood would be placed along the route. The steam-powered paddle wheelers had a crew of 22 and room for 100 passengers plus all the freight they carried for northern communities.

At 15 years both Edward and Gilbert Auger began their careers on the riverboats. Deckhands earned a dollar a day plus room and board and they were expected to load and unload the barges, haul wood and keep the decks clean.

Edward joined the army and saw active service in Italy where he was wounded in the knee. Although relieved of active duty he remained in the army and went to Medicine Hat where he was a guard for the 7000 German prisoners in a camp there. While in Europe, Edward said he carried photos of his nephew and niece, Grant and Merle Golosky, and this is what helped him through the tough times. He served with the 49th Royal Edmonton Regiment and proudly showed a *FOCUS* reporter his medals and a well-preserved army jacket from 60 years ago.

When Gunnar Mines closed on Lake Athabasca, Gilbert bought one of the houses and had it transported by barge to McMurray, and placed on a lot on Moberly Crescent. He recalled that his dad had paid $10 for his lot on the Prairie, and in 1968 Edward's serviced lot cost him $1,280.

Steel tugs and barges replaced the wood-burning paddle wheelers in the 1940s and both Edward and Gilbert became certified captains. Gilbert was the captain of the *Radium Trader* and Edward captained the *Radium Prospector*, both owned by Northern Transportation Company. In 1956 both captains' freight included supplies for the DEW Line construction. The Eldorado Mines at Uranium City and that thriving community received their supplies in the summer months from NTCL boats, as did Gold Fields, just east of Uranium City.

The *Radium Trader* was a steel tugboat with a thousand horsepower diesel motor and it would pull as many as six barges. The barges were attached to the tug by steel cable and were usually towed about 700 feet behind the boat. The river route was marked by buoys in the water and markers on the banks by the Coast Guard, who dredged the channel every year to provide a proper channel. The biggest danger on the river was shifting sandbars on which a boat or barge could be stuck.

When the mines at Uranium City were closed in 1983, NTCL stopped operating on the Athabasca River and took their boats to the Mackenzie system. Both the Auger brothers retired that year, although for a few seasons Gilbert captained the tour boat MV Echo for owner Bob Duncan.

Gilbert Auger died in February 2001 and Edward in August 2005. These men, honest, hard working and sincere helped create the rich history that is our city's heritage.

Captain Billy Bird,
A Legend In His Time

No one who knew Billy Bird will forget him. Even those who did not know him well were impressed by his courtly manner, intelligence and knowledge. His father Joe Bird had been a Hudson's Bay man and later captained the Northland Echo for James Cornwall's Northern Transportation on the Peace River.

Billy Bird was born in Fort McMurray in 1907. His charming wife, Ethel Fraser was born in Fort Chipewyan, a descendent of the famous Fraser family. They were married in 1934 in Fort Chip and moved to McMurray where they lived for more than 60 years. They had 12 children and they have been well-known citizens of our community.

A career on the riverboats was the aspiration of many young men during the first half of the last century. They could be assured of a dollar a day, a room, hearty food and were able to learn skills to eventually become a pilot or captain. Mr. Bird was said to be an expert in "reading the water," a necessity when navigating the wide river that could contain shifting sandbars.

Life as a riverboat captain meant long weeks away from home and family. One year the ice froze early in the Arctic and Billy was stranded; he was away from March until November and returned to make the acquaintance of a seven month old son.

In the winters of the early 1920s Mr. Bird transported the mail twice a month to Fort Chipewyan. He drove a four-horse team on the Athabasca River and on one occasion lost a horse through the ice. At about the same time, in the summer months, thousands of buffalo were taken on barges to Wood Buffalo National Park.

Freight and passengers were taken to Fort Chipewyan, Uranium City in Saskatchewan, Goldfields and also down the Slave River to Fort Fitzgerald where the freight was portaged around the *Rapids of the Drowned* to Fort Smith and loaded onto other barges. At times, Lake Athabasca could be very rough. From the Athabasca River there are several channels that flow into the lake that had to be crossed to get to Fort Chipewyan or the Slave River. Steamboat Channel was the one favoured by the captains because of the depth of water.

Captain Bird recalled the tragedy of the *Clearwater*, which capsized in 1956 during a violent storm on the lake with the loss of all seven crewmembers, and Captain Ken "Tiny" Holden. The ship was owned by Northern Transportation Company Limited (NTCL), the company that had virtually taken over all river transport. The Hudson's Bay Company and McGinnis Fisheries had previously operated steamboats on the river and lakes.

The Birds lived in a traditional log house on Franklin Avenue, which unfortunately burnt to the ground in 1974. They purchased a trailer overlooking the Clearwater River on the Prairie. The river was, after his wife and family, the love of Billy Bird's life.

Julian Mills,
Life On The Waters

Captain Mills came from a long line of sailors. His father, James William, worked out of Nova Scotia for many years and he was a master boat-builder as well. When he moved west to Winnipeg he built boats sailing to Norway House. He moved again, west and north, and while working for the Hudson's Bay Company in Fort Simpson he met his wife. She was the daughter of the Chief Factor of the Mackenzie River district, Charles Camsell, one of Alberta's most famous men.

Julian Mills was born in Fort Simpson in 1897, and when he was fifteen, like so many of the other rivermen, he became a deckhand on one of his father's boats. His river career was interrupted by three years of service during World War I. When he returned he settled in Fort McMurray. Years later he told historian Dorothy Dahlgren of a trip he made from Athabasca to McMurray during the summer on foot. Battling mosquitoes and black flies it took many days.

Mills went to work for the Hudson's Bay Company transportation department, first as engineer and then as captain. He stayed with the HBC for twenty years and in 1940 went to work for Northern Transportation Company Ltd. For 22 more years Captain Mills carried freight from Fort McMurray to points on Lake Athabasca, and to the Fort Fitzgerald Portage. Some seasons he did as many as 24 crossings of the lake.

In his book *Across the Sub-Arctics of Canada* J.W. Tyrrell writes of travelling by canoe from Fort McMurray down the Athabasca and meeting the steamer *Grahame*. To his surprise, his old friend and fellow-shipmate for two years in Hudson Straits, J.W. Mills was on board. Captain Mills had just been appointed to the command of the *Wrigley* on the section below Fort Smith.

Captain Mills recalled the terrible storm that saw the sinking of the *Clearwater* and the loss of all its crew. Mills had transferred just two weeks before from the doomed ship to the *Radium Queen*. He was crossing the lake towards Bushell, the port that served Uranium City. Captain Holden on the *Clearwater* and Captain Mills were keeping in touch by flashing their lights. When no response came, Mills thought Holden had gone on the other side of an island. When there was no sign of the ship the next morning Captain Mills went back to look for her and found the barges but no sign of the vessel. It had sunk in 135 feet of water.

The boats that Captain Mills commanded were known as floating libraries. For Mills carried books and magazines that he would loan to anyone interested at the lonely outposts he stopped at. His ship often took federal and provincial officials north on government business.

Mills was married to Phyllis Burke. In 1962 he retired from the northern rivers and moved to Edmonton. Here, for a few summers, he captained the *Klondike Queen* taking passengers on pleasure cruises on the North Saskatchewan River. He died in 1980 at the age of 82.

Captain Mills was another remarkable riverman who left us a rich legacy of history of our northern rivers.

The Wylies,
Riverboat Family

Listening to Les Wylie talk about river transportation and his family's role in the great northern rivers and the boats that plied the rivers is inspiring. It takes us back to the days when men worked five and a half to six months in the summer on the boats, just returning to their families after freeze-up. Back to the days when northern communities depended on the boats bringing their year's supplies to them each summer. We can imagine the excitement on the docks and riverbanks as the boats came into view, the first visit from the "outside" world for a season.

The Wylie family, like so many others of the Hudson's Bay Company recruits, came from the Orkney Islands in Scotland. John Wylie, Les' grandfather, came to work for the HBC at Fort Chipewyan. He married Levisa Fraser, daughter of Colin Fraser, Fort Chip's foremost fur buyer. Les Wylie is the proud possessor of Colin Fraser's safe and his shotgun.

Leonard Wylie was born in Fort Chipewyan in 1921 and moved to Fort McMurray with his wife, Christina Simpson and his family of five sons and five daughters. He worked for the Canadian Coast Guard that marked all the channels on the rivers for the tugboats and barges to follow. His boat was called the buoy tender; it put out buoys on the water and huge white markers on the riverbanks, so it was the first boat into the river after breakup.

The Coast Guard had four boats built in Vancouver; they were broken down, shipped to McMurray by the NAR and then assembled in the shipyard on the Clearwater River. Len Wylie was the first captain of each of these boats; he sailed three of them to Fort Fitzgerald to be transported over the portage and put into the Slave River again at Bell Rock for navigational use further north. The *Miskanaw*, which is the Indian word for *Trail*, or *Pathfinder*, was kept in McMurray and Captain Wylie used it every season to mark the channels in the ever-shifting sands of the Athabasca.

Les, after grade nine in McMurray, was put on his dad's boat as a deckhand. Brothers Wayne and Lennie also served their apprenticeship on the *Miskanaw*. The Wylies were born for the water, Les said. His uncle Horace was in the navy during World War II. Captain Len retired after 39 years of keeping our rivers safe for freight.

Les Wylie worked on the boats for 37 years; retiring from the Mackenzie River route in 2005. He spent his summers living on the Coast Guard boat, the *Dumit*, marking the channels for the boats and barges plying the mighty Mackenzie River. Just before freeze-up the buoys were pulled and he returned to McMurray for the winter. His crew of ten contrasted with eight that served on the *Miskanaw*. The crew of eight consisted of: captain, mate, engineer, cook and four deck hands. During later years the *Dumit* was equipped with a helicopter pad.

The *Miskanaw* is in Fort McMurray's Marine Park. Les has preserved memorabilia from his father's captain days and a Len Wylie room on the boat will house these artifacts, including his captain's uniform, log books, and many photos. When Len Wylie retired they pulled the wheel off the *Miskanaw* and presented it to him, and this along with life jackets and maps will be exhibited. Captain Len died in 2008 at 82 years.

When Les Wylie was working out of Hay River in the 1970s he was a bosun on a ship the *Nahidik*, which was brought from Vancouver through the Northwest Passage and down the Mackenzie to Hay River.

Captain Les knew all the old time boat captains and crew. He spoke fondly of Jackie Sutherland, brother of Sister Sutherland who taught at St. John's School in McMurray. He worked on the dredges and always had a smile and whenever he saw any children he would give them a quarter. Les spoke of the *Johnny B*, the fastest boat on the rivers that serviced Gunnar Mines.

Les Wylie's Aunt Florence was married to Vic Ingraham. One winter when Vic walked to Great Bear Lake from Yellowknife, he fell into the water and froze both legs and they had to be amputated. He has been immortalized by the *Vic Ingraham Trail* that stretches from Yellowknife to Great Bear Lake. NTCL named a vessel that did exploration into Great Slave Lake in his memory.

Captain Les told of the annual visit to Bay Chimo on Bathurst Inlet. The residents of this little settlement had no television, no radio. When the *Dumit* dropped anchor in port the community descended on the ship to enjoy a movie, pop and chips. A highlight for this northern community.

When Captain Wylie was asked of his best memories of the rivers, he said "the last pull, coming home after five and a half months."

Len Williams,
Everyone's Friend

Two of my great friends did wonderful stories of Len Williams, who when we came to McMurray lived beside the Hangingstone River in the area now called Grayling Terrace. I can't improve on their stories and so with their kind permission I'm reprinting them.

From The Place We Call Home, by Irwin Huberman.

There was no person more closely identified with the *Muskeg Special* than Len Williams. For almost 50 years, Williams was employed as the train's porter, serving as a host, caretaker and messenger to both passengers and residents along the rail line.

As the train regularly crept along the tracks from Waterways to Lac La Biche, Williams and crew would slow down as they approached trapper's cabins or small settlements and wait for a wave or a gunshot to signify that all was well. The crew would also deliver mail or gifts up and down the track, and would bring news of friends and relatives to those trapping in isolated areas.

When McMurray residents needed special medicine, fresh produce, dry cleaning, or even a tuxedo rental, Williams would gladly ride into downtown Edmonton and perform the favour. He was known as a sweet and caring man. But few knew about the background of hatred and violence that brought him to Fort McMurray.

Williams was born in Mississippi in 1885, and like thousands of other blacks, left the United States to escape the lingering hatred and racial violence that followed the American Civil War. Many blacks that remained in the south bore the brunt of vigilante groups such as the Klu Klux Klan.

In 1910 Williams watched from the forest as members of the Klan lynched his best friend. The following day, he borrowed money from his sister and headed for Oklahoma to join the "underground railroad" to Canada. Williams made his way to Winnipeg and west to Alberta where he first homesteaded near Wildwood.

By 1922, Williams had landed a job with the Alberta & Great Waterways Railway, and over his many decades with the railway remained a loyal and trusted employee. Children would remain in his gentle custody during the 28-hour train trip to Edmonton. For many years, any dignitary or important piece of cargo traveling between Edmonton and Fort McMurray would pass under his care.

He helped ship the original buffalo that would stock Wood Buffalo National Park. During the early days of oil exploration, Williams would also assist his friend "Sid" hauling oil sand by horse and wagon. Later, residents realized Williams was referring to oil sands explorer Dr. Sidney Ells.

Throughout, Williams remained tight-lipped about his Mississippi roots. His son, Gilbert, has spent a number of years piecing together his father's story, and notes that during his 65 years in Alberta, Williams refused to go back and visit his birthplace. "He didn't believe anything had changed," recalled Gil.

And excerpts from Dorothy Dahlgren's book "People of Our Past", published by Jean's Printing in McMurray in 1988 and now out of print:

Len Williams was a very big man, and when I met him in Fort McMurray in the mid-seventies, he was a very old man. He filled a large armchair in his daughter's living room to overflowing and his gnarled old hands were never still as he reminisced about all the things he'd done in Alberta – and all the changes he'd seen – since he first came here in 1908. He was seventeen years old at the time, and deciding to migrate to Canada had been a momentous event in his life.

Len Williams was born and raised in the United States and there'd never been much of a life for him there.

He landed in Edmonton that year of 1908 and at least one of his hopeful anticipations was realized right away. He found he could own some land of his own around Alberta, just for the asking and what he always referred to as a "$10 initiation fee." So he filed for a quarter section east of Athabasca Landing, and set about doing the required clearing which would give him a clear title in just three years. It was backbreaking work, all on his own. But he did it, as even then Len was a big boy for his age – and still growing. In between seasons he went back to Edmonton where it was a simple matter to find a job which would provide him with some needed cash.

He was hired by the Edmonton, Dunvegan and British Columbia Railway – later the Northern Alberta Railway – as a porter on the weekly train from Edmonton to McLennan to Peace River to Grande Prairie. Forever afterward he always spoke of its roadbed as the finest in the world. During wintertime, that is. Any other season of the year things were different though, because the rails were laid through muskeg most of the way. In really cold weather when the ground was frozen solid the train could chug along at all of 20 miles an hour without any trouble at all. But in warm weather, when the muskeg thawed you could actually see the rails rising up behind you if you happened to look out the back platform. It was no means of transportation for anybody with a week stomach. Many a passenger got seasick from the continual up-and-down movement of the train.

Nevertheless it was the quickest way of getting anywhere in the north at the time, and quite a fancy train, to boot. It sported the very finest of plush seats in the passenger coach; roomy sleepers and an elegant dining car complete with its own monogrammed china and silverware, and elaborate five-course meals were available for a dollar twenty-five. Len Williams even cooked some of those meals for the railway officials when they travelled north, in addition to being put in charge of their private car attached to the train. He recalled they always took their trips in wintertime when, as he put it "their digestive systems weren't in any danger."

There were other hazards in summertime on the ED&BC railway, quite apart from the temperamental trackage. Forest fires blazed away unconfined and unattended, with the smoke from them so dense the trains were often held up for 24 hours, right in the thick of it, as visibility along the right-of-way was down to zero; and when they finally did get going again it was necessary for a man on a speeder to ride ahead of them to lead the way safely into the next station. Most of the fires were started by sparks from the coal-fired train engines but some of them near the sparsely-populated settlements were sometimes ignited deliberately so the homesteaders could earn the dollar a day authorities were willing to pay anyone who'd help to put them out.

Nevertheless, it was an interesting career at the time, traveling on the railroad, because you never knew what was going to happen on a trip, and every trip was an adventure. You might have to stop en route if the wind was too strong, for instance. It might blow the train clear off the tracks. Or you might be held up because of a sudden emergency, like when the crew was called upon to act as midwives in remote communities. On those occasions – and they were by no means rare – train schedules went to pot. Len Williams always said the only real surprise was when they arrived anywhere on time.

After several years on the Edmonton-Grande Prairie run, Len Williams was transferred to the railway branch line that went from Edmonton to Waterways. And that was when he really fell in love with the north country. It was so wild and beautiful and unspoiled. He always made sure he could lay over in Waterways after spring breakup to travel on the first boat going down the Athabasca River into Lake Athabasca. "My annual thrill-of-a-lifetime," he called it. He booked his ticket early, too, as the boat was always filled to capacity, as the old stern-wheeler plied its way, offering the first taste of freedom and renewed life after a long winter of isolation in Waterways.

Len also made a point of spending his holidays in the north in spite of the fact his years of service on the railway entitled him to an annual free pass to travel on any other railway in the country. On those occasions he went prospecting on his own – right near Uranium City – not so far way on the border between Alberta and Saskatchewan. He enjoyed every minute of it but the claims he staked never amounted to anything. The north was in his blood, the railway was his life and he didn't stop being a traveling man around these parts until he retired in 1959. That was when he began to live permanently near the Hangingstone River in a small house he'd bought for $800 way back when any thought of developing the tar sands was still a madman's dream.

The place was comfortable enough, but Len Williams wasn't used to sitting around doing nothing, so he arranged for another job as night watchman of the Mounted Police barracks in the Fort. It wasn't arduous as McMurray was still a small town that was just beginning to get growing pains, but it was nice to think if there were any disturbances he'd been there to take care of things. It was a necessary job in a way, but it wasn't long before Len found that sitting around at night watching all by himself wasn't exactly his cup of tea, especially as it never seemed to lead to any physical activity. He'd been on the move all his life, now he had to face the unbelievable fact that he must slow down. He was suffering from painful arthritis, his eyesight was failing, and he could not be quite so independent any more. For a short time he felt that he was no longer of any use to anybody, and admitted he spent quite a bit of time feeling very sorry for himself.

The ever-resourceful Len, at 80 years old, found himself a job as night watchman at the Syncrude mine site during its early development in 1972. There he was given the place of honour by his fellow workers as "mayor" of the "New Town of Mildred Lake." This was a great day for Len Williams, born into a life he'd been taught had no value because he'd been born a Negro in the United States, but long ago became a Canadian citizen. Ever afterwards he wore the official Badge of Office to prove it.

Furbers,
The Train Family

For 28 years the Furber family of Waterways had their lives arranged by the Northern Alberta Railways schedule. Tim Furber first worked in Edmonton for the NAR, loading freight, and then in 1942 he became a brakeman and moved to Lac La Biche. In 1947 he was transferred to Waterways and moved his wife Gerry and young children to a house in the Saline Creek area.

Tim was born in the United States and came to Canada with his parents and two brothers to homestead in the Chavin area on the Alberta/Saskatchewan border. Mr. Furber, Sr. built grain elevators but soon returned to Wenatchee, Washington; his three sons remained in Canada.

It was in Chavin that Tim met his wife Gerry, whose father was a station agent for the railway. Soon after they married they moved to Edmonton where Tim delivered milk to homes with a horse and wagon. He recalled that the worst families to collect the weekly account from were doctors and lawyers; the poorer people always found the money for their milkman.

Northern Alberta Railways had a turbulent history; it had many changes of ownership and names, a government that fell over the rail controversy, and the most difficult terrain to build on. Building the rail tracks north from Edmonton commenced in 1914, reached Lac La Biche the next year, but it was not until 1919 when the rail reached a terminus six miles east on the Clearwater River from Fort McMurray. The muskeg, mosquitoes, mud slides, terrible living conditions resulting in a strike, all contributed to difficulties the contractors and men faced. A tragic accident in 1919 at Mile 276 saw five men killed when the locomotive and a flat car hurtled over a sliding embankment.

And so the railway was just six miles from Fort McMurray. In the summer, freight and passengers were brought into town by boat; in the winter the enterprising Mickey Ryan hauled the freight with his teams of horses. Understandably, McMurray residents were not happy with the station, named Waterways, being almost inaccessible and six miles from town. Finally in 1925 the terminus was moved to the confluence of the Hangingstone and Clearwater Rivers.

The name on the station, *Waterways* became the name of the new settlement, and *Old Waterways* was renamed *Draper*.

By the time the Furber family arrived Waterways was a settled and bustling community with this terminus the busiest on the entire NAR lines during the busy summer season. All the freight for the Arctic came through Waterways, by train from Edmonton, and then was loaded onto barges for the 2000-mile river journey to the north. Fish from Lake Athabasca and Great Slave Lake was brought south to the railhead and shipped east in refrigerated cars. Uranium from Saskatchewan was shipped to Waterways by barge and sent south. Salt from the salt mine, one in Waterways and one in Abasand, was hauled to markets by the NAR. And then there was the summer when the train brought in buffalo to be loaded onto barges to be released and populate Wood Buffalo Park in the Northwest Territories.

As brakeman, Tim Furber spent more nights at work than he did at home. He was the cook for the crew; his son Hugh recalls how he'd also cook for the family on his days at home. One summer forest fires raged near Baptiste Lake. The hot tracks expanded, the diesel went over and cars derailed. The trestle over the creek was out. A call was made to Dunvegan Yards in Edmonton by tapping into the telegraph wires. A crew came north to help repair the track damage.

When Great Canadian Oil Sands started building their plant so much freight came in for transshipment to barges that Furber remained in town to manage the yard.

The railway was not just about business to its northern customers. It was a social event. When the train blew its whistle on the approach to Waterways the entire community and many from Fort McMurray flocked down to the station to see who was coming in and to collect any packages they had ordered. The railroad men serviced the outlying native and trappers' needs by dropping off mail, medical supplies and even acting as bankers. Son Hugh says every Thursday he met the train, his dad would hand him a bunch of cheques from Bill Tatum's store in Janvier. Hugh would take the cheques to the old Royal Bank, cash them and his dad would deliver the money to the storekeeper on his trip south. The train made unofficial stops when it was flagged down by one of the isolated residents. There were even stories of a short stop so passengers could pick blueberries at the best spots on the line. The NAR and the men who ran it were the lifeline for this part of the north. Tim Furber said not only did he deliver mail but also over the years he delivered huskies, sleds, pigs and calves.

Despite his work schedule taking him away from home Tim found time to serve on Northland School Division Board and was a member of the Elks Club. He retired from the railway in 1975 and then went to work for a time at Syncrude. One evening in 1977 he visited the crew at the railway station and when leaving to go home, dropped dead of a heart attack on the steps of the station.

Until the 1960s steam engines were used. A high water tower sat beside the tracks not far from the station. Hugh says when he was very young he would walk with his mother when she went to fill two pails with water for the household use. At the time they lived in their home on Cliff Avenue, quite a walk.

Gerry Furber was a kind, friendly and well-loved community resident. She worked at Haxton's General Store for 19 years until a fire destroyed the Franklin Ave. building on Christmas Eve 1979. She was instrumental in working with the Waterways Women's Community Club to start the first library, and was an active member of the Anglican Women's Association.

Mrs. Furber enjoyed annual trips to Las Vegas with her best friend and neighbour Charlotte Mitchell, and Jerry and Elva Bussieres. Gerry never gambled but thoroughly enjoyed the sights and shows and most especially the shopping, most often coming home with a new purse. She died of cancer in 1999.

The Furbers raised six children in Waterways. Son Hugh was the only one to remain in McMurray, working at Suncor. In high school he was attracted to Joan Barclay, whose family came with the GCOS influx. They married and with their children and grandchildren the Furber family is in its fourth generation. Of such people is a community built.

We Take To The Air

Air flight has been said to have conquered the last frontier. The north, particularly the vast northern wilderness of Canada, has also been called the last frontier. Combine these two and we get some powerful stories. For the men who flew in those first decades in Canada's north were truly explorers, just like the men who discovered the new world, the men who traversed the continent, paddled the rivers to their source and crossed the great Rockies.

And Fort McMurray, in the first half of the last century was indeed the Gateway to the North. It was here, from the Snye, that pilots took off to deliver His Majesty's Mail to the northern posts of Canada's Arctic. Not only did those early pilots deliver mail, trapper's and prospector's supplies, but they mapped the Arctic. Much of the huge expanse of the Northwest Territories, beyond the great rivers, was blank on the map. Once the early pilots charted and mapped the area we found it filled with lakes and rivers.

The bush pilots were called heroes, and heroes they often were, but it was their engineers who kept their planes aloft. It had to be a team effort for the two to survive in the harsh flying conditions. During winter flying, the oil had to be drained out of the engine each night, warmed in cabins or outdoor stoves and returned in the morning.

These pioneers had no radio contact; they flew in open cockpits in the coldest of weather, and often had to pitch a tent in the wilderness to wait out a storm.

The City of Fort McMurray has honoured many of the airmen in a subdivision in Thickwood Heights. Wop May and Billy Bishop had streets named for them in earlier subdivisions. Fort McMurray can be proud of the Syne being used as a runway for these bush pilots; our young town was truly the gateway to the north. In winter, on skis; after breakup, on floats; these men made history from our doorstep.

Punch Dickins

The North Country was opened up and mapped by a new type of explorer, the bush pilot. Returning from World War I, many of these pilots still full of adventure and hope, found an outlet for their energies in the skies over northern Canada. One such pilot and a famous World War I hero was Clennell H. "Punch" Dickins.

Born in 1899 in Manitoba, he moved with his family to Edmonton when he was 10. He enrolled in engineering at the University of Alberta at 16 but left to join the Canadian Army and was shipped overseas. In England he transferred to the Royal Air Force and distinguished himself as a bomber pilot. He was responsible for shooting down seven enemy aircraft, flew 73 missions and was awarded the Distinguished Flying Cross and later the Order of the British Empire.

When the Great War ended Dickins joined the newly created Royal Canadian Air Force but in 1927 he turned his attention to the north. He was asked by the Edmonton Post Office to investigate and do a report on the feasibility of flying mail to the Northwest Territories and the Arctic.

In January 1929 Dickins landed at the Syne in a temperature of minus 52 degrees. He was on his way to Fort Simpson with the first airmail and he returned with a load of fur. With his mechanic, Lew Parmenter, he carried mail, furs and passengers in temperatures dropping at times to minus 60. He was pilot for Western Canadian Airlines, which had the first scheduled northern flights and landed in Fort Chipewyan, Fort Smith, Fort Resolution and Hay River. In 1928 the airline carried more passengers and express than any aerial transport on the North American continent. They logged 532,000 miles and carried 9018 passengers.

Punch Dickins was credited with a lot of firsts. He was the first pilot to cross the Arctic Circle on March 6, 1928. He made the trip from Edmonton to Aklavik in just 17 flying hours. He delivered the first airmail to the Northwest Territories; he was the first pilot to fly the length of the Mackenzie River, some 2000 miles. He was also the first pilot to fly the Arctic coastline and in 1926 he did a ten thousand mile aerial survey of Northern Canada.

In 1929 a great air search was carried out with pilots Dickins, May and Cruickshank searching for an oil exploration party that had gone missing. They flew 29,000 miles over unmapped muskeg and filled in much of the "unexplored" map of northern Canada.

When the Second World War broke out Dickins organized the British Commonwealth Training Plan and trained thousands of pilots, managing six training schools. He was instrumental in arranging for the United States government to build landing strips in the north, including Fort McMurray, to expedite the CANOL project at Norman Wells.

After the war Dickins joined the de Havilland firm. He was responsible in part for construction and promotion of the Beaver and Otter planes that were used so much in our area. He flew until he was 78 years old. He died in 1996 and his son John sprinkled his ashes over the Mackenzie River.

Some in the north called him *Snow Eagle*. He and his fellow pilots brought a new dimension of life to residents of the north. And like so many of his fellow bush pilots, Punch Dickins holds a well-deserved place in the Aviation Hall of Fame.

Wop May

Wilfred "Wop" May (1896 – 1952) was born in Manitoba and moved to Edmonton, which was then in the Northwest Territories, with his family at six years old. Wop and his wife Violet lived in McMurray at the corner of Franklin Avenue and Morrison Street for six years. May was, at that time, in charge of the base for Commercial Airways and flew mail to the north. His planes carried supplies, people and furs.

Like so many of the early bush pilots May was a hero of the First World War. He enlisted in Canada and then in Britain joined the Royal Air Force. He took part in an aerial dogfight just after his training. His guns jammed and he was attacked by the famed "Red Baron" von Richthofen. He credited his erratic maneuvers to his inexperience, but he led the Baron to his squadron leader, Captain Brown, who shot down the famous German's plane. May himself, in the few months left of the war in 1918, is credited with shooting down at least 13 enemy planes. He was awarded the Distinguished Flying Cross and then sent to train other pilots.

After the war Wop May wanted to continue flying. With George Gorman he rented the City of Edmonton's plane for $25 a month and started taking people up for rides. The field they used is known now as the Mayfield area. The RCMP hired him for the first aerial manhunt in Canada where they successfully arrested the suspect near Edson.

One of May's famous exploits was when he flew his plane under the High Level Bridge that crosses the North Saskatchewan River in Edmonton. City officials were not amused.

In 1921 May and Gorman flew two planes from New York to Edmonton. These were to be used to transport supplies to Fort Norman where oil had been discovered.

Perhaps the most famous of Wop May's flights was in January 1929 when he and co-pilot Vic Horner flew on a mercy flight that caught the attention of news media worldwide. A case of diphtheria, which is highly contagious, had been diagnosed in Fort Vermillion, 600 miles north of Edmonton. The local doctor requested serum to prevent an epidemic.

The three-day trip, in an open cockpit, was accomplished at temperatures of -30 and -45 with blowing snow. The plane landed each night on improvised airstrips marked by spruce boughs. At each stop the fliers had to be almost carried off the plane, as they were so cold. One report said Wop's hands had to be literally pried off the controls.

When the men returned to Edmonton after a successful mercy flight they arrived to a hero's welcome. Wop May was awarded the Order of the British Empire in recognition of his service. This was not his last mercy flight; many times over the years he was asked to fly medicine, sick people and food to outlying communities.

In 1929 Cy Becker of Commercial Airways Ltd. offered May a job ferrying men and supplies across the west and north. Here he set several new records; he was the first pilot to fly nonstop between two Canadian cities when he flew from Edmonton to Winnipeg. In December 1929, May flew farther north than had ever been done when he delivered mail to Aklavik on the Arctic Ocean. This successful trip resulted in a contract to fly mail into the north from Fort McMurray.

While in McMurray, Wop May was recruited to assist in the hunt for the Mad Trapper of Rat River. This man had shot and killed one Mountie and wounded two others. As well as dropping supplies to the search team May took a wounded policeman to hospital in Aklavik, thereby saving his life.

In 1934 May was promoted to Superintendent of the Mackenzie River District for the airline. In effect he was in charge of all the planes and flights for the entire north. More and more mining camps were being set up and his planes hauled everything from men to half-ton trucks to the camps.

When World War II broke out May was in charge of the air combat school in Edmonton. He trained over 2200 aircrews each month for the duration of the war. He initiated a plan for aerial rescue teams that could respond to a crash site. He worked with the US Army Air Force on this project and was awarded the American Medal of Freedom.

After the war he negotiated commercial flight contracts with foreign countries for Canadian Pacific Airlines. He always stayed ahead of the industry – from bush planes to jet planes, Wop May experienced it all.

Walter & Jeanne Gilbert

On New Year's Day 1930 pilot Walter Gilbert and his wife Jeanne, herself an accomplished pilot, arrived in Fort McMurray. Walter had been hired by Western Canadian Airways, which had been started by "Doc" Oaks and James Richardson in 1926. He was posted to Fort McMurray. Even in those days accommodation was hard to get in the town. After a few days in the Franklin Hotel they found a two-room shed just behind the hotel. The windows were covered with cardboard and although it had a stove and a bedstead there was little else. With Eaton's catalogue and air flights from Edmonton they managed to furnish it and buy the necessary cooking items.

Dorothy Dahlgren in her book *Tales of the Tarsands* tells how Jeanne had to rise in the pitch black winter mornings two hours before her husband in order to make his breakfast, all this done by a gas lamp. The waterman delivered water to the kitchen twice a week, but she melted snow to do the weekly washing, a job which took most of a week what with melting snow, washing, drying in the cabin and then the ironing.

I'm sure that Jeanne Gilbert was delighted to find as one of her neighbours, another bush pilot's wife, Violet May. "Wop" May was McMurray's resident pilot for Commercial Airways Ltd. and had acquired the Royal Mail contract to fly mail into Arctic posts.

Like so many young men during the World War I conflict, Walter Gilbert tried to join up at 18. He was rejected because of flat feet, but in 1917 enlisted with the British Royal Flying Corps who had set up a recruiting office in New

York City. He was posted to England to complete training but contacted Spanish flu and never fought an air battle.

Coming back to Canada after the war must surely have been a letdown for young pilots. Highly skilled, ambitious, and in love with flying, there were absolutely no opportunities. After a few years he finally landed a post with the Canadian Air Force flying forestry patrol in northern Manitoba. Then he applied to the new Western Canadian Airways, flew for two years in British Colombia's north and then was posted to Fort McMurray.

The Canadian government in 1930 commissioned an exploratory mission headed by Major L.T. Burwash, with Walter Gilbert as the pilot. They had a three-fold agenda: search for remains of the Franklin expedition, take aerial photos of the Arctic coastline and determine the location of the magnetic north pole.

At Victory Point on King William Island they found an abandoned campsite from the ill-fated Franklin expedition with artifacts scattered around the site. When flying over the southern tip of King William Island their erratic compass showed them they had located the magnetic pole. Apparently it is gradually moving north; in 2001 it was said to be at Ellesmere Island, and moves toward Russia 34 to 37 miles per year.

Walter Gilbert was awarded the McKee Trophy in recognition of this and other exploratory flights. He also was made a fellow of the Royal Geographic Society.

Gilbert flew freight out of McMurray for trappers, prospectors and mining companies. In March 1931, he and Punch Dickins flew the very first commercial flight to Port Radium on Great Bear Lake. The north country's wealth of minerals was just being discovered and the bush pilots were the transportation key. With Lew Parmenter in 1934 Gilbert flew from Great Bear Lake to Coppermine. Then aided by a stiff tail wind they flew south to Edmonton, 1374 miles in ten hours and 45 minutes. Breaking another record, Gilbert flew from Aklavik to McMurray in just 11 hours and 50 minutes.

Gilbert's flying skill was widely recognized. In 1931 Canada Press contacted him to fly one of their reporters to Aklavik to meet Charles and Anne Lindbergh who stopped there on a flight to the Orient. With his engineer Lew Parmenter they made the rendezvous successfully and assisted Lindbergh to get his plane, heavy with a full load of fuel, off the Arctic Ocean by creating a slipstream ahead with his plane.

After over a decade of carrying supplies and men into the north country Gilbert was made superintendent of operations for Canadian Pacific Airlines in Vancouver, and later of the Mackenzie District. He retired in Washington State after years of exploratory and freight flying, with never a mishap to his name.

Rex Terpening

Fort McMurray made its own contribution to the men who flew the northern skies. Rex Terpening, an engineer who flew with the famous pilots of Canadian Airways Ltd. lived 16 miles down the Athabasca River and went to school in McMurray. His father was employed by the Hudson's Bay Company at Tar Island Shipyards, a depot of Mackenzie River Transport, the marine arm of HBC.

Mr. Terpening Senior oversaw the first shipment of buffalo to be moved from Wainwright to Wood Buffalo Park. The animals were transported to Waterways on the Alberta and Great Waterways Railroad (later NAR) and then loaded onto barges and transported downstream to the Park on the Slave River.

The family moved to Tar Island in 1927 and Rex and his sister lived in a tiny cabin in McMurray during the school term. Rex haunted the Snye and the offices of Spence-McDonough Air Transport and helped with odd jobs and maintenance of aircraft. McMurray's schooling stopped at grade nine and as his family could not afford to send him to Edmonton to finish high school, Rex went back to Tar Island and worked his dad's trapline. One cold winter day, returning from checking his traps, he found a letter that a neighbour had dropped off for him. This was his passport to the future, a job offer with Spence-Mac doing maintenance on their planes.

When this job folded, John Sutherland, engineer on the steamship *Northland Echo,* offered him a job as fireman. Not only was it his responsibility to fire the boiler, but also the steam engines and pumps required constant checking and maintenance. The boat stopped every few miles to load up with cordwood that had been cut during the winter and stock piled for the boats. They burned about 36 cords of wood every six-day round trip, or a stack four feet wide, four high and 288 feet long.

Terpening's river career only lasted one summer but his wage of $60 a month, plus his fur sales gave him enough money to return to McMurray to work for his air engineer license. After two years apprenticeship, working with no pay, but with some of the most experienced engineers in the business, working on planes flying from the Snye into the north, he reached his goal.

In the 1930s there were generally a dozen or more aircraft on the Snye, winter and summer. The engineers were in charge of change over from skis to floats in the spring, and back to skis in the fall. During the winter months the fog and ice crystals often made it difficult to take off in the mornings unless the temperature was about fifty below zero.

While on flights in the north it was the engineer's job to drain the oil in the plane at night, warming and replacing it in the morning, doing any repairs while in the wilderness and warming the engine in the morning with a "blowpot". Often when away from civilization they would have to improvise repairs. On one such occasion, flying with Matt Berry, the "king of the bush pilots", a bad landing in fog at -63F resulted in a broken ski, damage to the fuselage and bent propeller blade. Not having a replacement ski they painstakingly made a new ski out of dog sleigh boards from the local Hudson's Bay store. All repairs were accomplished in a week.

Rex Turpening had the right hand seat and kept planes aloft for the best and most famous bush pilots. From his days as a teenager at the Snye base sweeping floors and running errands he rose to become responsible for all maintenance activities for domestic and international routes for his company, which was now Canadian Pacific Airlines.

In 2001 Fort McMurray held a Homecoming to launch Irwin Huberman's book *The Place We Call Home.* Many people who'd called McMurray home in past years came back, and Rex Turpening was one of them. He had just had his own book published *Bent Props and Blow Pots,* a marvelous read about our pioneering bush pilots.

In his book he sums up: "I had in my working lifetime spanned the technology from the tough-hewn aircraft of the bush flying years to the most advanced of modern airliners. I would say that the '30s placed the greatest responsibility on all of us as individuals. Those were the years when the equipment was untried, the facilities primitive, the terrain unmapped and mostly uninhabited, and we were largely dependent upon our own resources and efforts." What an amazing group of men, the bush pilots and engineers flying out of the Snye were.

The Snye,
A Northern Base

CY BECKER was born in 1895 in Medicine Hat, Alberta. In 1916 he joined the Royal Naval Air Service in Ottawa; training consisted of ground school and eight hours of flight training, which he did in one day. Lt. Becker was sent overseas and flew seaplanes on the Italian front. These planes were very primitive and equipped only with detonator bombs as weapons.

The Italians were fighting the Germans in World War I and British Empire troops and planes were deployed to assist in protecting the Italian coast. Cy Becker flew a Camel plane to seek and destroy enemy submarines. In the fall of 1917 the Germans launched an offensive and heavy bombing resulted. There was a lot of combat action and Cy Becker was credited with downing six enemy planes, along with three probable. He was shot down in late November, managing to land his plane but he was injured and sent to a hospital in Malta.

While in Malta Becker contracted malaria and was invalided to England on a hospital ship. The ship was clearly marked with a Red Cross and fully illuminated but was torpedoed by a German submarine in the Bristol Channel. He was rescued, along with most of the wounded and crew, by a small boat. Wounded once more he spent the next few months in hospital in Bristol. For the remainder of the war he was an Air Navigation Instructor in map and compass duties.

Cy Becker taught flying in the 1920s, but also attended the University of Alberta and graduated with a law degree in 1923. Along with Wop May and Vic Horner, he founded Commercial Airways. He participated in the first airmail flights to Aklavik in 1929, stopping in Fort McMurray to refuel at 40 degrees below zero.

Although Becker became a Crown Prosecutor and was senior partner in an Edmonton law firm, he remained active in flying all of his life. He died at 68 of a heart attack when he was on his way to the Edmonton Municipal Airport to catch a flight to Yellowknife.

ARTHUR MASSEY (MATT) BERRY was born in 1888 and raised on a farm near Ottawa. When World War I broke out he went overseas as a captain in the Canadian Expeditionary Force. Whilst there he was certified as a pilot with the Royal Flying Corps and later returned to Canada to train pilots.

Matt Berry was the first pilot to fly to and land on Baker Lake in the Northwest Territories and in 1931 he was the first pilot to fly the route from Great Bear Lake to Edmonton. Leigh Brintnell, along with Stan McMillan, chose him as one of the pilots for his newly formed Mackenzie Air Service. This company, which was founded with funding by the famed inventor Anthony Fokker, had the reputation of never being on the ground, except for loading and unloading.

In 1935 Berry found and rescued pilot Con Farrell and engineer F. Hartley who had been stranded for eleven days in the Barren Lands after a blizzard had downed their plane. Again in 1936, Berry was twice acclaimed for difficult rescue missions. He saved the lives of two RCAF airmen stranded north of Great Slave Lake. For this he was awarded the McKee Trophy.

The second rescue that year was of Bishop Falaise, three priests, a lay brother and an Eskimo guide. They were stranded and starving on the shores of the Arctic. On this mission, Berry and his engineer Rex Terpening, established a new record for the farthest flight north in the dead of winter.

In 1938 Berry left flying for a time and became manager of Northern Transportation Ltd. in Edmonton. But when World War II broke out, his expertise was called upon as a flight instructor. Also during the war he was instrumental in construction of many northern airports. He came to Fort

McMurray and oversaw the land clearing and construction of the airport, to be used by the U.S. troops, en route to the north.

In 1949 two Edmonton newspapers erroneously reported Berry as dead, and detailed his northern flying exploits. At the time he owned Territories Air Services and frequently flew in the north. He was in the far north, having failed to file a flight plan, when one of the firm's planes crashed in a small lake near Great Slave Lake. The pilot and one passenger were killed, but no names released. As Matt Berry had not been heard from, except from the people he stopped to visit with on his way to Fort Good Hope, he was presumed to have died. Both newspapers corrected their stories next day.

He was called "king of the bush pilots"; another great man to whom one of Fort McMurray's streets is named.

CONWAY FARRELL was chief pilot for the Mackenzie District for Western Canadian Airways and carried mail north from Fort McMurray to Aklavik in the Northwest Territories. Another hero of World War I he was awarded the Distinguished Flying Cross for his part in the Battle of Britain.

When Wop May left McMurray to take charge of the Edmonton office, Con Farrell took over this area. He was called the "Santa Claus of the North", probably because for the first time northern settlers received their Christmas mail on time. He was the first pilot to do night flying when delivering the mail.

Farrell was said to be the most intrepid and resourceful bush pilot with the heart and courage of a lion. On one trip he was set to return to McMurray from Aklavik when he was asked to look for Andrew Bahr, a Laplander. Bahr had been hired by the Canadian government to bring a herd of reindeer from Alaska, across the Yukon into the central Arctic. It was a five-year trek. The reindeer and all the herder's supplies were lost in a blizzard on the Mackenzie delta.

Farrell said it was like looking for a needle in a haystack. But he found the near-starving herders and delivered 1500 pounds of supplies. All in a day's work for the pilot whose name was a legend along the Mackenzie Valley and

Arctic coast. For he had hauled some unusual cargo in his time: two piglets to a northern restaurant owner from the NAR in Waterways to Fort Smith. And another shipment consisted of 50 day-old chicks. The plane was delayed, the weather was hot and he attempted to splash some water onto the chicks to revive them. The chicks, box and all, fell into the lake. Farrell pulled them out and laid them out on the wharf to dry; 43 of them revived and were delivered to their owner.

ELMER FULLERTON was engineer to pilot George Gorman. In 1921 they flew into the Mackenzie River area for Imperial Oil. With no maps, in open cockpits, on skis in winter, floats in summer, they followed the rivers to get to their destination.

Their first trip, from Edmonton to Fort Simpson, took four days. A rough ice landing resulted in a smashed propeller. Thousands of miles and weeks away from any source of parts, Fullerton and a local handyman fashioned a new prop from oak and birch toboggan boards and they put them together with glue made from moose hides and hoofs. They successfully took off for the return trip.

The sight of the "thunderbird" both amazed and terrified the local natives. At lower Hay River the natives shot at the plane and riddled the tail with bullets. But soon the locals grew excited to see the reoccurrence of the bush pilots and would line up for rides.

ALEXANDER (MICKEY) SUTHERLAND was born in 1910 in Edmonton. His father was an engineer who worked closely with Dr. Karl A. Clark on projects in Fort McMurray. Mickey got his pilot's license at 19 and two years later his aircraft engineer's license. He learned to fly under the famed Wop May. As his eyesight was not good enough for a commercial pilot he worked with many of the bush pilots as their engineer.

It was in 1931 that Mickey Sutherland came to Fort McMurray, working for Spence McDonaugh Air Transport. He flew north from McMurray with pilots Punch Dickins, Wop May and Lewis Leigh. He was chief mechanic for

Lewis Leigh, based in Winnipeg, for Canadian Airways. They flew all over the Barren lands.

In 1937 Sutherland married and he and his brother John went to work with Trans Canada Airlines. Here he set up maintenance shops and designed aircraft hangers. When he went to work for the Boeing Company in California it was to design equipment for them.

Years later he wrote: *It was bush flying out of Edmonton and Fort McMurray, starting around 1938 that opened up the Arctic. It made a tremendous difference to northern operations, and indeed, to the entire area 'down north'. Much of what we did then still provides benefits, even today.*

While the pilots got most of the adulation, the air engineers were there too. Bush flying was a team effort; it had to be if you wanted to survive....It was just not possible to operate alone on floats or skis; there were too many things that had to be done, such as mechanical breakdowns to be taken care of en route. We carried tool kits, survival gear, a spare cylinder, spare piston, a set of plugs and sometimes a spare magneto...

At one time on Great Bear Lake Mickey had to construct new landing gear, heat and bend a broken prop, and all at minus 50. Then the plane flew back to McMurray. He said, "Anyone who went into bush flying had no place there if he did not have the inventiveness to be able to figure out how to fix things; it was teamwork between the pilot and mechanic."

Like many of his peers, Mickey Sutherland was inducted into the Aviation Hall of Fame. His contributions and those of the other adventurous airmen of the north have left us a history to be proud of.

Z.L. "Lewie" LEIGH Like so many others of his fellow airmen, Lewie Leigh started his aviation career barnstorming over the prairies. His family had moved to Alberta from England in 1909. His father, a former member of the British Territorial Army, returned to Britain during the Great War, and when he returned his army stories and pride of his country deeply affected young Lewie.

His first air industry job was for $175 a month as manager, engineer, and pilot instructor in Lethbridge. By 1932, in the midst of the depression, Leigh was flying his own plane on charters out of Cooking Lake, just north of Edmonton. Some of the flights were to McMurray and providentially he was in town when Walter Hill asked him to take his wife, Gladys to Edmonton as her baby was coming. Son Kenneth Rowland Leigh Hill arrived in the Leigh's cabin just 10 minutes after the plane landed on the lake.

In 1934 Canadian Airways Ltd. hired Leigh, along with Mickey Sutherland, and his first posting was Fort McMurray, under chief pilot Walter Gilbert. At that time Canadian Airways was the largest airline in Canada, and one of the largest in the world. Lewie and his wife Lin settled into a small house; in the evenings he built furniture, their water supply was in a barrel in the corner, heating was a wood stove and light in the dark winter evenings was from Coleman or gas lamps.

Despite the depression business was relatively good in northern Canada due to mineral strikes and exploration. Flights took Leigh and Sutherland from Fort McMurray to Aklavik or Great Slave Lake with stops along the way. They flew from dawn to dusk. When the ice melted on the northern lakes they would pull their plane up on shore and change the skis to floats before heading back south.

Bush flying ended for Leigh when he was chosen to go to the Boeing School in California to take a course in instrument and night flying. He qualified as the first Canadian instrument pilot and then organized an airline training school to train the company's pilots.

Joining the Royal Canadian Air Force in 1940, Leigh was tasked with establishing overseas mail delivery to Canadian troops. He flew patrols on the east coast conveying ships into port. When World War II ended he stayed in the RCAF in the Air Transport Division and became the Commanding Officer. He was involved in the Korean airlift and supplying the DEW line in northern Canada.

Like so many of the pilots who flew out of McMurray, Lewie Leigh was awarded the McKee Trans-Canada Trophy, the top civil aviation award in Canada.

Bergeron,
Bush Pilot Extraordinaire

Contact Air was the name for charters in McMurray in the 1960s and '70s. Jack Bergeron had a reputation for being able to land his float plane anywhere on the rivers or lakes even if it was carrying unwieldy loads. Contact had planes at the Snye and planes at the airport and, particularly during the summer months, planes in the skies.

Jack Bergeron started flying in northern B.C. at 16 and received his pilot's license at just 17 years old. His dad was a partner in an oil field catering company and Jack found himself flying groceries into camps from Hay River to Yellowknife. By the time he got his commercial license he'd logged 2000 miles flying as an expediter. He got his night endorsement in Edmonton. When asked why he wanted to fly, Jack's reply was, "It was better than farming."

Jack's charter flying in the north took him to Inuvik, Alkavik and all the settlements on the Mackenzie River. In 1965 he was out of a job and heard of a charter service in Fort McMurray that needed a pilot and so south to McMurray he came.

Milt and Margaret McDougall had gotten a license for Contact Airways in 1961. They lived in a small house on Franklin Avenue next to Demers and had a base at the Snye. Mrs. McDougall had her engineer's license and was a pilot as well. Known for her forthright speech and manner, many of the youngsters in town were terrified of her. Jack said he always got along fine with her, and Milt was the kindest man you'd ever meet. The bridge across the Athabasca

River had not been built and Jack's job was to ferry people and supplies to the Great Canadian Oil Sands plant 20 miles down the river. Once a week they flew the Royal Bank manager, Vince Burke to the plant to distribute the payroll to construction workers.

After three months Milt McDougall told Jack that he should buy the business. The town, he said, already had 1200 people and it was just getting too busy for him. Jack's worldly possessions consisted of a pickup truck, a chest of tools and a trailer in Park Plaza Trailer Court. He asked his dad to back him at the bank, and $20,000 later he owned Contact Air consisting of one plane, three lots at the Syne and the Imperial Oil franchise.

It was a small town and it didn't take Jack long to meet Daphne who had come at Sister Cardinal's request to work at St. Gabriel Hospital doing admitting and records. She lived in the old nurses' residence on Franklin Avenue next to the hospital. Her training stood her in good stead as she kept the books for Contact Air until she turned them over to Mary Ann Warren. Mary Ann, a true McMurrayite, kept the Contact crew in their place and the Bergerons said, was the greatest help you could ask for and managed and kept a good office staff.

That summer there were lots of fires in the district and the Forestry contracted Jack's plane for their use. This meant the plane was on standby and could not be used for charters; this also meant there was no cash coming in. When Jack presented a bill to the Forestry office in Edmonton he was told they had spent their allotment for the year and he would have to wait for the legislature to sit before he could get paid. Jack and Daphne were being married in just a few days; they had bills to pay and no money. Jack spoke to his father who phoned a connection he had with the government and a day later Jack was handed a partial payment of $20,000.

While Jack and Daphne were on their honeymoon Contact had its first crash. The pilot Jack had hired had crashed with Claire Peden and son Torchy on board. All walked away unharmed.

Jack recalled his first air ambulance charter. Dr. Al Nicholson asked him to fly to Edmonton at night on a medical emergency. Jack's one plane was on floats, but Bill Leschasin offered Jack the use of his personal plane to do the medivac. It was quite a load, Jack said, to have as well as himself as pilot, Dr. Nicholson and the stretcher in a small four-place single engine plane. Another memorable medivac was when Jack flew Dr. Nicholson into the airstrip at a little isolated village and was met by men with a patient on a stretcher. They loaded him in the plane, Dr. Nicholson looked at his knife wounds, one on the arm and the other his scalp and set to work sewing him up. Much to the chagrin of the victim's friends, Dr. Al had him taken out of the plane and sent back home with instructions not to do too much activity for the next few days. The local doctor had done as much on the airstrip as he could have done for him in the hospital in McMurray.

For the first three years of Jack owning Contact Airways Milt McDougall was still in town and he was able to do all of the company inspections. When the day came that the McDougalls left town Jack knew he had to find a new mechanic. In 1968 he hired Chris Ritter. Chris is still in McMurray and was, to quote Jack, "one of the real true aircraft mechanics in the north." Several fine mechanics have apprenticed under Chris and they will all tell you that he was the best in the trade.

One of Jack's first pilots was Les Stalke. The Stalkes lived in Row Housing on Hardin Street, and Les was the pastor of the Lutheran Church on Franklin Ave. He loved music and was one of the originators of the Overture Concert Society. He also loved to fly and when he left McMurray he flew for northern missions and started LAMP (Lutheran Aviation Mission Program).

Al Furneau, a friend from NWT days, joined Jack as a partner. They soon had about a dozen planes, averaged about one medivac a day, flew charters to inaccessible communities such as La Loche, Janvier, Conklin, Fort Chipewyan, as well as lots of work for forestry during fire season.

Jack and Daphne said they had wonderful pilots and mechanics. They spoke fondly of them; Daphne said they were baby sitters, house painters, whatever needed to be done. Graeme Milne came on staff and flew for them for three years and then Jack and Al thought he was getting bored so they offered him a percentage of the business; Graeme stayed.

In the early '70s Contact got very involved doing work for the three main contractors working on the Mackenzie Pipe Line flying mainly out of Norman Wells, as well as working for the Polar Gas Pipe Line that was based out of Resolute Bay. For several years they had aircraft flying up and down the proposed pipeline routes as well as out of Old Crow in the Yukon checking to see what environmental effects the line would have on the animals in the north.

Because of their involvement in the pipeline studies Contact was successful in getting a CIDA contract to go to Kenya in Africa to work with a Canadian funded project to study the encroachment of wildlife into domestic land and also the encroachment of people into the wildlife territory. The contract lasted for five years and then was taken over by the World Bank. The project continued until 1996 and at that time it was turned over to Kenyan pilots. Andy Stephanowich remained in Kenya for 25 years before coming back to Calgary where he is still doing survey work, albeit a very different type.

The years in Kenya, Daphne and Jack said, were the best years of their lives. Wonderful people, beautiful country, and a delightfully slower way of life.

It was a shock to Jack when he returned to McMurray from Kenya to be handed a phone and pager and be on call 24-7. He went to Kelowna to visit his ill mother, liked it there and had Daphne join him to look at property that they promptly bought. Al Furneau also bought property in the Okanagan and the plan was they would alternate months running the business in Fort McMurray.

The day after they returned they were having coffee in the Peter Pond Hotel and Robert Vargo approached them. He'd heard they were selling and he had a buyer. A week of discussion followed and Robert Vargo and Fred Weatherup of Lethbridge made them an offer they didn't want to refuse. And so in 1980 two of our last bush pilots made the move to British Colombia.

This didn't end Jack's flying though. Over the years sometimes we'd see him back in McMurray, but he also flew for Don and Marlene Hamilton who had their fishing camp out of Cambridge Bay. This camp is now owned by their son Fred who flew for Contact for several years. Jack's children used to say, "Dad's gone to summer camp." Each and every summer he flew in the north that he loved so much.

Jack's memories of flying include some celebrities. The neatest person he flew, he said, was Gordie Howe and the most prestigious with the most security, former president of the U.S., George Bush, Senior. Jack got to fly President Bush on a one week fishing trip while working for Plummers Lodge out of Great Bear Lake.

Jack is justly proud of his air charter's record: they never hurt anyone in all their years of flying and he serviced the town and outlying areas well in the days of no roads. In 1971 Contact Air boasted more floatplanes than any other charter service in the province.

Nowadays Jack keeps busy with his hobby of restoring and showing old cars; Daphne has a collection of about 700 Old Dressup Hats. They say they were very happy to have lived in McMurray as it gave them a wonderful start in life with many great memories. They credit the wonderful people they met. Jack said, "Some of my earliest flying out of McMurray introduced me to several very interesting northern characters. Some of these were: DD Williams, Eddy Engstrom, the Faichneys, Ewashkos, Jeans, Budinskis, Ernie Aikin, Peter Norcliffe, Mrs. Pelton, the Yaniks and the public health nurse, Freda Vaness."

Jack and Daphne spend six months each winter at their home in Mexico. Al Furneau makes his home in Calgary but still flies and has a management position with Kelowna Flight Craft. Graeme Milne lives in Comox and is very involved with gliders

The Bergerons built the apartment building on the corner of Centennial Drive and Franklin Avenue. They sold the building after Bob Bergeron, a local electrician and pilot, was killed when his plane crashed in a "whiteout" in 1971. This was a heartrending time for the whole community as the local search and rescue people as well as the Canadian Air Force searched days for the downed plane.

In 2000 when Irwin Huberman was doing interviews for his book *The Place We Call Home* I phoned Daphne to see if Irwin could speak with them. She said, "You know, I've never been back. I've often said to Jack I'd like to go to McMurray again." This remark inspired me to suggest we have a Homecoming when we launched Irwin's book in 2001. Under the direction of the book committee, but particularly with the organizing skills of Anne Young, we held a wonderful reunion with people from the 1920s and '30s returning to the place they once called home.

Ray Ruelling,
Last Of The Bush Pilots

From a farm in northern Saskatchewan, with a dream of flying, to the last successful air charter business in Fort McMurray is the story of Ray Ruelling. Alert Airways operated from this city to many northern points from 1973 until 1996.

Ray was born and raised on a mixed farm south of Meadow Lake, Saskatchewan. His father had come from Germany, his mother from Finland and on the homestead they raised six children. School was good, Ray recalls, otherwise it was work on the farm. He attended the one room school along with about 20 other children in eight grades with one teacher. When an aeroplane (it was spelled this way in those years) flew overhead the teacher would let her students outside to wave at the pilot.

Along with his dream of becoming a pilot and having his own plane Ray worked on the farm and with his father and brothers did commercial fishing in Turtle Lake. High school meant boarding at the closest town of Livelong, and coming home on weekends.

Ray was an electrician and worked for Canadian National Railways for six and half years, mostly in Winnipeg. While there he was on the CN First Aid and Safety team. All teams from western Canada competed in Winnipeg and although Ray was the youngest on his team he was the captain. They took second in the competitions.

As soon as he could afford it he took flying lessons and bought his first plane for about $2000 in Winnipeg. It was a J3 Cub, 65-horsepower with a wooden prop, no lights and no radio. With this plane he courted Stella and they were married in 1966.

Soon Ray bought skis for the little plane and hunted wolves from the air in northern Ontario. There was a bounty of $25 on wolves in those days.

Meanwhile Ray's older brother Rudy was working as "smoke jumper" with the Saskatchewan Forest Service. The men would parachute into the region of the fires to put them out. Rudy quit the fire fighting and went flying for Johnny Midget out of Buffalo Narrows and La Loche, and soon Ray left his secure master electrician job to join his brother flying.

Ray and Stella started a successful store in La Loche. He purchased an advanced fighter trainer plane from Crown assets that boasted two seats and 600-horsepower. He flew to Hay River to pick up his brother and fly him back to Meadow Lake where his plane was. While there he got a job offer and so Ray and Stella moved north.

The flying was tremendous in Hay River, Ray says. He went on his own and flew fish from the fish camps on Great Slave Lake to Hay River and was able to pay for a 180 Cessna in just three months with his long hours in the air.

While flying out of Hay River Ray said there were times when he saw huge herds of caribou. One spring he landed at La Loche Lake, NWT and the waters were full of caribou. He sat on the plane's skis and shot enough to fill their freezer for the summer. The caribou did not seem afraid, sometimes Ray said you couldn't chase them off an airstrip. "They weren't tame," he said, "just stupid."

Discussing the talk of depletion of the caribou herds Ray's theory is that the caribou are being devoured by wolves. A few decades ago many trappers were shooting hundreds of wolves each season. Then the law changed and wolves couldn't be shot from snowmobiles and there isn't the same encouragement to hunt them. Ray said he's seen wolves stay with a herd of caribou and kill them at their leisure with a detrimental effect to the population.

"The best thing for conservation," Ray stated, "is hunters and trappers. They look after the wildlife as a resource, never depleting the numbers."

In 1973 the Ruellings moved south and Ray joined his brother Rudy and Brian Hardy in a partnership called Alert Aviation. They were both aircraft maintenance engineers as well as commercial pilots and so had all aspects of the business well covered. Two years later Rudy was flying on a scheduled airline to British Columbia to pick up a plane when he died of a blood clot. He was only 39. Soon after, Ray bought Brian Hardy's share and operated both from the Snye and a hangar at the airport.

The 1980s were crazily busy, Ray recalls. His planes were instrument rated and flying from the hangar he built in 1979 he could offer 24-hour service and often did. He had nine pilots and with no roads to Conklin, Janvier, Chard, Uranium City and Fort Chipewyan his planes were always busy. And then there were the government charters and the summer fire season flying.

Northern charter outfits had to have self-contained planes; they had to carry engine tents, heating systems, sleeping bags, emergency food and necessary tools. Pilots had to be able to land on rivers and lakes as well as primitive airstrips in the bush. They flew trappers into isolated cabins, flew supplies into fire tower airstrips, as well as taking hunters and fishers into camps. We often saw a floatplane with a canoe attached to the side; the pilot would land below Whitemud Falls and passengers would canoe down the beautiful Clearwater.

One of Alert's long time pilots was Ken Jones; he was as skilled landing with a canoe below rapids as he was taking off from the runway at the airport. Ken's wife Carol was a well-respected executive with an oil company. They now live in Kelowna. Brian Hardy returned to fly from here at times as well.

Colonel Saunders, of Kentucky Fried Chicken fame, was one of the interesting characters Ray had on board. Saunders flew with a fishing charter from La Loche to Lloyd Lake Lodge. He had just sold his Eastern seaboard franchise. "He was a great cook," Ray said. He stepped in at the fish camp kitchen and made some memorable dishes.

When the roads were built from Conklin and Janvier, and scheduled air service to Fort Chip instituted charter service was mainly to fishing and hunting camps and government work. Although the charter service was finished in 1996, Ray still owns four planes, one of which is on floats. He has a base at the Snye as well as the hangar at the airport. Ray and Stella spend five months of every winter in Yuma, Arizona, near the Mexican border. Summers Ray still flies, but now for his own pleasure.

Looking back Ray had two comments. He said he was lucky as the old experienced bush pilots were very helpful to the new pilots. He always had a word of advice for his own pilots: "See nothing, hear nothing, and say nothing." I'm sure he could tell amazing stories of some of the charters he took if it wasn't that he took his own advice.

On a summer day at the Snye we see a few floatplanes but miss the early morning and late evening landings that were so frequent just a few decades ago.

Newcomers

With the advent of easier transportation the North Country attracted more permanent residents. And the rail-river transportation system brought seasonal workers in; some brought their families and stayed. The motto of the town was "Where Steel Meets Keel" and men worked from dawn to dusk in the long summer days loading the barges with freight being shipped to the north.

And Fort McMurray had industry. There was the fish plant, the salt plant and always the dreamers attempting to wrest the secret of extracting oil from the sands.

There were three small communities, each with their stores, schools and post office. Fort McMurray boasted an established date of 1870, Waterways was created by the end of the railroad in 1922, and the picturesque town of Abasand was at the mouth of the Horse River, until a disastrous fire in 1945 destroyed the plant and the town.

Waterways and Fort McMurray amalgamated in 1947 as the Village of McMurray. In 1962 the word Fort was brought back, and for a time it had a special New Town status.

Many of the families that came to Waterways and McMurray remained and became the stable nucleus of the community, as it was poised for rapid expansion in the 1960s. In 1962 the population of Fort McMurray was 1,186 and in 1971 the population had swelled to 6,847. Those who had established their homes here made a stable base for this tremendous growth.

The Brooks Boys

There were some girls in the families too, but they chose to make their adult homes in other places in the country. The first Brooks family, that of Steve Sr. moved from Lac La Biche in 1942 to Waterways. At that time there were less than 250 people in the Village of Fort McMurray, while Waterways boasted about 500, including Steve and Thelma Brooks and their first five children.

Steve Brooks came to work for McInnes Fisheries. He was an engineer on the Norbasca during summer months and worked at a sawmill for McInnis at Draper in the winter. McInnis was the largest employer in this northern community. They had four logging camps up the Clearwater River, the farthest about 50 miles from Waterways. Each winter the logs were cut and stockpiled and in the spring floated down to the mill at Draper. Steve worked with his partner, Harold Livingstone, at a sawmill on Saline Creek, four miles up the old airport road out of Waterways. Steve and Thelma Brooks had nine children; the second youngest, Karen perished when their home in Waterways burned.

For many years Steve Sr. operated one of the first taxi companies taking passengers from Waterways to McMurray for fifty cents a person. He was elected to town council in 1959. He also fished commercially for a time. Mrs. Brooks always raised a huge garden and canned vegetables and berries. Steve Brooks died in 1990 and his wife Thelma in 2002.

When Steve's nephew Bobby Brooks received his discharge from the Canadian Army after the end of World War II he arrived in Waterways to work for his uncle.

Bobby Brooks was born in Lloydminster in 1924; he enlisted in the Canadian Scottish Regiment in Edmonton at 18. He went with his regiment to England on a ship that was later sunk by a German U-boat. He was stationed at Aldershot and then onto the beaches of Normandy on D-Day eight hours after the first troops went ashore. Advancing with the army toward Paris, Bobbie was wounded and sent back to hospital in England. He had shrapnel wounds in his back and shoulder, and spent six months in hospital. When released he was sent back to Canada on the liner Queen Elizabeth, docking in New York and taking the train to Calgary.

Bobby told me his memories of England are of the blackouts, the pubs and the friendly people. When he arrived home he took a 30-day leave and went to San Francisco to visit an aunt, then on to Lac La Biche. His Aunt Thelma persuaded him to travel by train with her and the children to Waterways. Bobby said, "I had a drink of the water, and stayed." He says our people are great and so is the climate; this he told me on a winter day at minus 40.

Bobby went to work along with his Uncle Steve for McInnis Fisheries. He said the McInnis enterprises kept the town of Waterways going for many years. Not only did they operate the fishing enterprise, sending pickerel from Lake Athabasca to Boston and New York, but also they maintained a fleet of boats for transporting the catch and did logging for their sawmill in the winter.

Bobby Brooks became foreman in the fish plant yard supervising about 20 natives from La Loche who came each summer to unload the fish from the barges onto the railway cars. Filleting and packing of the fish was done at the Crackingstone fish plant on Lake Athabasca where about 30 people worked. In Waterways the fish boxes were loaded into reefer box cars prepared with ice and rock salt and shipped south and then to eastern points.

In the winter, ice was cut on the Clearwater and hauled to a 100 by 60 foot icehouse on the bank at Waterways. Six to ten men made up the ice cutting crew with two on the saws. The icehouse was packed tightly with chipped ice as they found that sawdust, which was so often used in icehouses, was too messy when they needed to use the ice in the summer. And then in the summer an electric ice crusher allowed the men to shovel the ice into the big boxes that kept the fish cold on the trip east. Lake Athabasca fish was in demand in Chicago and New York. Bird's Eye Food bought whitefish, pickerel and trout from the McInnes plant.

The company, which had been established in 1916, had about two-dozen fishing boats on Lake Athabasca and at the close of the season they were brought to the Waterways' shipyard, where Swanson's mill was operated in the 1960s. Most of the fishermen were from Gimli, Manitoba and so were the people who worked in the Crackingstone fish plant. The company operated first on Peter Pond Lake, near Buffalo Narrows, and in later years they operated as far north as Great Slave Lake.

After McInnis closed their fish plant Bobby worked for Northern Transportation at their docks at the Prairie. He also worked for a time at Gunnar Mines on Lake Athabasca, 35 miles from Uranium City. He spent two summers on the tug JohnnyB as second engineer hauling sulphur to the mine to make acid to break down the uranium.

After Great Canadian Oil Sands opened Bobby went to work for Catalytic and thus began a 28-year stint at the oilsands plant. He and his wife Thelma had seven children; all made their homes in McMurray. Bobby Brooks died in 2007, one of the last of our heroes from World War II.

Bobby Brooks may have come to Waterways to join his Uncle Steve but his life-long friend was his cousin Steve.

Steve Brooks Jr. worked for Demers Contracting along with cousin Archie, and on the boats for McInnis as well as in their logging camps up the Clearwater River. He married a local Waterways' girl, Shirley Mitchell, and went to work for George Sandulac at an electric power plant near the Hangingstone River.

Like many small communities the magic of flicking a switch and getting lights did not come to Waterways and McMurray until the 1930s. In 1933 a ten-kilowatt generator, owned by a Mr. McNeill and sold to storekeeper Mr. Boisvert, supplied Waterways with power from dusk until midnight. Every day that is except Monday, the traditional wash day, when it was operated in the morning for any resident lucky enough to have a new wringer washer.

In 1935 a diesel-powered plant was built in downtown McMurray. Cost of electricity was 25 cents per kilowatt-hour. Then in 1940 he built a new plant, along with an office building, at the Hangingstone River and in 1942 with the arrival of the American Army installed a three-phase line between Waterways and McMurray.

George Sandulac bought the plant in 1954 and increased the capacity with a generator from the now closed Waterways salt plant. It was at the Hangingstone plant that Steve Brooks went to work and not only read metres but also often collected payments at the same time. He recalled that they had 300 customers.

In 1957 Canadian Utilities, later Alberta Power, bought the plant from Mr. Sandulac and part of the terms of the sale was that his employee Steve Brooks would be guaranteed work with the new company. Steve went on to make a career with Alberta Power, first in Hay River, then High Level, and back to Hay River where he was active in the community, serving on the town's council for several years. The Brooks home in the summer port of Hay River was on the banks of the beautiful Hay River. When Steve retired after 37 years with Alberta Power they came back to McMurray.

Recalling his growing up years here, Steve said he had wonderful memories of living in Waterways beside the creek, swimming in the river and building rafts.

Archie Brooks, born in Lloydminster, Saskatchewan, went to work as a young man at Norman Wells in the Northwest Territories. In the fall of 1950 on his way south he decided to visit his relatives in Waterways and his cousin Steve induced him to stay. With Steve he went to work for Demers Logging, and later for the new airport. He met and married Marion Deep and has never regretted his choice of McMurray as home.

The Brooks family lived at the airport along with about ten other families, all who worked for the facility. Highway 63 had not yet been established; access to town was by a rough, steep and winding road behind Waterways. The children living at the airport had to be bused to school and Archie and Art Hoehne shared the bus driving. As well, with two boys in hockey and a girl in Guides, Archie said he made many trips to town a week.

Until 1974 Fort McMurray had a volunteer fire department and Archie had been a volunteer for several years. He and Joe Gauthier were the first permanent fire fighters hired by the town, with fire chief Roy Hawkins. He remembers the drastic fire of Christmas Eve 1979 when Haxton's Store burnt to the ground. Another notable fire in those years was the original Plaza I when the Islander Inn, Garvin Real Estate and Harry's Food Market burned.

The Athabasca River breakup was a momentous event for the community. The Elks Club, of which Archie was an active member, sold tickets on date and time of breakup. For many years Archie was the one who placed the barrel and timer into the river to correctly record the time; when the ice broke, it stopped the clock. On one occasion a well meaning resident in the Syncrude towers saw him lower the barrel and thought he was preparing to jump. They called the police who responded with lights and sirens. The annual breakup sweepstake was an exciting event for many years.

In 1986 Archie retired and became very active in the Golden Years Society. He and his wife Marion have a beautiful garden at their home in Beacon Hill. Their grandchildren make the fourth generation of Brooks to call McMurray home.

David and Fern Brooks are a couple who contributed much to Fort McMurray, together and individually. Dave was five when he came to McMurray and went to the Waterways School (where the Legion is located) until grade nine when he attended McMurray High School. He worked for Northern Alberta Railways for 15 years and when NAR downsized in 1971 he went to work for the hospital. He retired after 30 years there.

David and Fern were both avid curlers and great ball players. Dave was pitcher for the McMurray Hardware Lynx team. When Fern quit playing herself she never missed a game as she kept score for the guys' teams. There was great competition in sports, both between Waterways and McMurray, and later baseball teams from Alberta and the Northwest Territories competed in the Blueberry Festival Tournament.

Fern Ulmer came to McMurray in 1958 as a brand new teacher. She taught grades seven to nine, and immediately realized the lack of books in the community.

When Gunnar Mines in Uranium City closed, the town bought a collection of about 2000 books. Fern was hired to catalogue the books and then run the library for two dollars an hour. The books were here, but no place to set up a library until the town partitioned off a part of the maintenance garage. There was no heat and fumes from the garage often seeped through to the library. The library was open on Saturday afternoons and Thursday nights and well appreciated by the newcomers who flooded the town in the late '60s.

Fern worked many unpaid hours at the library that changed locations five times in ten years. This would necessitate Fern, and her assistant Edna Kelsey, packing, carrying and trucking the books to their new location.

Books and learning were Fern's passion. She taught the Write Break program at Keyano College for a time as well as working for both school districts as teacher and librarian. Fern always encouraged me to research and write this book, hopefully recording some of McMurray's interesting history.

In a bold move Fern opened Moberly Hall, a private school offering a small, specialized environment for students. Starting with just grades seven and eight, it soon grew to encompass grades one to nine with emphasis on core subjects. Parents and students alike have praise for the institution that unfortunately closed its doors in 2008.

Dave and Fern relocated to St. Albert in 2002, but their time in Fort McMurray has had long-term benefits for our residents.

Harold and Grant are two other brothers who remained in town, both working for the newly developing oilsands industry. Harold was a volunteer at the soon to be opened Marine Park, helping Torchy Peden refit the vessels. As a board member of Heritage Park he spent many hours volunteering in both parks.

One of the Brooks boys, who in this book shall be nameless, became infamous for maiming a friend. He and his very best friend lived across the road from each other. One day when they were playing, probably chopping kindling, young Brooks said to his friend, "Put your finger on the chopping block and I'll chop it off." Trustingly, his friend obeyed, down came the hatchet and off came the finger at the first joint. There was no such thing as reconstructive surgery in those days and so the young friend went through life with a constant reminder of his good friend from across the street.

Third generation Dwayne Brooks recalled a comment his grandfather Steve Senior often made when discussions during family gatherings centred on the opportunities in the new oilsands plants. Grandpa Steve would say, "We had a living here before the tar pits."

The Incredible Mrs. Mitchell

Charlotte Mitchell was probably the most loved McMurray resident during the last half of the past century. When the Royal Bank celebrated 50 years in town, it was Mrs. Mitchell that former manager Bill Bannister recognized as one of his first customers. When she walked from her home in Waterways to church in McMurray on Sundays, taxi driver Chuck always tried to be there to give her a ride. She'd drop off a box of her delicious squares to Mayor Guy Boutilier or to the staff at The Print Shop. Her sense of humour and love of dancing gave enjoyment to those who attended parties with her.

It was in 1910, when Charlotte was two, that the Maier family moved from a small town near Boston, USA to Alberta. Two sisters came together with their families; they cleared land and settled onto homesteads near Colinton. The next year her father gave an acre of his land to the School District for a school, and Charlotte and her siblings and cousins started school. She was seven. It was a one room school with grades one to eight and one teacher; a typical farming community school. Mrs. Mitchell recalled that one family walked five miles to and from school every day; she only had a mile to walk.

Mrs. Maier had trained as a nurse in the United States and was often called on in the community to deliver babies and for other medical emergencies. The family had milk cows and it was Charlotte's job to help with the milking. She had a cousin who was a constant tease and one time she dumped a whole pail of milk over his head! Then she was in fear and trembling that her mother would notice that only six pails, rather than seven, got to the separator. Somehow her mother never noticed and her cousin was much more respectful after that incident.

More settlers came into the area to take advantage of the 160-acre purchase for $10 that the government was offering. One of these was a handsome young man from Ontario, Albert "Ab" Mitchell. In 1934 he and Charlotte were married, and while in Colinton two daughters, Shirley and Elva were born.

Ab's brother, Bill Mitchell had moved to Waterways and opened a café. Early in 1943 Charlotte and the girls caught the train in Boyle planning to have a ten-day visit with their relatives in Waterways. They never left. Charlotte, who had never been sick before, or since, developed rheumatic fever and was flat on her back for four months. She told me her poor sister-in-law, Dorothy had to run back and forth between the café and house to feed her and look after the young girls. Miraculously Charlotte recovered. Ab had come up to check on his family and they decided to stay in Waterways and sold their farm and animals in Colinton.

Ab worked for the American Army until they left town; also for the McInnes fish plant, and the salt plant, until these enterprises closed. He also worked for Imperial Oil and the town. Mrs. Mitchell recalled they bought a house on the hill from a couple returning to the east. They had a garden on Lawrence Tolen's land, and although Mrs. Mitchell was raised on a farm she doesn't have fond memories of gardening and said she tried to get Ab to do most of it.

Meanwhile the family was enlarged with the birth of Corinne in 1951. Mrs. Maier, Charlotte's mother, moved from Colinton to a small home next door. She died in St. Gabriel Hospital in 1969.

In 1950 some cult had announced the end of the world would come to pass in January 1951. Corinne was born in the early hours of the morning on the ninth of January. The Mitchell house was near the road and Shirley was awakened by a rumbling that shook the house. She immediately woke sister Elva crying that the end of the world had come and they hadn't yet seen the new baby. Elva commenced wailing as well; they woke their dad who wasn't happy that all the fuss was being made just because the town grader had gone by on the nearby road.

Christmas was always an important day in the Mitchell home. Ab invited Olaf Meyer, a bachelor who lived in the bush near Saline Creek, to share their festivities. He refused to come saying it was a family day. And so Mrs. Mitchell prepared a dinner and Ab delivered it to him every Christmas for many years. After Mr. Mitchell died in 1971, Christmas Eve festivities were moved to daughter Elva's home. But Mr. Meyer wasn't forgotten, the meal was prepared and son-in-law Jerry delivered it.

In 1970 a fire totally destroyed the Mitchell home and all contents. With her usual positive outlook, when talking about this disaster, Mrs. Mitchell concentrates on how good everyone was to them. Neighbour Bobby Brooks spearheaded donations for the family.

In 1967 Mrs. Mitchell worked in the meat department of the Red and White Store. I recall how friendly she was to a shy newcomer and how she recommended best economical cuts for a large family. In those years, with a huge influx of workers and families arriving, I'm sure the patience of the locals was stretched. Mrs. Mitchell was one who always had a kind word and a smile for all; her courtesy went a long way to welcome many.

Soon Mrs. Mitchell went to work for Alice Haxton in the hardware department of Haxton's General Store. Her great friend, Gerry Furber, looked after the clothing and dry goods section. Mrs. Mitchell said, "We were well suited to our jobs; Furber wouldn't have known what a hammer was, and I'd have been hopeless with lace and fabric!" These ladies were neighbours in Waterways, and in later years travelled many times to Las Vegas with Mrs. Mitchell's daughter and son-in-law.

The day before Christmas in 1979 the Haxton Store on Franklin Avenue caught fire and despite efforts of the fire department all was lost. Mrs. Mitchell worked for Mrs. Haxton for 18 years and said she was a most wonderful person to work for.

When the bus system was established in Fort McMurray, Mrs. Mitchell enjoyed its services. For many years, however, she walked the three miles from Waterways to McMurray several times a week. Perhaps that is part of her secret of old age. In 2008 a large gathering of family and friends celebrated her 100th birthday. At the time this is written she is still, at 103, a very gracious, well spoken and I often say, is a much smarter lady than either her daughters or me. She delights to play crib with her daughters and grandchildren and most often wins. Amazingly, Mrs. Mitchell can read the fine print of the newspaper with no eye-glasses.

Fort McMurray's grandest lady, Charlotte Mitchell, was an example to us all.

Just after this story was written Charlotte Mitchell passed away with family by her side. Until the last week she was able to play crib and do her crosswords. Her funeral, a celebration of a wonderful life, was attended by many friends, the nurses who gave her such loving care, and her family. We will not soon see her like again.

Mrs. Mitchell wrote poetry, often for birthdays and special occasions. In 1987 her family compiled many of them into a book. With her daughters' permission I'm including one favourite.

McMurray Then and Now

Mukluks and memories, scenes from the past,
Time marches on, but memories last.
Following the trapline, happy and free.
Back to the cabin, for bannock and tea.
Fond memories forever that last.

The traplines become a bucketwheel trail,
Turning out black gold – still causing no gale –
Maybe a little bit lost, still many a gain.

A bit of nostalgia, an old song refrain.
Again McMurray comes through without fail.

So instead of bannock and tea for chow,
Instead of doing the trapline now,
We're digging the oil from out of that sand.
The intake and profits add up to a few grand –
Again McMurray – we love you and how.

Bussieres,
Faithful Town Servants

For decades the name Bussieres for many people indicated the town, then the city, administration. A father and son served ably in different positions for the municipality; one being the longest serving city clerk in the whole province.

Tony Bussieres, his wife Marjory and children Gerald and Gordon moved to Waterways in 1952 from the Peace River country. Northern Alberta Railways transferred Tony to Waterways as Charge Hand in 1951; he was responsible for looking after the steam locomotives and getting them ready for the return trip south the next day.

Tony immediately became active in the curling community. He was president of the Waterways Curling Club for a number of years and helped raise funds for a two-sheet curling rink that was built in 1957.

In 1956 Tony was elected to the town council and appointed by the province as a Justice of the Peace. As there was no resident judge in the town, a JP held court on cases under a summary conviction. His first term on council was during the time of controversy as to whether McMurray should install water and sewer lines. A successful plebiscite was held and services installed in 1963.

NAR decided to transfer Mr. Bussieres to the Dunvegan Yards in Edmonton. He had worked for the railway for 17 years but after a few months decided to resign and return to Waterways. He became involved with the experimental plant of Great Canadian Oil Sands, and then supervised Engineered Homes

(GCOS' builder) work camp during the construction period of the late 1960s. For some years he managed the Park Plaza Mobile Home Park.

Mrs. Bussieres passed away in 1970; she was being ambulanced to Edmonton hospital by Contact Air and died enroute. Mr. Bussieres enjoyed his grandchildren; one memorable trip with his son Jerry and wife Elva and grandson and granddaughter took them by car to Texas, Florida, and Boston and to Quebec City where they visited Tony's brother. In 1976 he was a passenger in a car involved in an accident and was instantly killed.

Tony's eldest son Jerry started work for the Town of McMurray as secretary-treasurer in 1960. He was the only employee in the office, and three years later the council applied to the province for New Town status. In the mid-1960s with the construction of Great Canadian Oil Sands (Suncor) the pace of town business changed dramatically. Until 1963 water was delivered to homes from Saline Creek and treated with bleach to Provincial Health standards. The streets were not paved, sidewalks few. Athabasca Realty Company Ltd, the housing arm of GCOS, and the New Town created subdivisions for employees who were arriving to work at the new plant. Engineered Homes started building houses and the first GCOS employees were sold houses in Block X (Alberta Drive area).

With the New Town status the province appointed a Board of Administrators as the Council. The first Board, appointed in 1964, was comprised of two government officials and the former mayor Claire Peden. In 1965 Mr. Peden resigned and Mac McCormick was appointed as chairman. Then more members were added and the government appointees flew in once a week and a meeting would begin and go on often until three or four o'clock the next morning. These were truly boom times and at the centre, keeping records, finding information, answering to board members and soothing taxpayers, was the Town Clerk, Jerry Bussieres.

In the first half of the 1970s we published the weekly newspaper, *McMurray Courier* and during that time reported on the long, sometimes boring, sometimes heated, weekly meetings. There were times in those board meetings when tempers flared and blame was put on anyone convenient and available. Through any crisis Jerry was, outwardly at least, calm and in control and did his job quietly and efficiently. He was always courteous and even-tempered and never critical of anyone, no matter what the provocation.

Jerry's good memory and knowledge of events was an incalculable asset to the town, and then to the city we became in 1980. When he retired in 1994 after 34 years with the municipality we lost not only a dedicated employee but also a valuable resource. Ask Jerry any question about a period of the city's growth and he'll have the answer, or be able to find it.

The Bussieres loved to curl; Jerry learned this skill from his dad. All winter in the '50s and '60s there was fierce competition between Waterways and McMurray teams. Hazen Holmes, who curled with Jerry, said, "There was no better curler than Jerry. He was a 'thinking curler'; he thought about every rock he threw." Once the curling ice was gone, sportsmen turned to fastball. Nowadays Jerry's sport is golf on the MacDonald Island course.

The wealth of knowledge Jerry acquired through his municipal job and time in the community was most valuable when a volunteer group published Irwin Huberman's book *The Place We Call Home.* Irwin called on Jerry often, once to wife Elva's dismay on Christmas morning, to verify some fact or other. The pictures in this wonderful book about our city were collected and chosen by Jerry and his long time friend Ken Hill.

Heritage Park has seen the benefit of Jerry's knowledge as he helped Tammy Plowman with the Time Line, a valuable resource. Jerry and Elva both volunteer at all Park events.

No chapter about the Bussieres family would be complete without a word about Elva. Daughter of wonderful Charlotte Mitchell, Elva with a seemingly rough exterior is one of the kindest people you could ever hope to meet. If she knows of anyone sick or in need she is the first there to help. She speaks her mind, has a wonderful (inherited from Mrs. Mitchell?) sense of humour and is a kind and true friend to many.

Jerry and Elva like many other retirees have travelled to many places in the world – China, Egypt, the British Isles, Italy and many cruises, some with Lance, Luana and their five grandsons. These grandsons mean everything to Jerry and Elva. With their grandparent's example to go by, we can only speculate on what their future contributions to the community will be to enhance even more the Bussieres' name.

Dim Silin,
Our Russian Aristocrat

One of McMurray's most notable and colourful characters in the mid-1900s was undoubtedly Dmitri Silin. For those of us who remember him coming to town in a wagon behind his grey horse, Spider, it is a cherished memory of the early boom years when the pace was considerably slower and the way of life of the trader-trapper years had not completely disappeared.

Dmitri and Anna Mae Silin came to Fort McMurray in the late 1940s and Anna Mae purchased 340 acres of land from the Department of Veteran's Affairs. The land stretched from the Athabasca River up to what is now known as Thickwood Heights. When Athabasca Realty (GCOS's housing arm) purchased the land in 1971 for $125,000 it was McMurray's largest land deal to date.

Dmitri, or Dim as locals called him, was born in Russia in 1909. His parents were of the White Russian nobility involved in the fur trade in Siberia. His older brothers were officers in the Czar's army. During the Russian Revolution the family fled to China and in Mongolia retained their fur trade connections. Dmitri was sent to Heidelberg to study the fur industry when it was at its zenith.

His travels took him to Africa where he became a hired mercenary. He was captured by an enemy tribe and held hostage but managed to escape and return to Europe. He went on to China and eventually came to Canada, living in Vancouver. Jim Rogers, who was a young friend of Silin's in the '60s, and is now a colourful character himself, told me Silin married a lawyer in Vancouver and was later divorced.

Travels next took Mr. Silin to Kelowna where he worked in a logging camp. Here he met Anna Mae Wegren who was the camp cook; they married and soon moved to Fort McMurray.

Mrs. Silin was in the Canadian Airforce in World War II and travelled throughout Canada and part of the U.S. She was a gold medalist in sharp shooting. Although she left school after grade eight she was very intelligent and well read. She was more than able to hold her own with her well-educated husband, who spoke four languages fluently.

The family lived on the trapline across the river until daughter Judy started school. Then Mrs. Silin, Judy and Ruth moved to town living in a large house just across the back alley from the Hudson's Bay store (present day Morrison Centre.)

There was no bridge across the Athabasca River and they used a canoe with a small motor, going from the trapline to their home in town. A team of horses, Dick and Molly, served as their transportation, and later it was their offspring Spider that pulled the wagon.

In winters Mr. Silin cut firewood and with his team brought it across the frozen river to sell in town. The area around Uranium City was in its high days, with prospectors and geologists seeking their fortunes, and Mr. Silin spent several months there at different times.

The Silin girls at first went to school in Waterways, three miles away, and then when the Peter Pond School was built they were in town. Mrs. Silin took in boarders and cooked for the Northern Transportation crews. In the '60s she cooked for Alberta Government Telephone crews, Hudson's Bay men, and the "bank boys."

Daughter Ruth recalls her mother cooking for 26 regular boarders three meals a day; the men ate in two shifts.

When the Morimoto family came to town, Dim Silin would play Mah Jong with the father all the while conversing in Japanese. A skilled trapper, Mr. Silin was a favourite with the youth of McMurray who were eager to learn his skills and enthralled by his stories. He was an excellent shot and devoted to his animals that had been taught to respond to his words. Mr. Silin often slept in the day as his early experiences of war and death often kept him awake at nights.

Mr. Silin, as the saying went, did not suffer fools gladly. Irwin Huberman in his book *The Place We Call Home* tells of Silin's encounter with an oilman walking across his property. The man kicked one of his dogs and said he represented an American oil company and needed access to study the deposits. Silin warned him never to touch one of his dogs again and said the company was behind in its easement payments. He was ignored and the man continued down the trail.

Moments later the oilman saw the trapper with a shotgun and witnessed him shoot out the headlights of his half-ton truck, then the windshield and finally the four tires. The man dashed off the property and sent a tow truck to pick up his vehicle. Later that week the overdue easement fees arrived in a special delivery envelope.

Fern Brooks, the town's librarian, recalls the many books Dim Silin borrowed from the small library attached to the town hall, always on a variety of topics.

One afternoon in 1968 teenagers, Stephen Anderson and Mark Jean, hiked up to the Silin cabin on the west side of the river to drink tea and listen to his fascinating tales of travel and trapping. While they were chatting at the table, Dim Silin collapsed and died instantly from a heart attack.

From the life of an aristocrat in a far away land, to the simple life of a trapper who enjoyed all nature, and with so many adventures in between, Dim Silin knew the world as few ever will.

Caouette,
Construction Of The 1960s

Some years ago George Caouette walked into my office and gave me a document that he had entitled *Ramblings and Recollections, 1956-1974*. From this mine of information I have been able to put together the story of George and Mavis Caouette's pioneering times in our community.

On January 3rd, 1956, with a temperature of 52 below Fahrenheit, George and Mavis with their two children, along with partners George Waterhouse and Elmer Johnson and four employees, arrived in Waterways on the Northern Alberta Railways' weekly train. With them they brought logging and sawmill equipment.

The two local taxis, operated by Steve Brooks, Sr. and "Snoose" Moore met the train and one was hired to drive the group to the town of Fort McMurray, three miles away. First on the order of business was lodging and the taxi driver told them Curly Jewitt had a house big enough for nine people. They rented it on the spot.

After some months Mr. Caouette bought an old condemned restaurant in Waterways, put logs under it and skidded it with two trucks to property he owned at the corner of Morrison St. and the highway.

George recalled a day in 1963 when J. Howard Pew, owner of Sun Oil, came from Philadelphia to inspect the work at the future oilsands plant. He said Joe Fitzgerald hired the Caouettes to set up a big tent in the bush, complete with a red rug on the floor. The menu for lunch was beefsteak and turkey but Mr. Pew claimed the best part of the meal was Mavis' homemade bread. He later wrote to her and thanked her for the great "in the wild-north meal." He asked her to make 20 loaves of the same kind of bread for him and he would have the Sun Oil airplane pick them up. She obliged.

George Waterhouse and Elmer Johnson set up a mill and George Caouette's company subcontracted the log skidding to the mill and hauled the lumber to town. It was a busy time for his company; he hauled lumber to Beaver Lumber at the end of Franklin Avenue and graveled the streets for the Town of Fort McMurray, all done by hand with pick and shovel. That winter he began delivering coal to St. Gabriel Hospital, churches, homes and the Oil Sands Hotel, which Mike Kolowaski and Jack Wagner owned.

In 1959 a Mr. Bill Gallup hired Caouette Transport to go to the Great Canadian Oil Sands site and pack samples in five-gallon pails for shipment to Philadelphia. George carried all the tools into the site and then, along with the pails of samples, carried them back down the hill to the river and brought them twenty miles upstream to Fort McMurray by speedboat.

These were busy times in the growing community and Caouette's competition in the construction business was the company owned by Hector Demers and Albert Lacombe. George did not feel threatened by Demers Contracting, he said there was enough work for all; in fact as his business got too big for Mavis to handle all the bookwork he hired Hilda Demers (wife of Ernie) to do his books.

A tugboat and barge had been added to the list of equipment of Caouette Construction and soon George rented a large building from Gus Hawker and brought in drilling supplies for Amoco Oil. Fuel had to be trucked into the drilling rigs on winter roads. Demers supplied companies that used Esso products, sold by Mac McCormick and Caouettes had the contract to supply the B.A. Oil fuel. A few years later Jim Mutton arrived in town and opened the Shell Oil bulk plant on the prairie and Caouettes hauled their fuel to Tri City Drilling.

George's company built the first ice bridge across the Athabasca River so that heavy equipment could move to the other side of the river. Located where the Grant MacEwan bridge is now, during the winter equipment and men moved across it into the bush and down the river to GCOS. That winter the company acquired a large log-hauling contract for Swanson Lumber; this required a new big loader.

Mr. Caouette said that every road in the lower town site was built by his company, either as a sub-contractor to a Vancouver firm or directly. They built the road dam across the river to MacDonald Island. Over $4000 worth of preparation work was done on the Miskanaw Golf Course, to be traded as shares. He neglected to pick the shares up right away and when he retired and sought to use them found to his chagrin that the city had taken over the golf course but not the share obligation.

The biggest construction job undertaken in those years was building Reidel Street out of the bush. A six-inch water line, a gas line and sewer were installed and it was graveled and paved. With the advent of Athabasca Realty, George Brosseau's Park Plaza and Norm Simons and Siggi Lukas' trailer parks there was a great deal of work to be done.

Before the town's water system was installed, Mr. Caouette wrote, water was delivered to homes with a one-ton Chev by Harry Pilkington. He went from house to house to fill the barrels and put a quarter cup of bleach in each barrel. At this time Albert Reidel was mayor and he and the Tolen brothers both hauled freight to town from the NAR station in Waterways. Also of note, was Russ Denholm, a government public works superintendent, who built the wing dams along the Clearwater to keep the banks from washing into the river. Mr. Denholm was a boat builder by trade and he built scows in his spare time, including one for the Caouettes.

When George and Mavis Caouette retired to B.C. in 1974 he gave a small bucketwheel that had been used to test oil sands at GCOS to Heritage Park, as well as the barge he had used to haul freight on the river. He still had 85 pieces of equipment that he hauled to the south. Eighteen years of construction in the community; George Caouette helped turn a village into a town, and a booming one at that.

The Mysteries Of Eddie Engstrom

A quiet, tidy man with a sense of humour, Eddie Engstrom bequeathed his house and lot at the corner of Fraser Avenue and Hardin Street to the Scouts and Guides. It was a small pink house, surrounded by a pink fence and with a colourful flower garden. During the winter Eddie lived on his trapline some fifty miles up the Clearwater River.

Born in Sweden, he came to Canada in 1928 and joined the Canadian Army during the Second World War, serving in the tank division. He went overseas and visited his homeland for the last time. He was a machinist by trade and was very proficient with hand tools and carpentry.

Eddie liked children and sometimes took boys to his cabin for a few days fishing. He built a huge scow in his back yard and often had an audience of half a dozen boys. The scow had a cabin and an inboard motor. When he finished it he set fire to his old boat down at the Snye. He used the new scow a couple of summers but after getting stuck on the sandbars on the Clearwater he sold it and went back to his freighter canoe.

Before the bridge across the Athabasca and the road to the Great Canadian Oil Sands plant, Eddie sometimes took passengers to the development. Occasionally he took people to Goldfields on Lake Athabasca.

Eddie was not a big talker and his youthful visitors knew when to keep silent. He was a very exacting man, possessive and a perfectionist. He was said to be the nicest guy when all went well, but could be obnoxious at times and had a quick temper.

Both his summer and winter homes were neatly kept. In his home on Fraser Avenue he had many furs, samples of everything he had trapped over the years. Eddie had a real love of nature and imparted his knowledge and love to the youngsters who visited him. He kept two large dogs that he used in winter on his trapline.

He built a new log cabin, using pink paint on the interior, at *The Big Eddy* on the Clearwater River. It was his private domain; he had a "Private – Keep Out" sign on the path from the dock and a chain stretched across the path. It annoyed him immensely if people walked onto the pristine snow around the cabin.

Eddie Engstrom left us with at least three mysteries. He had a wife and child in Sweden. Why did he leave them to come to Canada and never send for them?

The second mystery was a story that made headlines across newspapers in Alberta in 1973 and involved the largest RCMP search to have been held in this area.

Eddie sister, Gretha Engstrom, came from Stockholm, Sweden to visit her brother in June 1973. He took her by canoe, with his dogs, up the Clearwater to see his cabin. We can only guess what happened on the trip as he told conflicting stories to the police.

According to Eddie, at the head of an island the canoe tipped, the dogs drowned and he and his sister got to shore. They attempted to walk the last five miles to the cabin but the bush was too thick. Eddie suggested they get in the canoe and drift down to the Crees' cabin (about 20 miles) for help, as his motor wouldn't start. They became separated and Eddie told conflicting stories as to why they did.

Eddie drifted down to the Cree cabin, had tea with Elmer Cree and went to sleep for the night. The next morning he told Elmer his sister was up river and they should go and find her. They returned to the site and fired off shots but did not find her. The accident occurred on Wednesday afternoon; it was late

Friday afternoon before Eddie and Elmer went to town and notified the RCMP of the missing woman.

The local detachment, headed by experienced river and bushman Sgt. Don Rumpel, immediately began a search. A helicopter was used as well as a police dog brought from Edmonton. A camp was cleared out of the bush on the high riverbank opposite the island and 12 policemen and local trappers made an exhaustive search in a ten-mile radius.

Sgt. Rumpel told The Courier, "The search was conducted in the most difficult terrain, thick bush, dead falls, swamps, hordes of mosquitoes, black flies and torrential rain…" The RCMP camp that was cut out of the bush by a 17-year old friend of Eddie's was later developed by the forestry and named "Engstrom Campsite."

The police and residents had many questions. What would make the canoe tip? Engstrom was an excellent river man and the current was neither strong nor rough at that part of the river. Why did he have the dogs tied in the canoe? Why did Miss Engstrom refuse to get back into the canoe? Was it because of the teasing Eddie admitted he did on the way up river about the dangerous and violent Indians?

Why was a body never found? The RCMP went back in the fall and did another search and still no body. Why did Eddie not tell Elmer until next morning? Why did he wait so long to report the accident to the police? Is it just possible that the brother and sister argued and a death resulted? We'll never know the answers.

After his sister's death Eddie changed; he became morose and drank heavily. In early September of the same year Tom Weber saw his canoe drifting down the Clearwater. His body was half out of the canoe with his face in the water; he had suffered a heart attack.

When Sgt. Rumpel went to Engstrom's Clearwater cabin he found a manuscript of a book Eddie had written, along with a holograph will. He left his town property to the Scouts and Guides and his cabin, trapline and canoe to his friend and neighbour D.D. Williams. Relatives from Sweden contested his will but the court upheld his wishes. His home on Fraser Avenue was sold and the money used to develop the campsite at Engstrom Lake.

Bob Duncan, who was keenly interested in the community's history, arranged to have the manuscript published, entitled *Clearwater River*. The book is a delightful read but one wonders about its accuracy. We gave a copy of the book to D.D. Williams the winter it was published. A few weeks later when we stopped to visit, D.D. pulled out the book and said he'd underlined all the garbage parts – the book was full of red inked pages!

In any event, true or not, the last mystery Eddie left us with is in his book. He tells of hunting beaver in a creek one winter and said he found chunks of rocks that he thought might be uranium or silver. He sent samples to the University of Alberta and they verified the samples were the purest silver. In the spring he went back to try and find the source of the mineral. While he was chipping rocks, a slide roared down the mountainside and boulders fell on his leg. He was able to make his way painfully back to base camp, started a fire that was reported to forestry and then he was rescued by helicopter. He never did go back. He wrote, "But every time I set out, instead of prospecting, I fished the creeks and watched the sun rise and set, too happy to spoil all that beauty with thoughts of mother lodes and lousy wealth."

It is fitting to close the story of Eddie Engstrom with the dedication in the front of his book. *To all the lowly, the lone and the humble, who take to the bush in the fall to follow the trails with traps and snares, and with rifle over their shoulders to hunt for the meat they need in order to live – to all the honest to God bushmen, I dedicate this little book. Just Eddie.*

D.D. Williams,
The Big Eddy

Ask any of the aspiring young trappers and dog mushers of the 1960s who taught them the most bush skills, and I'd venture to say they'd name D.D. Williams.

He was a man who lived in Waterways and worked for Imperial Oil for 26 years, trapping every winter. His trapline was about five miles below the Cascade Rapids on the Clearwater River and stretched to the Saskatchewan border.

D.D. and his twin brother Dwight were born in Saskatchewan and he lived for a time with a fur trader in the northern part of that province. He came to McMurray sometime in the 1930s. Mrs. Williams was born in La Loche and the couple adopted her sister's son when he was two months old.

When his neighbour Eddie Engstrom died he left a hand written will bequeathing his canoe and his cabin and trapline to his friend D.D. Williams. So Mr. & Mrs. Williams moved seven miles downriver to the Engstrom cabin. Son Archie stayed for a few years in the old cabin and every Sunday walked down to visit his parents and get a week's supply of bannock from his mother.

Mrs. Williams could do more than bake bannock; she picked blueberries and raspberries and made jam every year, and more than once shot a moose. One winter when she was in her 70s, a moose strolled down the river in front of the cabin. She took out the rifle and felled it with one shot. She left it for Archie to skin and butcher and haul to the meat house.

When Archie was a baby Mrs. Williams paddled 60 miles to town from the Cascade Rapids, and all in one day. Joan Lewis, a great friend to her, once asked her how long it took to walk and snowshoe to Waterways in the winter. Mrs. Williams replied, "Two sleeps if there is a trail, and three sleeps if we have to break a new trail."

Mrs. Williams tanned moose hides and did wonderful beadwork. Art Hoehne wore a moose hide jacket she had made for him for over 30 years.

D.D. was an expert and efficient trapper; his furs always got top prices due to the quality of skinning. He never begrudged sharing his knowledge and trapping skills with his young friends, even to telling them where the best fishing spots were. He saw his way of life change from using dogs and toboggans to skidoos, and of course in summer it was a canoe with a "kicker".

The site of the Williams' last cabin on the river was known as *The Big Eddy,* a spot where the full force of the river waters curled around a big rock. Over the years the channel has moved, the rock has somewhat disappeared and it no long has the big swirl.

A southern Alberta farmer remarked that in the 1930s a trapper with a dozen traps and a good line could make more than a farmer could on two sections of land. And many from all parts of North American flocked to the north to earn a living by trapping.

To this spot on the river came many adventurers and trappers. The history of some of the residents has been lost to time but we do know that in the 1930s at least six cabins were occupied by families. Bertha McBryan, who now lives in Hay River, tells of living there with her parents, Claude and Mary Watt and her three siblings. Her family had a large cabin overlooking the river; smaller cabins were clustered on either side. Two Swedish men lived in one cabin, her Uncle Blake in another and Jean Poulin and Gunnar Boutie also had cabins.

Luke Short, the famous American western writer, was just one more wanderer who came to the north to survive by trapping. He spent time at *The Big Eddy* from 1931 to 1933. Mrs. McBryan, then a little girl, remembers seeing him writing in his cabin. We don't know how successful he was at trapping fur but certainly his vivid imagination eventually gave him a good living. D.D. also recalls Luke Short, whose real name was Frederick Dilley Glidden.

Claude Watt would get an abundant harvest of furs each winter, his daughter remembers, and sold them to free-trader Sam Kushner in Fort McMurray. In the summer the family grew a large garden. Bertha particularly remembers the huge cabbages and that the Swedes and Mr. Boutie made sauerkraut. Because the Watt cabin was the largest it was often a communal dining room with a very large table. The cabin roof was made of birch bark.

In summers the family would make a trip to McMurray and Bertha remembers the rapids, with her dad lining the canoe down and the rest of the family walking the portages. Mr. Watt tended an oil derrick on the river. Mrs. McBryan does not know just where it was located but it was on the same side of the river closer to town. The owner of the derrick would bring prunes and raisins for the children – a real treat.

In time all the families left *The Big Eddy* and Eddie Engstrom built a new log cabin there. And then for many years D.D., Mrs. Williams and Archie called that beautiful spot on the river home. Many changes in many lives, but through all the years, the river still runs on.

George Deep, The Man From Syria

At just 15 years of age George Deep came with his father from Syria to a new land. His father went back but George stayed, working first in Quebec and Ontario and gradually working his way across this vast country.

He became a peddler and also bought fish and sold them to housewives. It was in his role as country salesman that he met his future wife. She was just 15 when they married; Mr. Deep was 32. They settled on a farm southeast of Lac La Biche but in 1941 after their farmhouse burnt they moved to Fort McMurray. The Deeps had 13 children in all, but when they travelled by train to Waterways the oldest was away in the army, and the youngest son had not yet arrived.

A house on the Prairie was their first home, and later they moved to Waterways. Mr. Deep worked for the U.S. army during its time here in the 1940s. They were loading freight from the incoming NAR trains onto barges for shipment to the Norman Wells Canol Project. An estimated 5000 American troops were camped on the Prairie area, along with all their equipment, offices, bunkhouses and mess halls. Many of the local men, including George Deep found employment with them.

George Deep's peddler days must have given him a taste of salesmanship because he opened the Venice Café and Grocery on Railway Avenue. It was a popular gathering spot for the local poker players who had their own back room. He also cooked on the Hudson's Bay Company boat, the *Northland Echo*.

Mrs. Deep, while raising her 13 children, found time to have a large garden and can all the vegetables, which were put down in the cellar. As well she was an amazing cook. Her daughter Marion recalls going to the garden on the Prairie, pulling weeds, hoeing and picking and hating every minute of it. And now Marion has one of the most beautiful gardens in Fort McMurray.

Recalling her childhood days, Marion says some of the best memories were riding the train to Anzac and picking berries. Of course the berries, which were abundant each summer found their way to the Deep's cellar for tasty winter desserts.

Marion Deep married Archie Brooks in 1953 and they raised their daughter and two sons here. They bought a log house from Andy Fossen for $500. It is now in Heritage Park and is used as a caretaker's cottage. In summers Archie and Marion enjoyed traveling the rivers by canoe and later by boat.

Two of the Deep sons made their home here as well. Lester worked at Suncor for 33 years and in retirement volunteered at the Golden Years. Arthur logged in Lac La Biche for a time and also ran a grader for the town.

George Deep never went back to his native country. He spoke four languages fluently: English, French, Cree and Syrian. To leave one's homeland in their teens and venture across the ocean and the continent to establish a new home must have taken courage, stamina, endurance and much faith.

Haxtons,
A McMurray Tradition

For two decades Haxton's Store was the place where you could find anything you needed or wanted in Fort McMurray. The enterprise, run by Alex and Alice Haxton, sold groceries, dry goods and hardware. In the neatly stacked shelves, residents could find everything from sewing thread to snare wire and traps.

When the store burnt on Christmas Eve 1979 it was not only a local landmark that burned but also a source of convenience and supply for so many citizens.

Alex Haxton was a Scot who flew with Canadians in a bomber during World War II. They were shot down over the Mediterranean, and floated for nine days on the sea before being picked up by an Italian Red Cross ship. He spent the rest of the war as a prisoner, first in an Italian POW camp and then two years in a German camp. The camp he was in was liberated by the Russian army.

When the war was over Alex Haxton moved to Canada, working for the Hudson's Bay Company, first in Winnipeg and then in Yellowknife and northern B.C.

Alice Haxton was born in Winnipeg and worked as a seed analyst for Federal Grain. On a trip to Yellowknife she met Alex and the couple married in 1953.

In 1955 the Haxtons moved to Fort McMurray and worked for the Hudson's Bay Company. The experience gained in northern Canada as a fur buyer for the Bay was invaluable a few years later when they purchased Ed Hanson's general store across the street from the Bay. They soon built the Caledonia

Building next door to add groceries and dry goods to their retail mix. In the late 1960s while the Dr. Clark School was under construction, classes of the public district were held upstairs in the Caledonia Building. The library was based there for a few years in the '70s.

When telephones were in most homes in Fort McMurray the Haxtons devised a unique advertising technique. Each year they printed a card listing all the numbers; this was given free to each household and was a prized object. They are now collectors' items.

In 1972 when the Clearwater Subdivision was cleared of bush and subdivided into lots the Haxtons bought a large lot and built their dream home. Their flooring was traditional plaid carpet brought all the way from Scotland.

The Scottish heritage was important to both and they were prime movers in the annual Robbie Burns dinner that was such a popular evening every year in town.

On a trip to Edmonton in 1974 Alex Haxton suffered a fatal heart attack. Mrs. Haxton, along with her teenage son Keith kept the business going, including buying and selling furs. Many of the natives had a close rapport with Mrs. Haxton; she helped them with correspondence, gave them advice and sometimes loans. They looked to her for a fair price for their furs and were able to purchase their needed trapping supplies.

Tragedy struck the Haxtons on Christmas Eve in 1979 when the store burned to the ground. A smoker accidently ignited a macramé hanger and the fire soon engulfed the whole building. Charlotte Mitchell and Gerry Furber, the two clerks escaped out the front door, and anxiously wondered where Mrs. Haxton was. She had grabbed the store's ledgers and ran out of the back door. These books not only had financial records, but daily weather information and notable events taking place in the town.

The wooden building was built in 1922 by Swedish brothers Henry and Sven Swanson. It was occupied by Sam Kushner, a trader and then by Ed Hansen's General Store. At the time of the fire, Mrs. Haxton had run the entire retail business of hardware and dry goods from this location. They had sold the grocery store to Red & White store in 1966 and when this grocery store closed they rented the Caledonia Building.

After much deliberation Alice Haxton decided not to rebuild for retail but built to lease; she had constructed a modern three-storey office and retail in a prime location.

Mrs. Haxton travelled extensively to many parts of the world. She contributed to the community by serving on various boards, including the hospital board, the recreation board and the Board of Human Rights. She was very active in getting the Family Y started in McMurray and was the first woman president of the Chamber of Commerce. The Haxton Centre in Borealis Park has recognized the family.

Son Keith took his schooling in McMurray and went to the University of Alberta for further degrees. When he decided to open a bar and restaurant in the city on family property Mrs. Haxton found another interest, and became a valuable asset to The Tavern on Main.

The Haxton family has been an integral part of the business community for more than half a century. For some, there will never be another store like Haxtons, the store where you could find whatever you needed or wanted.

Claire Peden,
A Man Of Opinion

One was never in doubt about Claire Peden's opinion on anything, whether it would be the introduction of metric, dykeing the Snye or installing sewer systems in the town. And most often time proved him right over and over. Some agreed with Mr. Peden's opinions, some were just as verbally against them, but all respected the man.

Claire Peden came to McMurray in 1956, opening up the winter road from Wandering River. He was born in Manitoba and began work in the construction industry at 15. He was part of the crew that built the first highway cloverleaf bypass in Niagara Falls, Ont. In 1941 he married Edith Moulson; they had three children, Ray, Diane and Jack (Torchy).

The famous Alaska Highway, a difficult and speedy construction job by the U.S. Army Engineers, provided a northern challenge for Mr. Peden. In 1943 he joined the Royal Canadian Engineers and spent 39 months in the army. After the war he returned to construction in Manitoba and in 1950 made the move to Alberta.

Starting his own firm, C.H. Peden Construction Ltd., he started building bush roads for oil exploration companies. This brought him to Fort McMurray building a cutline from Wandering River and then in 1955 he built trails north of town for another oil company. Mr. Peden shipped his cats and trucks in by train and barged them north to the Shell site. Work for heavy equipment seemed to be in the north and so he moved his family here.

Peden's Point, across from MacDonald Island at the confluence of the Clearwater and Athabasca Rivers was developed and settled by Claire and Edie. During the Great Canadian Oil Sands construction years many barbecues were held there. Visitors would cross from the Snye on barges provided by NTCL. Mr. Peden and Archie Brooks would dig a pit and roast the beef overnight and when the pit opened the aroma and taste were never forgotten.

Mr. Peden became involved in the politics of the McMurray Town Council, and was elected as mayor in 1961. He served also on the Fort McMurray Town Council and on the New Town Board of Administrators. Fort McMurray was partially administered by the province from 1964 to 1980 when it became a city. Two members of the board were appointed by the province and the balance elected; the board chose the chairman.

In earlier years a debate raged in the community as to whether sewer lines should be installed; some felt taxes would increase too much. Mr. Peden, with Bob Duncan and Mac McCormick loaded an outhouse and a new toilet on the back of a truck and drove it down Franklin Avenue to demonstrate and question which system the citizens preferred.

When J. Howard Pew came to McMurray in 1963 it was on Claire Peden's skiff that the entourage went down river to the Great Canadian Oil Sands' site.

Mr. Pew, chairman of Sun Oil, had faith in the development of the oilsands and became a firm friend of Mr. Peden's.

With the decision of Sun Oil to go ahead with GCOS it appeared McMurray was on the brink of rapid expansion and an influx of new residents. The ice jam and resulting flood during breakup in 1963 convinced the province that a dyke should be built across the end of the Snye to MacDonald Island. Mr. Peden violently opposed this and predicted it would become a swamp. The province did install culverts to let the water flow through but the heavy silt from the Athabasca soon filled them in. Once again time proved Mr. Peden to be correct and while we lost the free flow of the Snye we have had several major floods since the dyke was built.

I think it was about this time that Mr. Peden voiced one of his most entertaining critical observations. Speaking of engineers and consultants he said, "They are men educated beyond their intelligence." During council meetings every time a new consulting firm was proposed he would voice his displeasure. Over the years we have been, to quote him, "consulted to death." He called the consultants "insultants." Councillor Peden believed in common sense and practicality, often traits that seemed to be missing in the experts who came here to tell us how we should do things in our town. Mr. Peden cared about the community and the ordinary people; his decisions and influence were not for himself but for those who lived here.

When the metric system was imposed on Canadians, Mr. Peden was violently opposed. He often said Canada fought and won the war but lost our identity with the introduction of the metric system. He had a sign on his lawn on Fitzsimmons Ave., "Protect your heritage, Think miles."

When he retired from construction and then from the political arena he still took a great interest in the community. He made a large collection of scrapbooks, recording all the milestones of our town and its residents. He travelled often in his camper, and in later years had a local print shop print a sign he could put in the window asking for help for a senior. He never needed to use it. He died of heart failure in 1985. I doubt whether our city will see his like again.

While Ray Peden, who joined the RCMP, and Diane (Veldhouse) left the community to make their homes elsewhere, the youngest of the Peden children, Jack (Torchy) followed in his father's footsteps as a community supporter and booster. Born in Manitoba, he came to McMurray with the rest of the family in 1956 and went to school here. He worked for his dad in the construction business and later for Keyano College before turning to Syncrude for employment. For many years Torchy managed the bison herd for the oilsands company.

Torchy and Mary Jane Pullar, a girl from Uranium City, were married in 1967 and when the construction business was sold in 1970 they purchased a café and the Hudson's Bay Store in Fort McKay. Mary Jane and her mother ran the business and Torchy did expediting for Shell. They sold *Little Arrow Enterprises* to the McKay Band in 1979 and returned to Fort McMurray with their children.

Torchy retired from Syncrude but didn't stop working. The Marine Park, along Clearwater Drive, has been his dream and project. He has been instrumental in arranging to have the vessels moved, repositioned and conditioned and ready for show. Many companies donated their services to place the ships and help restore them. At times Torchy was joined in his efforts at the Marine Park by long time McMurrayites, Harold Brooks, Neil Marlowe, and Philip Jean. Always Torchy was there and involved in every aspect.

The Marine Park ships include: the *Radium Scout*, an NTCL yarding boat; the *Miskanaw*, a Canada Coast Guard ship that marked river channels; the M*iskanaw* barge; *Dredge 250; McMurray,* a tugboat; a *Fuel Barge*; and *Kris,* a small runabout. Many artifacts are included on the vessels; these have been inventoried and conditioned.

The Pedens not only created history in our town but they are helping preserve it.

Bob Duncan,
Preserver Of History

In the early 1970s a proposal was made by the town's electrical supplier for the town to use street numbers rather than names. The power company offered to provide a grid plan using all numbers. The town garage had a quantity of street number signs on hand. *The Courier*, among others, objected to losing the historic names and we've been adding more ever since.

As names such as Hardin, Hill and Demers were added to the street map, Bob Duncan, manager of Canadian Utilities remarked, "Nobody is going to drive on my name." According to his son Danny, he wasn't too happy when the signs appeared on Duncan Drive.

Bob Duncan was born in Edmonton in 1915, finished his schooling in Peace River and spent time on the west coast before heading north to work in the mines in the North West Territories. In 1943 he started working for Canadian Utilities, later Alberta Power, and installed the first power plant for the company in Fort St. John. From there, with the company, he went to Grand Prairie and then in 1957 to Fort McMurray.

Bob and Helen Powers were married in November 1939. The move to McMurray included all their eight children: David, Sylvia, Dennis, Diana, Phyllis, Richard, Danny and Dale. The children first attended school in Waterways beside the Legion.

As the small towns of Waterways and McMurray grew so did the need for power. The family lived in a house near the power plant, across the road from

Heritage Park. As lots were developed during the GCOS boom they built a house on Crescent Heights.

Bob Duncan and Ken Cochrane owned the very first trailer court in town. Built in 1964, it was called Keel Trailer Court.

Work for the utility company was fast paced with hiring new crews, putting up new power lines, and occasional power outages. The power outages often lasted several hours and always seemed to be on dark late winter afternoons. With all that went on, Bob Duncan still found time to give back to the community. He was president of the Chamber of Commerce, served on the town council, on the Advisory Council to the Northeastern Commissioner, a member of the Elks Club and a prime mover of the Fort McMurray Historical Society.

It was Bob Duncan's dream to preserve the history of our region. He was instrumental in starting Heritage Park and having many of the buildings moved onto the site. He had a vast collection of artifacts and his wife Helen was quite relieved when some of the park buildings were opened and they could be moved from her basement. His vast fur collection, with every northern animal represented, gave the family rumpus room a distinction.

Equal to his love of history was Bob's love of boats. He always owned boats, as well as one time, a barge. His son recalls they were wooden hull boats that needed lots of maintenance, and summer for the Duncan boys was painting and repair time. Just before he retired he bought a large boat called *The Echo* and took passengers on trips down the Athabasca River. His friend, Captain Billy Bird, was captain. Mrs. Duncan had a favourite plaque: "A boat is a hole in the water, surrounded by wood, into which your pour your money."

Friends of the Duncans recall entertaining evenings in their home. Mrs. Duncan was a phenomenal piano player and Bob would join her on the mouth organ or violin. Not only could Helen Duncan read music but also she could play anything by ear after just hearing it once. Helen was a wonderful cook, a quiet gracious lady. Although Bob could be called a "firm" father, he always let the children figure things out for themselves. They said he never got angry when they made mistakes and he gave them lots of flexibility.

In 1980 Bob Duncan retired from Alberta Power and in 1992 the Duncans left their home on Crescent Heights and moved to Edmonton. Bob died in 1995 and Helen four years later.

Bob Duncan's sense of humour is captured by a story in Irwin Huberman's book *The Place We Call Home*.

In 1962, a petition was circulated demanding that a water and sewer system be installed. There were divisions in the community. At times, the debate took on a carnival atmosphere as Bob Duncan and Claire Peden attached an outhouse and a toilet on a flatbed truck, and rumbled down Franklin Avenue asking residents to compare the comforts of current and future options.

As pioneers of our boom years Helen and Bob Duncan contributed to the growth, stability and history of our community.

Art Hoehne,
Came To Build An Airstrip,
Stayed To Build A Church

Construction and church work. That is what brought Art Hoehne to Fort McMurray. A 22-hour ride from Edmonton, on the Northern Alberta Railway, saw Art and two of his fellow Bible College graduates from Vancouver, arrive in Waterways at five a.m. They were immediately put to work by the superintendent of Dawson and Wade, who had recruited them to work on construction of the airport runway expansion. The year was 1955.

Born and raised in Minitonas, Manitoba, Art attended Northwest Bible College in Vancouver, along with a fellow schoolmate, Bruce Mateika. Art's future wife, Ella had just completed her nurse's training and she was rooming with Helen, who later became Bruce Mateika's wife. The Mateikas lived in Fort McMurray during the Syncrude boom years in the 1970s.

Expansion of the McMurray airport, originally built by the American Army, was completed in August 1955. The crew slept in tents and the dining room was a large tent with Edna Bacon as chief cook. Art tells of his job as "grease monkey" working out of a pit dug in the ground with logs over it. The cats and graders had to be greased at night so they were ready for work the next morning. The mud and grease combined were so discouraging he wanted to quit after three weeks, but his boss talked him out of it. When his fellow students returned to B.C. at the end of the summer Art stayed to start a Baptist work in Waterways.

Art and Ella were married in 1956 and made their home on Hughes Avenue. The need for a church was great and Art bought the Hawker store property. A church in Vancouver shipped an Armco building by train, in seven boxes. Art and Dave and Jack Leirdal put the "tin" building together in one week. Now half a century later it serves as Waterways Community Centre.

Art had a variety of jobs to supplement a meager allowance as a northern pastor. His first job was for the Hudson's Bay Company, loading barges in the busy summer months. He drove a school bus, did janitor work and managed Swanson Lumber for eight years. He worked for George Caoutte in the winter driving a truck to supply oil rigs at Birch Mountain. The route took them down the Athabasca River (no bridge or road), up the bank by the Supertest Hill and on through a bush road to the rigs. He later drove the mail and express truck for Ken Cochrane.

Swanson Lumber, known as the King of the Spruce Industry in the World, had a big sawmill in Wood Buffalo Park. The lumber was shipped by barge to Waterways where it was transferred to boxcars for shipment all over North America. Located near the outlet of the Hangingstone River, Swansons employed eight men and a manager to load the boxcars. One summer, Art recalled, they loaded fourteen and half million board feet. The men were paid 22 cents each per thousand board feet and averaged about $1.70 to $8.50 per carload and loaded between two and three carloads a day. Payday was Friday and sometimes it was Tuesday before Art could get his crew back to work. He persuaded some of them to bank their cheques with Frank Hume of Hume's Store until the season ended. This benefited them all; Swansons had their crew, Hume had interest free money, and the crew had a stake at the end of the shipping season.

Ella was busy at home with her young family and as well was always available when help was needed in the community. Randy was born at St. Gabriel Hospital in 1957. Two years later twins Garry and Terry arrived and some years later Cheryl, and then Lois rounded out the family.

In 1964 the Hoehnes started a new venture – chicken farming. They leased property on the highway near Centennial Park. Each spring PWA would fly in up to 2500 baby chicks. In the first years Art would drive to Plamondon for grain on a winter road that later became Highway 63. It was a 24-hour trip each way. The Hoehne chicken farm supplied the community with fresh eggs for a few years.

When Fort McMurray boomed with the construction of the Great Canadian Oilsands (Suncor) plant, the town expanded rapidly and the little tin church could no longer hold the congregation. Sunday services were moved to the Community Centre on King Street, now site of Composite High School. Sunday School classes of about 200 children were divided into three venues. Land was purchased at the corner of Alberta Drive and Franklin Avenue and construction of a permanent church began.

When the GCOS plant was under construction and with no bridge across the Athabasca or road to the plant, one of the local clergy were flown out on Sundays to hold services for the camp of 450 workers. Rev. Hoehne had a turn once a month. Both Art and Ella were driving a school bus and running the chicken farm. They had a Boys' Club, Crusader Girls' Club, Youth Group and every summer held a church camp on Ted Walter's farm at Anzac.

In 1961 Art was elected to Town Council and he also served on the Public School Board. The Lions Club sponsored the Fort McMurray Band and Art played the tuba in the band. When the Athabasca Bridge officially opened the band performed as they marched across the new link to the north.

After seeing the Fellowship Baptist Church established, the Hoehnes felt a call farther north. In 1970 they moved to Fort Chipewyan and built a log home overlooking the lake. A winter was spent in Prince Albert attending a Cree language school. This enabled them to better understand the elders and went a long way to establishing friendships. Art worked with the Junior Forest Wardens, was on the Volunteer Fire Department and the provincial Advisory Board for the community.

In 1979 the Hoehnes moved to Bonnyville and established a church there. Looking to retire, a home was purchased in Westlock in 1997. As always they involved themselves in church and community as well as growing large gardens and each fall Art usually had a very successful hunting trip, often with his sons.

Ella and Art Hoehne have been true partners. Their faith, family and community were important to them. They enjoyed northern nature; Art delighted to take his boys and other youngsters on fishing trips. Ella gardened, canned and sewed. A true neighbour she would always drop everything to help someone in need.

Many lonely families who came to Fort McMurray with the GCOS boom were welcomed in the Hoehne home. For a young couple to choose to make their home in an isolated northern town, not to seek their fortune, but to dedicate themselves through their faith to the people of the community is rare indeed.

The Chinese Influence

Wherever areas opened in western Canada there would come into the area the Chinese immigrants who were ambitious, hard working and good citizens. They saw opportunities and took them. The very first Chinese to come to Fort McMurray, according to records of the Chinese Cultural Society was **David Mah** who came in 1915 and built the Union Café and operated it with his brother Charlie. The Union Café, near the present day bridges, burnt down around 1934 and the brothers operated The Club Café on the present site of the A&W until it too burned in 1949.

Hume's Meat & Groceries and the Liberty Café, next door to each other on Bulyea Avenue in Waterways were run by **Frank and Ying Hume,** with help from sons Benny and Huey. The very busy store was established in 1955, and kept the family working long hours until they sold it in the early 1970s. The Tony Bussieres family lived next door in the early years and Jerry and Benny were great friends; Jerry recalls a cup of coffee in the café was ten cents and a full meal just 75 cents. Benny's son, Kenneth, born in 1959 was the first Chinese baby to be born in Fort McMurray.

Dr. Steven Yung was enticed to this community by GCOS and the Department of Indian Affairs in 1964 and for some time was the only doctor in town. He was joined by Dr. Allan Nicholson, who had practiced in Uranium City, and they opened a clinic at the corner of Main and Morrison. Dr Yung, a skilled physician from Hong Kong, soon became involved in the construction of apartment buildings for the ever-increasing need of housing for the growing population. A leasing office in the basement of the new Hill Building, managed by Elva Bussieres, was often a first stop for newcomers. Sadly, during the downturn in the late 1970s Dr. Yung lost his apartments, and McMurray lost a good doctor.

In 1968 Georges Brosseau expanded the Park Plaza strip mall and Dr. Yung opened The Islander Inn with a Polynesian décor. Soon after he turned it over to Jean Gower and Ed Croft and in 1969 they sold it to Jack Wong.

Jack Wong and **The Islander Inn** were fixtures in the McMurray business scene for many years. With friendly staff, attractive décor and excellent food The Islander was the place to dine in Fort McMurray. Bert MacKay recalled that GCOS (now Suncor) even featured the restaurant on their recruitment brochure. When the mall burned in 1973, McMurray Imperial rebuilt the mall and The Islander reopened in a larger space.

The Islander Inn's Christmas parties were the social event of the year; looking at those old photos gives us a record of the "Who's Who" of our young vibrant city.

Jack had come to McMurray in 1960, emigrating from Canton province in China at age 15. He joined Wayne Chow in his restaurant at the Oilsands Hotel and later in the laundry. And then he bought The Islander. Soon he was joined by his father, Frank, who had operated Frankie's Restaurant in Edmonton. Sons Sam and Alan came to McMurray from Hong Kong and went to Peter Pond High School.

Jack and his wife May had three children, Cindy, Della and Raymond. And then in 1976 Jack's mother, who had raised Sam and Alan in Hong Kong, joined the rest of the family in Canada.

In 1975 on December 26th a planeload of McMurrayites flew to Edmonton for the celebration of Jack's mother's 70th birthday and his parents' 50th anniversary. Contact Airways' plane was chartered and about a dozen couples flew out, dressed in their best, enjoyed the party in Chinatown, and flew back at midnight. Cost was $50.00 each.

Jack Wong was a generous contributor to many local organizations. The wishing well at the entrance of the restaurant collected coins and for many years the funds were sent to the Canadian Institute for the Blind and later to the Salvation Army. Each year he made a beautiful Christmas dinner for the seniors, and this tradition was carried on by **George and Jennifer Chou** when they purchased from Jack in 1993. The Chous had come from Taipei, Taiwan in 1986 to work in the restaurant. When Jack retired and moved to Vancouver in 1993 the Chous took the opportunity to buy The Islander. They also served the community's needs, with good food, good service, and many donations. Sadly on December 31, 2003 their lease expired and The Islander Inn closed its doors.

There are over 60 million Chinese in the world with the last name Wong and several families of the name, albeit not related, have called Fort McMurray home.

Chow's Variety, on Franklin Avenue, is the longest running retail business in Fort McMurray. **Wayne Chow**, at 15, left Canton Province in Southern China to join his father in Boyle, Alberta. He spoke no English but that didn't stop him from teaching himself how to drive his father's car. When his father caught him driving the car he told him he'd better get a driver's license. He went to Alex's Store and ordered a license that cost him all of $1.10 including postage; that was back in 1950 when you didn't need to take any driver's test.

His father moved to Whitecourt then to Drayton Valley as Boyle was a very small town and business was not great. About a year before Wayne and Anne were married Wayne's father and Anne's uncle set them up on a date in Calgary. Anne had come to Canada via Hong Kong with her mother by boat, first to Vancouver and then on to Calgary. Wayne and Anne's wedding ceremony was conducted in both English and Chinese, and Wayne said it went on for far too long! In 1958 Wayne and his new bride joined his father in Whitecourt to assist him in a very busy restaurant in a town experiencing an oil boom.

After a disagreement with his father, Wayne and Anne moved back to Calgary. One day Wayne told his cousin Danny that he wanted to go for a ride and check out possible restaurants for sale. They started driving and ended up in Lac La Biche. They heard a train was going to McMurray and decided to take it and check out the town. They made an offer of $3500 to Audrey Girard for the restaurant in the Oil Sands Hotel. This was in 1959 when a Canadian Pacific flight from McMurray to Edmonton cost just $17.50.

And so in 1959 the Chows were full time in the restaurant business in Fort McMurray. Anne said it was long hours, from breakfast served for 75 cents, until after midnight when the after-show and beer parlour crowd arrived and left. Wayne bought Benny out and then looked farther afield for opportunities. And he found the opportunity just across the street in a vacant lot.

For $1000 the Chows bought the lot and in 1964 had Carlson Construction build a cement block building, a first for McMurray, to house a dry cleaners and laundry. They did laundry for the hotel, GCOS and Bechtel. There were 7000 sheets a week plus the kitchen laundry for the plant camp. Long days and hot conditions. Wayne also opened a jewelry store in the same building. In the early 1970s he sold the jewelry store to Dod Gibbon, who with Ted Pundy, owned the Esso Service station down the street.

A few doors down the street was the old pool hall owned by Leo Gaudet and Lawrence Ulliac which Wayne rented and in 1965 opened the Fiesta Confectionery. As well as convenience foods, such as bread and milk and the necessities for the young shoppers such as bubble gum and comic books, you could also get keys cut. In 1968 he purchased the property and renamed the store the W. Chow Confectionery.

In the '70s another name change occurred and it became Chow's Variety. That's where hunters and fishers could buy their licenses and others the latest newspapers and magazines.

In 1992 Wayne and Anne sold and now in summers instead of turning the key to the store, Wayne turns the key to his golf cart and both he and Anne golf at the course on Macdonald Island every day all summer, weather permitting. After many years of downtown living they now live in Wood Buffalo Estates and enjoy time with their children Lorraine and Collin, and their three grandsons.

Wing Wong and wife Eleanore like so many others of the period, moved to McMurray in 1969 when the population was about five thousand. He was transferred here by AGT but they soon decided to stay and go into business for themselves. They opened McMurray TV and later took on the Radio Shack franchise. A hard-working family; the store on Franklin Avenue is now run by sons Jerry and Darryl.

Harry Loo was another Chinese immigrant to run a successful business in Fort McMurray. Harry's Meat Market was definitely the place in town to buy the best meat from 1971 until it closed in 1997. A daily truck from Edmonton assured shoppers of fresh produce.

Harry came to Canada in 1949 and having heard from Wayne Chow about the opportunities in the northern community opened a store in Plaza One at the first opportunity. His son Ken finished high school in Edmonton and then joined him in the business. Mrs. Harry, although speaking almost no English, always greeted customers with a sweet smile. Ken's wife May also worked in the store making it a truly family business.

Friendly customer service, along with the best meat and variety of product made shopping at Harry's a weekly pleasure for me.

Dr. William Yeung and Dr. K.P. Wong were two of the doctors from the Chinese community who served Fort McMurray patients well. They opened an office on MacLeod Street. A husband and wife team from Taiwan, **Dr. Ting and Dr. Wong-Ting** practiced here for many years as well. McMurray has been so well served by the Chinese doctors who came to our northern city. In the 1980s almost one third of the medical doctors were of Chinese origin.

Bill and Pauline Wong gave McMurray residents a brand-new deluxe eating establishment in 1976. They came from Golden, B.C. with their two little girls, Nancy and Wanda. Bill had come from China to B.C. in 1952 and Pauline had come from Hong Kong.

The Wongs hired Kit Leitch of Green Forest Builders to construct a building on MacDonald Avenue. They started building in May 1976 and the official opening in November of that year saw a gathering of most of McMurray business people.

At the Cedars, Bill's role was planning meals and organizing, while Pauline looked after the front desk and the bar. Open seven days a week, with great food, it gave residents an alternative place to socialize, but created long hours for the Wong family. Now occupied by Long Shots, a sports bar owned by long time residents Gord and Lianne (nee Dutka) Pederson, Bill still has a role.

Nowadays Bill can be found at one of the meat markets he operates along with the wholesale meat division that he has been running for 20 years. He employs eight butchers and his home made sausage and jerky are in high demand. Cutting and wrapping game for hunters has been a boon to many local outdoorsmen. Bill credits his success in his wholesale business and meat markets directly to taking care of his customers' needs.

Bill and Pauline love to travel and have taken many cruises. Pauline's favourite was to northern Europe and the Balkans. Bill's best relaxation is in his trips to Las Vegas. He loves to gamble, Pauline loves to shop and so they both pursue their interests in that city.

In 1980 the **Chinese Cultural Society** was established, with Dr. William Yeung as the first president. In 1983 a Chinese school was begun on Saturdays in the Peter Pond School. Seventy-five students were enrolled. Adult classes in the Chinese language were taught on Sundays for a time.

A continuing special event of the year is Chinese New Year when the Chinese community welcomes their friends from all other nationalities in a celebration of their traditions and the best of Chinese food.

The French Connection

Many of the French-Canadians who settled in Fort McMurray came from Plamondon, a small hamlet three hours drive south. A man of that name who hailed from Michigan settled Plamondon in 1908. Many of the residents of the small town came from Quebec and from farms in Michigan. The Gauthiers arrived in Plamondon in 1908 and 1909. They travelled by train to Edmonton, then by horses or oxen through Morinville and Lac La Biche to their destination. They farmed and fished and to them it was the Promised Land.

One of the first to come to McMurray from Plamondon was Clarence Gauthier, father of fire fighter Joe, who was a timekeeper at Max Ball's enterprise, Abasand Oils. He worked at the plant at the mouth of the Horse River, just over the banks of the present Abasand subdivision, for three years. A fire totally destroyed the plant in 1945. After a first fire in 1941 the plant was rebuilt and actually produced oil and a very smelly gasoline that was used by locals in their cars. The 1945 fire not only destroyed the extraction plant but the entire little settlement including a school and store.

Joe and Pauline Gauthier moved to Fort McMurray looking for work in 1965, and for a time Joe drove taxi for John Sandulac. They left the farm because in Joe's words "it was a place to go broke slow." He went to work at the Suncor fire department and was a member of the local volunteer fire fighters. In 1974 he became the second paid fire fighter in the town's new department under Chief Roy Hawkins. The original team of the Fort McMurray Fire Department included Chief Hawkins, Archie Goodwin, Joe Gauthier and Archie Brooks. Joe became captain in charge of training until he retired in 2002. The family lived on Rae Crescent and after the new fire hall was built he walked every day to work over the bridge that crossed the Hangingstone River.

Before hiring on with the new fire department, Joe took on the job of dog-catcher for the town after Mr. Silin gave it up. One winter, he recalls, he caught 218 dogs in the small town of two thousand people.

Joe also recalls the disastrous freeze up at GCOS in 1967. Thanks to farmers who had been hired to work at the new plant they got it thawed out and avoided a total shutdown.

Some of the major fires Joe remembers are the Abasand forest fire in 1979 when flames could be seen from Franklin Avenue. It was also in 1979 on Christmas Eve when Mrs. Haxton's store burned. There were the fires at Park Plaza and Swanson Sawmill fire near Waterways.

Since retirement Joe has competed in the World Fire Fighter Games and took a Gold Medal for his cooking skills in New Zealand in 2002.

Joe's other passion is hunting. He received his first rifle at 12, a gift from his older brother, and he still has it. Along with his brother in-law, Norm Dube he went on an African safari and has trophies to show for it. Nowadays he hunts only for the table and every year bags a moose for the freezer. As well Joe is an accomplished trapper and he describes the skills and shows the furs to schoolchildren who take part in Heritage Park's school programs.

The **Dube Family** arrived in Plamondon in 1913. After completing her schooling in Plamondon, Pauline Dube took business administration in Edmonton.

Pauline and Joe were married and after they moved to McMurray Pauline worked for two years for the forestry. After their first child was born she stayed home and became very active as a volunteer.

In the 1960s and '70s the Catholic Women's League, of which Pauline was a member, were the best cooks in town. Each Friday and Saturday night there were parties and dances in the basement of the Catholic Church; the food was unequalled. Many wedding receptions were held there as well. Father Beauregard was anxious to finish the church basement and the catering efforts helped bring this to reality.

Pauline's volunteer efforts, and she's never learned to say "no", have included Alberta Summer and Winter Games, the 2001 Homecoming, the California Bingo Association and a cause dear to her heart, that of the Association Francaise de L'Alberta – Wood Buffalo.

When it is election time, whether it be federal, provincial, municipal, or the native bands, Pauline is sure to be a part of it. She has been Returning Officer for many elections and as the city has grown her responsibilities have increased. Staffing is always an issue and she calls on her long-time friends and acquaintances to help man the polls.

Joe and Pauline have done much traveling in recent years. As well as the African safari, they have been to Saudi Arabia, China, Israel, Egypt and Jordan. Holidays included Hawaii and Mexico and fishing in the Northwest Territories.

It is hard for an outsider to sort out all of *The French Connection*, but in chatting with Joe and Pauline we recalled some of the people from early days.

Joe Gauthier, the bus driver came to McMurray in 1957. He was such a kind man, and would wait on the corner for tardy youngsters. At one time he had nine buses; he sold his bus business and retired to Kelowna with his wife Edna.

Jerry Gauthier, best known as *The Mad Trapper*, doesn't live in Fort McMurray, but has come several times to do his act. He dresses the part, has many jokes, often at the expense of the audience, and has performed before at least two Lieutenant Governors and several premiers. He delights to poke fun at politicians.

Urban and Jeanne Gauthier had triplets. The three little girls were adorable and they were the only triplets in town. Euclid Gauthier is the son of the family. They came to McMurray in 1964.

St. Jean Brothers were builders in town in the 1960s. They also operated an ambulance for a time.

Leo Larose was a very competent secretary-treasurer for the Catholic School District. He spoke little, but worked hard, and I remember, always made sure the accounts were paid on time. His wife Rita managed the Sears store for many years.

Andre (Andy) and Yvette Gaudet arrived in Waterways in 1956. Yvette's cousin, Eddie Plamondon, had been working for Northern Transportation for some years; his wife Anne worked at the Hudson's Bay Company and this was what drew them to the community. The Gaudet family had originally come from Montreal to Plamondon.

Andy and Yvette were married in 1949 and lived in a tiny house three miles south of Plamondon. Andy was attempting to farm with his dad, as that was what one did in those days, but they were very poor. Andy said, "I'm not going to be a poor farmer all my life", he went to Lac La Biche, caught the train for a 12 hour ride to Waterways. Cousin Eddie introduced him to the NT foreman and he was hired that very day. When winter came, all NT employees were laid off; not Andy, they kept him on to fix all the equipment that was shipped from the north to the Waterways warehouse for repair.

Andy had a reputation in Fort McMurray. His wife Yvette expresses it best: "There was nothing he couldn't do. He was the smartest man that ever lived." Not only was he a brilliant mechanic but he was very generous and would take young people "under his wing", to quote Joe Gauthier. He became a trustee of the Catholic School Board and was a member of the active Knights of Columbus.

After seven years with the Northern Transportation Company, Andy decided to branch out on his own and opened a full service station at the corner of Main and Franklin. It was the only gas station in town at one point, and as young people came from Plamondon looking for work many ended up pumping gas at Andy's Garage.

Andy was looking for space for a larger shop. Joe Gauthier was also looking for land. Claire Peden had two lots he was willing to sell; one faced

Franklin and the other toward the river. To decide who would get which lot the two friends played crib, Joe won the first hand, Andy the second, and Joe the last one giving him his choice, which was on the main street. Andy and Yvette lived next door to Joe and Edna for many years.

In 1978 Andy built a large, beautiful five-bedroom home on Deep Road in Thickwood and they lived there until he decided to retire at 51 years old.

Yvette had raised six children, four of which were born in Fort McMurray, and had never worked outside the home although she had competently kept Andy's books all these years. She decided she would go to work. Leo and Rita Larose lived next door to the Gaudets and Rita offered Yvette a job at Sears. Andy laughed at her and said she'd never stick it. Yvette says she would have quit after the first few days of unceasing telephones and hurrying customers but was bound to show Andy she could do it. She worked at Sears for eight years.

When Andy decided to sell his shop and retire back in Plamondon Yvette did not want to go. They had a cabin on Bayview Beach and Andy, in his usual competent manner soon had it all fixed up, including a two car garage.

Tragedy struck the Gaudet family in the fall of 2005. Always Andy and his boys went on an annual hunting trip to fill their freezers with moose meat. Their favourite spot was some 100 miles down the Athabasca River, inland on Moose Lake. They set out in Andy's home-made jet boat, took their quads into the lake. They had a small canoe and Andy had borrowed a kicker (small motor) and he and a friend were to set out on the lake. The kicker wouldn't start and Andy pulled and pulled for about 20 minutes. All of a sudden it started and threw both Andy and Herb out of the boat. Herb made it to shore but couldn't see Andy. Divers found his body four days later; the autopsy showed that the heavy exertion followed by the very cold water had given him a heart attack. He was 78.

Yvette is a charming, intelligent lady who still keeps active in Plamondon. She stayed on at the lake for a year and half and then moved into town to

L'Manoir Renaissance. Yvette, at 81, still drives, raises an abundant garden and volunteers in the community.

Germain and Marie Routhier arrived in McMurray early in 1967. Germain to take up duties at GCOS (Suncor), a job he didn't leave until 1987 when he retired as supervisor. Marie was busy with her seven children, four boys and three girls.

They had been farming near Lac La Biche, but the revenue from their mixed farm of pigs, chickens and cows wasn't enough to support the family so Germain went to work for Hamilton Construction, skidding logs to the river for the Swanson's mill in Waterways. Hamilton Construction was sub-contracting to Canadian Confer and they went broke and did not pay the men. The logs that had been skidded to the Clearwater River about 15 miles upstream from Waterways just stayed on the bank. Germain eventually got paid but Hamilton did not.

By 1957 there was a push to get a road into Fort McMurray. That winter Germain ran a cat knocking trees down to facilitate this. The men stayed in a bunkhouse that they moved every few days as they cleared areas further north. That winter they cleared from Crow Lake to the Algar Tower and also built the airstrip at the Algar Tower. Germain took the train home in the spring.

In 1961, working for the forestry, Germain hauled gravel for the winter road to Stoney Mountain and Anzac, and later to Fort McKay. It was a hard life for the family as their dad was away most winters, but he was never assured of work. With rains in the spring there was no construction work; they could only depend on freeze up. And so when GCOS was interviewing prospective employees in Lac La Biche, Germain applied and was offered a job.

Marie said it was almost too good to be true. They were offered $3.00 an hour, a house to move into for $16,800, no down payment, and this house had a stove, fridge, washer, dryer and dishwasher. To a growing family from a non-productive farm this was wonderful. The Routhiers are still in their home; they raised a family that has contributed to Fort McMurray in many ways.

When the children were all in school Marie worked part time for *The Courier* and then for 21 years for the Catholic School District; 18 of these years in the library of Father Beauregard School.

Germain and Marie have given back to the community. They both volunteer at the Golden Years; both have been recognized as Senior of the Year. The Routhiers are a shining example of the folk who moved to this town in the late sixties and were given an opportunity. They took advantage of the opportunity and have given so much back to the town they adopted.

Roger Ulliac is a man who proved it can be done. He says, "God didn't give me a brain, so I had to use my hands." Use his hands he did, but his story will show just how wrong the first part of his statement is, as he proved to be one of McMurray's cleverest entrepreneurs.

Roger's first trip to McMurray from Plamondon, a distance of 170 miles took nine hours. This was in 1966; he was with his parents, on a holiday, coming to visit the Gauthiers and the Lords. Their car had to be pulled by caterpillar tractors on some sections of the road.

Then when he was just 18 he came back to town to work for Poole Construction building the pump house on the Athabasca. Working outdoors at minus 30. After two years with Poole, Roger bought a truck and started in business. He was a dab hand at concrete construction, having learned at 16 in northern B.C., so he started pouring basements. He had 20 guys working for him, all older than he was, and he poured basements for ARC (GCOS) and Northward Developments (Syncrude). Abasand, Thickwood and Beacon Hill all have Ulliac built basements.

In 1980 Roger started buying properties and built his first warehouse in Mackenzie Industrial Park, a warehouse he still owns today. In 1984 with the great recession in town, businesses folded and people left; Roger bought more properties.

His real estate includes warehouses, malls, hotels, motels, houses and condos, totaling over 40 pieces.

During these busy years, he still found time to chair the board of the City Centre Business Revitalization Zone for two years with valuable input.

British Columbia may be a depressed area for some but Roger has found lots of opportunities, building executive homes in Winfield, Kelowna, the Shuswap and Campbell River and employing about two dozen people.

And then five years ago Roger suffered a stroke. He was born with a muscle problem in his heart and this coupled with bad blood resulted in a very dangerous stroke. He couldn't walk, he couldn't talk and all his muscles from his feet to his cheeks were racked with pain. Doctors' prognosis was not favourable but Roger's determination kicked in. He pushed himself, no physio, just determination and hard work and within a few weeks was walking. Speaking took much longer, but today he just sounds like the old Roger.

After the stroke Roger decided to go to Mexico to recuperate and there he saw lots of opportunity. Even with the handicap of not being able to communicate fully, he started construction on the west coast of Mexico. He has built houses and condos on the beach and has 30 guys working for him there.

Roger is a "hands on" person. When I phoned him for an interview he was on a bobcat; the next time I called he was fixing someone's plumbing. Never having had training in any trades, he is still capable of all plumbing, electrical and carpentry. He employs over 90 people and maintains three offices. He's not in McMurray much anymore, perhaps just two months out of the year. Every fall you will find him in Plamondon harvesting on his and the family farm, now run by his brother.

Roger's brother Ron lives in McMurray, and cousin Marcel has worked for the municipality for many years.

About employment in McMurray, Roger said, "Anyone who tells me there is no work here, never got up in the morning. They need to be up and ready for work at seven o'clock."

Certainly Roger Ulliac's ambition, skills and hard work have paid off for him. This is the story of the success of a young man from a farm, with a will to work hard, take risks and seize opportunities to become one of McMurray's wealthiest landlords. And then to battle back from a devastating stroke and find more opportunities. It shows us that with a will, it can be done.

Leo Robert was a man who couldn't say no. In the years Leo was in business in Fort McMurray the donations and sponsorships from his company were phenomenal. Whether it was for a sporting event, for the seniors, for the schools or for any community organization the answer was always "yes."

A French-Canadian, Leo was raised in a small village near Timmins, Ontario. He trained as a mechanic and worked for Ontario Paper at Manitouwadge, on the north shore of Lake Superior. In 1974 he had some months off and rode his motorbike to Alberta. He liked the province and when his buddy Steve Jarvis described the opportunities in Fort McMurray it didn't take long for Leo to join him. It was 1975 and the Syncrude plant was under construction. This meant lots of work for tradesmen. Leo put his name in at the union hall and was soon living in camp on the site and working for Bechtel.

When the Bechtel contract finished Leo worked in Peace River for a few months for Marine Pipelines. Coming back to McMurray, in 1980, he joined Al Askeland and four other partners in Bobal Enterprises, a heavy equipment construction business.

1980 was a banner year for Leo Robert. He met Debbie while they were both working for Bechtel and they were married that year. They formed a company, L. Robert Enterprises Ltd., and invested in the Bobal partnership. In 1984 they sold Bobal to Neegan Development Ltd. and under the contract Leo stayed on to maintain the equipment.

The role of the Robert's business was equipment maintenance. They worked for the plants, for all the contractors and had a site at Fort McKay to service the plants as well as an in-town office and shops. When the new in-town four-building complex was opened, a distinctive sign read, "World Headquarters, L. Robert Enterprises Ltd."

L. Robert Enterprises had over 100 pieces of equipment, including trucks, loaders, and welding units. At peak times they employed 450 people. Getting staff was always a problem, and the company trained many apprentices. Leo sat on the provincial Apprenticeship Board for about 15 years, and at any time would have about 60 apprentices on staff. Many of the mechanics and welders now working at Syncrude and Suncor got their start in Leo's shop.

The growth of the company must have been a challenge to Debbie who raised a son and daughter and oversaw the administration and accounting of the very busy office. She also found time to dedicate to the community, she was instrumental in starting a Business and Professional Women's Club and acted as chair.

Probably Debbie's most valuable contribution to the community was the role she played at Keyano College. She served on the Board of Governors for six years, the last year as chair, and then chaired the Keyano Foundation for five years.

In 2006 it was time for a change. Leo and Debbie sold their business and moved from the community they had helped build. From a town of about ten thousand to a bustling city of 70 thousand, they'd seen immense changes and helped make many of these for the better. One thing that never changed was Leo's constant endorsement of the Montreal Canadiens.

In Kelowna now, Leo says he keeps busy with his three-acre orchard, cutting grass and caring for the apple trees. Debbie, of course, has found volunteer work to do. They spend much of the winter in Palm Springs.

Recalling their days in McMurray, Leo said he has millions of good memories, mostly of people and how the community would come together to accomplish any project they undertook. Debbie echoed these sentiments and added how far the community has come in the past four decades.

When I told Debbie I was including the Robert story in *The French Connection*, she agreed, that as always, she'd just have to go along with Leo.

The French people who made Fort McMurray their home were hard-working, honest, caring, good citizens. Our city's history has been richer through their contribution.

Father Brown,
The Priest Remembered

The Catholic parish of St. John the Baptist has hosted some remarkable priests in the 100 years it has maintained a presence in the community. Both Father Turcotte and Father Beauregard have schools named for them in the city; a street is named for Father Mercredi. Father Turcotte and Father Beauregard were here in the boom years and the lean years of the latter half of the past century. Both were exceptionally fine men of God. Father Beauregard, particularly was a people person and did not limit his hospital visits just to his own parishioners.

Having spent many years in the north where he had to fend for himself, chopping wood, carrying water and doing his own housework, he told us once that he felt guilty being in a warm home with heat, lights and running water.

And as for Father Brown, he is now lay clergy, lives in the high Arctic and is an artist of renown. Although no longer owning the title, to long time McMurrayites he will always be remembered as Father Brown. I never had the privilege to meet Father Brown but have gleaned some history from his outstanding book *Arctic Journal*.

Born in Rochester, New York, Bern Will Brown was in love with the north from an early age. He joined the Oblate order and from the first said he wanted to be posted to the north. And to the north he went and always said Fort McMurray was not far enough north for him.

Young, handsome Father Brown drove a two-ton truck with medical supplies to Edmonton, loaded his truck onto Northern Alberta Railways and reached Waterways. The truck and supplies were loaded onto Northern Transportation's barge but Father Brown caught a ride with the McInnes Fisheries plane to Fort Smith.

Father Brown's duties took him all over the North West Territories and the Arctic but he did spend four years down south in Fort McMurray, all the time wishing for a post farther north. Fort McMurray was the most southerly post in the Mackenzie Vicariate. Over the previous years Father Brown had served in posts along the Mackenzie River and the Arctic coast as well as on Lake Athabasca. He had built numerous churches for the parishes.

Father Turcotte met Father Brown off the DC3 at the McMurray airstrip in July 1958. It was a hot and humid summer with many forest fires. As well as pastoring the churches in Fort McMurray and Waterways, he often went by helicopter to Stoney Mountain and to Anzac.

The priest's duties also included being administrator as well as chaplain for St. Gabriel Hospital, a brick building at the corner of MacDonald Avenue and Hardin Street, and ably run by the Grey Nuns. He was also secretary-treasurer of St. John's School. As well he was appointed as Regional Superior of the missions north and south of McMurray. This involved traveling to Fort McKay, Fort Chipewyan and Camsell Portage, where he had previously built a church.

Father Brown was not just interested in the spiritual needs of his flock. At heart he was a developer and seized on many opportunities for the good of the parish. The original Old Mission, a log building, had been sold to a man who planned to use it for firewood. Father Brown traded him for another building and moved the historic log building to a spot behind the church. At this time the church was at the corner of Franklin and Hardin; each Sunday morning its bell pealed out the invitation to mass. After the new church was built on Hospital St., this church was moved in the early '70s down Franklin Avenue to the corner of Alberta Drive and converted into the Lutheran Church. The Old Mission, saved from destruction by Father Brown, was moved to Heritage Park.

About this time the DEW line station at Stoney Mountain was being dismantled. Father Brown purchased several buildings from Crown Assets for $150 each and had them moved to town. This gave the parish a carpentry shop, extension to the hospital laundry, a garage and an apartment building for hospital staff. He remodeled the hospital kitchen and built a new septic field.

One year on the seven acres surrounding the church (now the Peter Pond Shopping complex) Father Brown grew potatoes. They harvested 500 hundred pound sacks but were not able to sell them all. The next year he planted alfalfa, as by this time he had acquired a horse.

A true northerner, Father Brown had a freighter canoe, and a dog team that he acquired while in McMurray. He was an avid hunter, both for ducks and geese and for moose, and he fed his dogs with fish he netted in the rivers. When his mother and brother visited from New York he took them up the Clearwater River for a few days.

One winter, when it turned 50 below in January Father Brown built a proper igloo on the grounds of St. John's School. He organized a Boy Scout troupe and boys' hockey games.

Because he always wanted to be a cat-skinner (bulldozer operator), Father Brown persuaded Hector Demers to loan him a TD9 to practice with. He moved some buildings and then skidded in logs to place under the Old Mission. McInnes Fisheries loaned him two TD18 Cats to move the Old Mission to the church property. Today it is in Heritage Park.

The parish published a weekly bulletin and as the town had no newspaper, Father Brown added, each week, local news and events.

It was the priest's opinion that the hard working sisters in both the hospital and school would benefit with having a place of their own; a quiet retreat in the beautiful woods on the church property. He drew plans, had Bill Malcolm cut 50 logs at two dollars each and construction started on the hillside just above the roadway (now Highway 63). It was a beautiful structure with a cedar shake roof, stone fireplace and front porch. Many peaceful evenings, and many happy parties were held there by the Grey Nuns and their friends.

The opening of Chateau Gai (now in Heritage Park) coincided with the 50th anniversary of the Catholic Mission in McMurray. The building was dedicated to the Grey Nuns in recognition of the selfless work they had done for the community.

That fall the Bishop wrote to Father Brown asking him if he would construct a church in Nahanni Butte. The logs for the church had been cut three years earlier and were well seasoned. He built the church and then went back to New York state to visit his mother.

While there he recruited five young men to come back with him. In July they left McMurray in his freighter canoe, with his dogs, and travelled to Norman Wells on the MacKenzie River. From there he flew into Colville Lake. And in that small community he has stayed for almost 50 years.

In 1971 the Catholic Church released Father Brown of his vows of poverty, chastity and obedience. He remains a clergyman, but no longer celebrates mass or hears confessions. Bern Will Brown and Margaret Steen were married by Bishop Piche. Father Brown's love of the north, his explorations by river and by his plane were now shared with his wife.

Four short years in our community, but what a lot this man accomplished and what stories old timers can relate of his time in our town.

Father Brown's many adventures and building projects are well told in his book *Arctic Journal*. Copies of some of his amazing paintings are also in the book as well as a photo of Bern and Margaret with Prince Charles and one with Prime Minister Trudeau, both visitors to Colville Lake.

Father Brown's life story is part of the history of the north he loves so much.

The Robert & Marnie Grant Family

Marnie Grant is a remarkable lady in many ways. When well into her eighties she tended a large garden, made pickles and jams and picked berries. A musician and singer, she kept a journal for years and turned it into the story of her husband's life and their remarkable days on a trap line on the Athabasca River.

Robert and Viola (Marnie to her friends) Grant were both born to farming families in Alberta. Robert and his father obtained a homestead at Athabasca Landing, but at 14 Robert went trapping; he got about four cents for each squirrel pelt, and sometimes got the odd fox and weasel. Marnie's book says: "I walked for miles carrying my equipment on my back. My pack consisted of traps, an axe, one blanket, a large pail for making tea, salt and my skinning knife. I fashioned my own stretchers to dry my pelts on. Thank God wildlife was abundant, so I didn't go hungry for meat." This was a 14 year old, alone in the bush making his living.

A few years later, trapping in the Territories he had a team of huskies and was able to sell marten fur for $120 and beaver for $80. Then the war came along and Robert joined the Edmonton Fusiliers. One night at a dance he met his future wife. Marnie had graduated from high school and gone to work in Edmonton. She and her friend entertained soldiers in the Empire Theatre and they sang before audiences of five thousand soldiers.

During the war the Grants were moved several times in western Canada, at the will of the army. Robert cooked for the officers and trained other cooks.

When Japan finally surrendered in 1945 the lure of the north, its woods and its trap lines brought the Grant family first to a trap line at House River and then in 1950 to one on the Athabasca River 100 miles north of Fort McMurray. By this time they had three daughters, later another daughter and five sons.

In Marnie's tale of their life she tells of the unusual caribou migration in the spring of 1951. Caribou herds were migrating by the hundreds past their cabin; they completely covered the Athabasca River that was half a mile wide at that point. Old timers tell of them being on the streets and back yards in Fort McMurray, and they were so thick airplanes could not land on the Snye. The herds of caribou have not come that far south since, but that year the meat at their back door must have been a blessing for the residents.

Life on the trap line, Marnie told Anne Young of *FOCUS* magazine, was hard work with hauling all their water from the river, keeping a big garden, and teaching the children. She taught five children by correspondence in the cabin, as well as looking after her pre-schoolers and doing all the normal family housework. But they enjoyed the lifestyle they had chosen.

The children had many pets; Robert was given an orphan moose on his sixth birthday. Marnie had a collection of rabbits that would come for the vegetable peelings she saved for them. And one spring the children placed three chicken eggs in a partridge nest, the three chicks soon disowned their mother to follow the girls around. Marnie taught all the children to dance, they always had a bedtime story and although they were isolated and rarely had visitors each traditional holiday was a special time for them.

Robert had arranged for a plane to stop in once a month; bringing supplies to them and taking furs and mail out. But for four months of the year they were totally isolated when planes could neither land on floats or skis. But their root house bins were full of vegetables; they had 200 jars of canned berries as well as vegetables and pickles. And as always, plenty of good wild meat.

The Grant family moved to Fort McMurray in 1961 and what a change that must have been for them. Adjusting to locking their house door, traffic and a classroom with strange children was something that they all got used to quickly.

As with all families the Grants had their share of tragedy and sadness. One little boy disappeared when they lived at the trap line, whether he drowned or was lost in the woods was never determined. Eldest son Robert, at 12, drowned at the mouth of the Clearwater trying to rescue a friend, and son James died suddenly in 1986. Daughter Muriel was very sick one year at freeze-up, which made it impossible to get a plane in to take her to hospital. Marnie nursed her constantly and one night prayed to the Great Physician that her daughter would be healed.

The next morning the little girl began to mend. When they were able to get her to a doctor he told the anxious parents she had lived through Infantile Paralysis.

When the Grants came to Fort McMurray in 1950, Marnie's story says there were 800 people here. What changes they witnessed, but still their love was for their cabin on the river and the great outdoors. Bob trapped each winter with his sons until he died of cancer in 1992. Mrs. Grant still lives in Waterways with her son Glenn and family. Her story of the family's life on the trap line shows a woman of great understanding of life, one who enjoyed every aspect, and was gifted with amazing talent. With Mrs. Grant's permission, this is a poem she wrote in memory of her husband Bob.

A Trapper's Retreat

I don't care for city sights,
No better bed was ever found
Motel rooms or glaring lights,
Than scented spruce boughs on ground

Or jostling crowds near exhaust-filled streets,
A waterbed could not compare
All I need is my retreat.
For I sleep like a babe in mine so rare.

I'd rather hear a wolf's lone howl,
Turn your TV on, view violence and fights
Hamstringing moose along the trail
I prefer watching the Northern Lights,

To step on cushioned moss beneath my feet.
Where the air is pure and I'm free to roam
I think God for my retreat.
The great outdoors my home sweet home.

Enjoy your drinks in pubs and bars
I love to sip spring water, cool and sweet,
Lose your lives in speeding cars.
And listen to the birds near my retreat.

Live your way, I shall not blame
I wouldn't change my way of life
While I brew tea o'er a campfire's flame.
For that in the city of stress and strife.

I love to view the golden sunset in the vast northland
I see God's works on either hand
At this time of evening a wood thrush thrills,
I know he is walking among these hills.

Developers

Like any growing community Fort McMurray and Waterways had industrial development that spurred the economy. This section includes individuals who either themselves, or on behalf of a company, undertook enterprises that had a far reaching effect on our city.

Before the successful oilsands developments, two major industries provided work for the people in the area, taking the place of the traditional seasonal fur trapping - salt and fish.

While drilling for oil at the mouth of the Horse River in 1906 Count Alfred Von Hammerstein discovered a huge salt deposit. His various oil explorations came to naught, and in 1925 he and a partner started the Alberta Salt Plant. It only operated until 1927. The salt produced had to be hauled all the way to the train depot in Waterways and coal hauled back. This proved to be too expensive.

In 1936 the Dominion Tar & Chemical Company started a plant in Waterways. The rock salt is 150 feet thick but is 960 feet below the surface. Water was pumped down one well, pushed to an adjoining well and pumped to the surface. Pumped into tanks, treated with caustic soda and put into one of six evaporators, 60 feet high. Then the liquid was drained out the bottom and the crystallized salt was bagged into 50 and 100 pound bags. The boilers were steam powered and run by coal which was shipped in and delivered throughout the plant by wheel barrow.

The plant employed both men and women, and Waterways residents set their clocks by its whistle. The workers had eight-hour shifts and were paid between 57 cents to 60 cents an hour. Although the plant produced, at peak, 110 tons of salt a day, once again, freight costs made the plant unprofitable and it closed in 1950.

McInnes Fish Co. not only caught and sold fish but also operated its own fleet of boats and barges, and had a fish processing plant on the Clearwater River close to the rail access. They also logged up the river and produced lumber to make fish boxes. In winter they cut and stored ice for the summer transport needs.

The fish caught on Lake Athabasca were gutted and graded on barges at the south end of the lake, packed in ice and then brought by boat to Waterways where they were loaded onto the train. *"In just ten days*, Huberman's book says, *"after being plucked from Lake Athabasca, northern pike, pickerel, lake trout and white fish were on the tables in restaurants and homes in New York, Chicago and other urban centres."*

These two industries, along with logging, and sawmills, the railway, and trapping provided families with incomes before the oilsands booms. As the town developed with the influx of workers, other developers made their mark. These are their stories.

Ewashkos,
The Sawmill Family

If the Fort McMurray area didn't have the mammoth oil sands developments, we would showcase with pride the Northland Lumber Company industrial wonder. And indeed it is a marvel, being for some years one of the most modern sawmills in all of North America.

The Ewashko family, like so many of the city's residents, came to Fort McMurray for a better opportunity in the 1960s. For the same reason, Roy's grandparents left their home in the Ukraine in 1933, travelled by ship to Halifax, and across the continent by train till they spotted an area with many trees at Evansburg, a village west of Edmonton, and decided this was the spot in which they wished to settle. For in the "old country" most of the trees had been cut down and the sight of the forest was enticing to them.

From the train station they walked to Tomahawk to take possession of their quarter section and proceeded to build a one room log house. That winter three families lived in that home, six adults and nine children in all. They cleared the land, built more homes, and farmed. Roy was born in that cabin in 1934. He was the fourth child in a family of eight. Eventually the family moved to Keephills, where they built a new house and barn and settled into farming. There, Roy coached a girls' softball team with Keith Porter, and fell in love with Keith's sister, Beverly. The feeling was mutual and Roy and Bev married in Edmonton when she was 20. Roy was operating a portable sawmill near Whitecourt but in 1964 moved it to the McMurray area for the winter.

The winter of 1966 saw Bev and first son Howie join Roy in a bush camp near Fort McMurray. Here Bev cooked for 30 guys and shopped for the groceries once a week at the Solo store in the Park Plaza Shopping Centre in Fort McMurray. Trucks hauled the rough lumber out to Edmonton and would also bring supplies back. They also shipped to the Primrose Mill, near Draper. The Primrose Mill would plane the lumber, put it on the train and send it to the Edmonton markets.

This first mill site was half way between GCOS (now Suncor) and Fort McKay, with a road going through Lower Camp, later part of Syncrude. A fire destroyed the mill in 1968, the first of three fires the family business was to experience.

The following summer, Roy returned and used his equipment to clean up the radar site on Stoney Mountain.

In 1971 the family, now joined by daughter Kim and younger son, Craig, made a permanent move to McMurray. They bought and lived in one of the five trailers in a small area rented out by Siggi Lucas and located near The Heartbreak Hotel, on the Prairie region. Bev has fond memories of those years. She said Alfred Gauthier, who lived next door, used to say you could knock on the wall and ask your neighbour to pass the ketchup. Bev said, "Living so close together, if you didn't like your neighbours you'd be in big trouble."

Roy was able to purchase another portable mill and began sawing timber for George Waterhouse. He eventually bought the Waterhouse timber quota and so was ensured of a more stable source of timber. The Town of Fort McMurray was expanding and because there was timber on the land destined for expansion, Roy was asked to clear the land. He moved the mill onto a site in the Gregoire Industrial area and then to a site where Burnco Rock Products is now situated. From there the trees in the Thickwood and Timberlea area were cleared. They were able to get a contract to provide all the mine timbers for Uranium City and shipped all the lumber and timbers north by barge. Bev, at this point did all the bookkeeping, sold lumber and filled in as a cook when necessary. Because all the children had become involved in competitive swimming, she was also very involved in the swim team as well. She was one of the original founders of the Fort McMurray Swim Club and served as its president for nine years. For four years she also was on the provincial board of Swim Alberta. She became a Master Official and travelled all over Canada as a swim official as well as to the Universiade Swim Meet in Edmonton in 1983.

In 1981, the mill burned again when an oil pump overheated and exploded, and the workers ran for their lives. Up until now Ewashkos had operated portable mills. Now they felt it was time for a permanent mill and in 1982 leased 20 acres from the Alberta government to build a partly steel mill. Bev became the sole person in charge of sales as well as in charge of accounting and administration. Their product was in demand all over North America and as well they shipped as far as Japan, China and Great Britain. Roy was invited to go with an Alberta Government delegation to tour and give advice to the Russian forestry industry. He also travelled to South America on a government fact-finding mission.

Sons Howie and Craig bought shares in the company in 1995, and Roy and Bev, though still active started to phase out of the business. The sons work as a team with Howie looking after administration and sales and Craig running the mill and looking after purchases and installation of equipment.

The third devastating fire, in 1996, was thought due to faulty electrical equipment in the sawmill and saw it totally destroyed. The planer mill and the office did not burn. They rebuilt the sawmill with the very newest technology available and it became a state of the art mill, with industry people from all over North America coming to view it. The mill is totally operated by computers that are so efficient they can decide how to get best value out of each log processed.

The office was built in 2001 with all local wood and is a beautiful workplace. The power and heat for the complex is generated by the waste product from the mill. Nothing is wasted, in fact. In 2011 Northland Forest

Products started shipping shavings to Texas for bedding for cattle. The mill has green certification, one of the first to do so in Canada.

In 1999 Roy was diagnosed with cancer and fought it until 2004. Earlier in 2004 the family had hosted a party celebrating Bev and Roy's 60th and 70th birthdays respectively and their 40th wedding anniversary, and invited family and friends from all over the country. Roy spoke of life and the joy of a life filled with good people and hard work that he loved.

Fort McMurray can be justly proud of this family, who came to make a living, found a good life for themselves and their children and have enhanced our area's reputation throughout the forestry world.

Bob Lamb,
The TV Man

Over the past years many entrepreneurs have come to Fort McMurray with the intention of investing and capitalizing on the boom times. Most of those who made profits left after a few years and took all their dollars with them. Not so Bob Lamb. Although he never lived in McMurray Bob Lamb was more generous to our community than almost any other businessperson I can think of.

Bob Lamb came to Fort McMurray and set up his cable company in 1970. His company did extremely well over the years in the oilsands city, and he invested in the community and gave lavishly to many causes including the United Way, Keyano scholarships, and local clubs. The 911 number came into existence here through his contribution. His gift to Keyano helped fund the training centre that bears his name and Borealis Park is home to the band shell he funded.

Through the years ABC Cable promoted many events. There was coverage of all the parades from a spot on top of the Professional Building on Franklin Avenue. Every Friday evening local news, sports and community events were broadcast in a live program done from the studio in the Professional Building. Ron Morgan did a rundown on the week's sports and upcoming ones; I did a synopsis of the week's news events and Maureen Billings talked about community events, interviewed local residents and kept McMurray viewers up to date on the social side. Our local group was there when anything of note happened in the community; I remember interviewing Bob Stanfield, leader of the PC Party when he came to town.

Robert William Hugh Lamb was born in 1923 in Lashburn, Saskatchewan and raised in the small town of Waseca until he was 12 and moved with his family to Edmonton. At 13 years old Bob had a ham radio license – the youngest person in Canada. When he was 15 he worked on equipment for CFRN during the summers. He and his future wife Betty both went to Oliver Elementary in Edmonton and Victoria High School.

Bob was not able to serve in the armed forces during the war due to his emphysema, which plagued him all his life, and so he was put in charge of all radio communications for Air Observations in Edmonton.

Television was just a dream in Alberta in the early 1950s and Gordon Love of CFCN radio in Calgary made it into realization. He sent Bob Lamb and two other technicians to Rochester, New York for three weeks of training. When they returned they built the first TV station in Calgary. This necessitated Betty, who had married Bob in 1942, and their young son David to move to Calgary from Edmonton. Daughter Marion, later involved in the cable business in B.C. was born in Calgary.

Every Christmas morning in Calgary Bob, along with others, broadcast live by radio from the Alberta Children's Hospital. For 20 years youngsters in hospital at Christmas could sing along with the radio crew, and say hello to their parents, some in distant parts of the province.

When Mr. Love sold his stations to McLean Hunter Bob stayed on for two years to run them and then he left to branch out on his own. His first project was with cable television at Rainbow Lake and High Level. The Chamber of Commerce in Fort McMurray contacted Bob to put cable into our town. The result in 1970 was Alberta Broadcasting Corporation, headed by Bob Lamb, with partners Bob Dawson and Jim and Bill Love.

In 1970, with a hard working team of Larry Biswanger, Grace Dafoe and local staff, underground cables were laid, houses connected, tower signals erected, and Grey Cup 1970, albeit snowy, was seen live in Fort McMurray. What an undertaking it was to get television up and running in this town. Muddy streets, inches of rain, towers on Highway 63 breaking down at inexplicable hours made every day a challenge for Larry and Grace. It was not unusual to see lights burning in the ABC offices in Norm Simons' Professional Building long past midnight.

Bob Lamb brought a service to our town, he reaped the profits of a successfully run business and he returned to the community probably more than any other individual and yet his home was in Calgary. His early hometown of Waseca, SK was given a sound system for their community centre, a curling rink, and had the cemetery fenced thanks to his generosity.

When ABC Cable sold to Shaw Cable Bob retained shares in the company but as well gave shares to his immediate and extended family members. Larry Biswanger and Grace Dafoe, the early hard working and long time employees of ABC were given shares. As well as northern Alberta the Lamb cable empire extended to Prince George, the interior of B.C., to Red Deer and to Vancouver Island.

In 1970 Bob and Betty Lamb purchased property at Rancho Mirage, a gated community near Palm Springs in California. They spent most winters there because of Bob's health but he was always back and forth to Alberta even then.

In December 1996 Bob had a fatal car accident in California. He was buried in Calgary from St. Mark's Church, where he had supplied the sound-system.

When we asked Mrs. Lamb about Bob's hobbies she said, "His whole life was his work. He loved photography and his ham radio. His heart was in Fort McMurray."

Bob was a great friend to all, and especially to the citizens of our city.

Lawyer-Developers, They Filled A Need

In the years leading up to the GCOS boom Fort McMurray had two bright, personable lawyers who came weekly from Edmonton to see clients. With very different personalities and very different practices, both of these men had faith in McMurray's future and invested by building shopping centres, apartment buildings, homes, trailer parks and other commercial ventures.

Without Georges Brosseau and Norman Simons, the ordinary people who came to Fort McMurray to work in the businesses that supported the oil companies would have found no place to live.

Norm Simons with his partner of some years Siggi Lukas, were responsible for several trailer parks, many apartment buildings, a kitchenette motel, and the famous men's lodging, the Heartbreak Hotel. The first elevator to be installed in town was in their four-storey apartment on Charles Avenue.

Simons and Lukas owned most of what is now the Abasand development and at one time planned to develop view acreage lots. Town council turned the project down as being too "elitist." For many years a ski hill down to the Horse River was maintained on their property. Siggi Lukas was tragically killed when a private plane he was travelling in crashed at the City Centre Airport in Edmonton.

Norm Simons had an amazing repertoire of stories and a great sense of humour. It was always a delight to cover council meetings when Simons appeared with a new proposal.

With the downturn of the economy in the '90s both Syncrude and Suncor decided to divest themselves of their houses and apartments. With the vacancy rate already the highest ever this put Simon's apartments in jeopardy. His entire McMurray empire collapsed, and such were the intricacies of his financial assets and liabilities that the bank that put him into receivership, hired Norm Simons the lawyer, to do the work as no one else could understand the inter-company transactions. Although he lost his holdings in McMurray, Simons' practice in Edmonton was intact and flourishes today.

Georges Brosseau, of a longtime St. Paul and Bonnyville family and with a law practice in Edmonton, also saw a future in this northern town. One of his first projects was Plaza One, a shopping centre on Franklin Avenue, midway between the new Peter Pond Shopping Centre (built by Dr. Allard) and the Riviera Hotel at King Street. It was here that McMurrayites had a choice of grocery shopping with the Solo Store and then later Harry's Food Market.

Into the 1970s Mr. Brosseau saw the need for more commercial space and built Plaza 2 (now renamed River Centre) that gave us two storey shopping with the first escalator in town. He also built several apartment buildings to accommodate the growing population.

Roland Chalifour managed the properties for Brosseau for many years, and was followed by Paul Hartigan. Through the lean years of the '90s with extremely high vacancy rates the company managed to keep afloat.

Today, Georges Brosseau, who was born the same year as the author, still maintains an office in Plaza One and commutes to McMurray every other week. His partner and daughter, Dorothy Brosseau takes a turn in the law office alternate weeks.

These two Edmonton men saw a future for our town when its main street was mud, or dust; there was no radio, no television and natural gas and electric lines were just being dug into the ground. Due to government policy, the oil companies provided housing for their workers; many of the "others" found their place to call home in a Brosseau or Simons apartment. Their foresight and their gamble on what was a town's very uncertain future must be recognized.

Dr. Karl A. Clark, Oilsands' Pioneer

No name is as widely recognized in the development of the Athabasca oil sands as that of Dr. Karl Clark. He is credited, after many years and trials, of unlocking the secret of how to extract the oil from the bituminous sands. Many books and scientific articles have been written of Dr. Clark and his work, not least the two books by his daughter, Mary Clark Sheppard. *Oil Sands Scientist* is a collection of his early letters and *Athabasca Oil Sands* contains letters from 1950 to 1966, both edited by Mrs. Sheppard.

Of Scottish ancestry, Karl Clark was born in 1888 in Toronto. He studied for his B.A. and Masters in Chemistry at McMaster University and went to the University of Illinois to take his PhD. Unable to join the army because of poor eyesight when he left university in 1915 he worked in Ottawa with the Geological Survey of Canada.

Dr. Clark married a school teacher, Dora Wolverton, from B.C. in 1919; both had a keen interest in education and the outdoors.

A report by Sidney Ells on the *Bituminous Sands of Alberta* sparked his interest as a research scientist. Samples of oilsands were sent to Clark's Ottawa laboratory in 1920; he was to determine if they would be suitable road building material. In 1920 Dr. Clark was offered a post as research professor in what was to become the Alberta Research Council.

The tar sands, then so called, were looked upon as a source of road surfacing material. Dr. Clark felt that the oil could be separated from the sand and began a long process of experimentation until he perfected the method. In his efforts he was assisted by Sidney Blair, a returned serviceman who had studied petroleum engineering at the University of Birmingham. The two remained lifelong friends and worked together for many years. They were the first to use detergent in the separation process at the Dunvegan test plant near Edmonton.

In the fall of 1925 Clark and Blair made a trip down the Athabasca for about 80 miles, exploring its tributaries and collecting samples. They travelled as far as Fort Chipewyan by canoe and returned on one of the steamboats with all their gear and samples.

Sidney Ells had established a quarry on the Clearwater River between Waterways and Fort McMurray. Clark and J.A. Sutherland moved the experimental extraction plant from Dunvegan to the site of Ells' quarry. In the summer of 1930 this plant, remains of which can be seen today, produced 15,000 gallons of good, clean, dry oil. This Clearwater plant proved it could be done.

There was much interest in the oilsands during the first half of the century with scientists and entrepreneurs like Fitzsimmons at Bitumount, Max Ball with an Abasand plant and Count Von Hammerstein who drilled for oil and found salt.

In 1949 the provincial government commissioned Sidney Blair to make a study of the different separation methods, their economic viability, and potential sale to refineries. Completed in 1959, Dr. Clark's scientific analyses were included and this led Cities Services Limited and Great Canadian Oil Sands to make application to the Alberta government to build commercial scale plants.

Dr. Clark had a great love of the outdoors, was an avid canoeist and loved camping. Although trained as a chemist he understood mechanics and the principles of engineering. He was an accomplished musician.

The development of the vast oilsands is due in a great part to the role played by Dr. Karl A. Clark. He was present for the sod turning of GCOS, the very first oilsands plant, but died in 1966, just months before the project was officially opened. The growth of the Town of Fort McMurray commenced when Dr. Clark's extraction methods were introduced to the Athabasca Valley.

J. Howard Pew,
A Man Of Faith

If it hadn't been for J. Howard Pew the development of Alberta's oil sands might have taken many more years. When no other oil company, no government, was willing to invest in the gamble of the Athabasca tar sands, and against the opposition of the majority of the board of Sun Oil, Mr. Pew took that gamble. He had faith in being able to produce oil from the sands; he had a strong faith in God and was a man who lived by his Christian principles.

Mr. Pew's family had left Wales and settled in the colony of Virginia in 1640.

His father, born in 1848, invested in real estate and the new discoveries of oil. He started Sun Oil, named after the largest of the heavenly bodies, and soon started delivering oil to Philadelphian homes.

In 1882 John Howard Pew was born to parents J. Newton and Mary Catherine. His brother, Joseph N. Pew became his business partner and his sisters were involved in the Pew Charitable Trusts.

By the time he was 18 Mr. Pew had finished college and enrolled in M.I.T. taking advanced engineering. By 1912 he was president of Sun Oil.

"This unique man," wrote Bert MacKay in FOCUS magazine, "made his character known at an early age. He had a memory that could recall all employees of Sun Oil, their families and children. He was a man who could entertain endlessly with a large collection of limericks; a business leader who introduced stock purchases for his employees; a man who was known to visit any worker in hospital who was injured or seriously ill and a man who arranged necessary expenses and wages for the family."

During Mr. Pew's leadership of Sun Oil the company grew almost forty times over. During World War II they supplied most of the lubricating oil and aviation fuel for the Allies. Little emphasis has been placed on the company's ship building industry; they built 550 ships, including forty per cent of the U.S. oil tankers.

Sun Oil began to be interested in northern Alberta's oil deposits in the 1940s. The crucial reports by Sidney Ells and Sidney Blair, as well as the advanced engineering done by Dr. Karl Clark convinced Mr. Pew of the opportunities for development of the sands.

In 1962, against the wishes of the Sun Oil board, the company filed an application for a commercial oil sands project. By September 1967 the Great Canadian Oil Sands (now Suncor) plant opened, there was a newly constructed bridge across the Athabasca River, and a dusty 20-mile road led to the plant, as well as a fleet of busses carrying workers to their shift. Athabasca Realty, the housing arm of GCOS, constructed homes in Block X (Alberta Drive area) for workers' families. Five large homes were built at the site itself for the top executives; these were later moved into town.

The town of about 6000 boasted the only Sunoco gas station west of Ontario. Located at the corner of what was King St. (now Hardin) and Franklin Avenue it was open to serve customers 24 hours a day. Keith MacLeod was the first manager, followed by Glen Ellert. In the late 1960s and early '70s the station sold more gas than any other outlet in Canada. It didn't just sell gas though; rough roads necessitated many muffler and gas tank repairs and as it was open all night it was often a meeting and shelter place for workers.

The two characteristics that stand out in Mr. Pew's life are his belief in hard work and free enterprise and his devout Christian beliefs. No doubt his work ethic is what made him a good friend to both Claire Peden and Dim Silin on his visits to Fort McMurray. Alberta's Premier Ernest Manning and Billy Graham were close friends who shared his Christian faith.

In 1950 speaking to the National Council of Churches, he said, "We must strive constantly for honesty in government, in politics, in business, and in our private lives. We must rededicate ourselves to the service of God, and be ready at all times to give a 'reason for the faith that is in us.'"

When GCOS officially opened in 1967 J. Howard Pew was there to see the culmination of his dream of oil from the tar sands. He died in 1971 at 89 years.

Whether he drove the dusty road to the plant site, or went down the Athabasca River in Claire Peden's boat, this very first oilsands plant was the finalization of Mr. Pew's vision.

Frank Spragins,
He Had A Dream

An American by birth, a Canadian by choice, as an employee of Imperial Oil Ltd. Frank Spragins was tasked with investigation and recommendations about the feasibility of development of the tar sands in northern Alberta. In 1965 Syncrude Canada Ltd. was founded and Frank Spragins was the first president.

Franklin Keller Spragins was born in Natchez, Mississippi in 1914. The family moved to Texas in 1923 and Frank earned his electrical engineering degree from Rice University in Houston. Employed by Imperial Oil he moved to Calgary and met his wife Nell McGregor. He became a Canadian citizen and they raised a family of three boys and one girl.

Bert MacKay wrote in FOCUS: "It was clear from the beginning that Frank was a visionary; he saw the downturn in the conventional oil patch, and proclaimed the importance of the oilsands as a key energy source in many national and international conferences. His technical papers were precise, he was persuasive, and most of all he was highly respected. His personal friendships with people of all working levels endeared him to all."

For several years Fort McMurray people waited anxiously as the Syncrude project was an on again, off again dream. It was felt that a second plant would not only benefit the business community but also bring stability to the town. Finally in September 1973 it was announced that Premier Lougheed would be making a major announcement on Tuesday the 18th of September. Mark Jean and Gordon Butte of the local weekly newspaper, *McMurray Courier,* "hitched" a ride with a charter plane checking the GCOS pipeline, and attended the press conference in Edmonton.

Next day the *Courier* headline, in red, said "Syncrude Goes". How happy everyone in town was. Frank Spragins told *The Courier,* "Our employment needs will be enormous and we will train every man possible." It was estimated 11,000 Albertans would be employed. "All we want is for the federal government to leave us alone," Spragins said. The government of Alberta was to receive fifty per cent of the profits of the new plant.

Frank Spragins had been working toward this day for many years; it was eagerly anticipated by the town's folk. He had been involved in Alberta Newstart and was instrumental in starting programs for people of the First Nations. His vision has resulted in Syncrude being the largest employer of aboriginals in Canada.

Oilweek magazine named Mr. Spragins as "Oil Man of the Year" in 1973. In 1974 Premier Lougheed presented him with the Provincial Achievement Award.

The Syncrude plant, under Spragins, brought in draglines rather than the bucketwheels that GCOS had used. Construction of the plant started almost immediately. My last memory of Frank Spragins was with a media group at the plant site just as the slab was poured for the administration building. He suggested, as I was local media, that my handprint be impressed in the concrete.

Jack Shields and Frank Spragins were friends. Jack was chair of the Public School Board and had the new school in Abasand named for Mr. Spragins. Sadly the name of the school has since been changed. Do we forget so soon those who helped make our history?

Frank Spragins died just six weeks after the official opening of Syncrude Canada. His home was in Calgary, but part of his heart was in McMurray.

Charest & Morton,
The Radio Guys:

Growth and progress was coming quickly to the Town of Fort McMurray in the late '60s. But media was not keeping pace with the rapid influx of residents. In 1967 when the population first swelled, there was no television, sporadic reception for CBC radio from Edmonton and two competing weekly papers, one published by Pat Switzer and another by Clint Buehler, both soon to disappear.

By 1969 we enjoyed four hours of "canned" CBC television one week later than the south of Canada. The programming was sent to Jim Pauls who arranged the transmission to the quickly bought television sets in the homes of McMurray. And then in 1970 Bob Lamb and his team dug through the mud in constant rain to install cables to the local homes and we had cable television. Earlier in 1970 the Jean family started a weekly newspaper, *The McMurray Courier,* that sold to become the *Today* in 1974. And then radio came to town.

On January 1, 1973 at one minute past midnight CJOK came on the air, at 630 AM on the dial, and entered the homes and vehicles of Fort McMurray. Two personable, handsome, ambitious young men moved into offices on the second floor of the Hill building and with two more full time and two part time staff gave McMurray their first radio station.

Roger Charest had a keen interest in radio all his life. At 12 years old, he'd sit at the breakfast table reading the newspaper aloud. His mother used to say, "You sound better than the announcer on the radio." In high school he was a football player, but one day entered a contest for "DJ for a Day" sponsored by CFRN between 15 to 20 high schools north of Red Deer. At just 16 years old, Roger won, and radio has been his life ever since.

During high school he did a Saturday show for CFRN television called *Teen Parade*. From 1963 to 1968 he worked for CFRN as a disc jockey and afternoon and evening announcer. He was in Fort Smith for a time and met Father Turcotte; then they transferred him to Yellowknife where he met Father Beauregard. To his surprise when he came to Fort McMurray, both priests were here, and he stayed at the rectory while researching station prospects.

Roger also had other connections to McMurray. Through family ties he was connected to the Bird family and Captain and Mrs. Bird befriended him. From working at CFRN he knew Dick Rice well; he was a friend of Walter Hills. As was Mr. Hill's custom, the lease on his building was arranged by a handshake.

In the mid-sixties Roger applied to CRTC for a license to open a station in Calgary. He was turned down. When he asked why, they said he had no management experience and he was applying in a place that was well covered by radio. And so he went to work for CHQT as program manager, to gain experience, and did the morning show for them also. He asked the CRTC board if Fort McMurray would qualify as a place that needed a station; the answer was yes.

Roger recruited Stu Morton from a station in Red Deer and together they got the station up and running. Soon the financial structure was changed and Stu Morton became a partner. The initial crew at the station, as well as Roger and Stu, included Clare Stewart and Ron Kahlin, who also wrote a sports column for *The Courier*. Janet Morton worked part time and John Shields, still in high school, did the six to midnight shift. John went to school in the day, worked at his dad's A & W in the afternoon, and did radio at night. He is still with the Victoria station that Charest and Morton started, and later sold to the Jim Pattison Group.

Meanwhile, Roger looked farther afield and started stations in St. Paul and Westlock. Later on, the OK Radio Group started radio stations in Edmonton, Calgary, Vancouver and Victoria, as well as obtaining another license for Fort McMurray for KYX 98.

Roger was away much of the time; Stu was very busy and they decided they should hire a general manager. Roger felt radio was very male dominated and chose Judi Dicks, a smart, hard working saleslady. Other managers over the years included: Dan McAllister, Brian Blackburn and Kelly Boyd. Charlie Olivier was Chief Financial Officer for the company and looked after all the locations from Fort McMurray.

Roger and Linda retired in Edmonton, still being very active. Roger ran marathons several times, including in McMurray, now they take long walks, he does woodwork and they travel. Winters are spent in California.

Stu Morton was intrigued with radio from a very young age. He and his mother lived in Red Deer with grandparents and dominating their living room was one of those beautiful old floor model radios. Young Stuart would sit in front of it and absorb all the programs; even as a pre-schooler he loved that radio. Sitting in grandpa's big chair, he'd listen to the "Happy Gang"; listening to Tarzan he would have visions of great African adventures.

Stu says radio is personal, it fires the imagination, images are generated in the mind by listening to radio – it is a "one on one" communicator.

The family moved to Edmonton when Stu was eight; they lived on 124th Street and one summer during high school years, Stu and his buddies set up his equipment complete with microphones and broadcasted from the front lawn. This included whistling at the girls who went by. After this was reported to her Stu's mother confiscated his equipment for the rest of the summer.

Edmonton CFRN was where Stu got his first job and where he met Roger. Stu worked part time as an operator for remote location broadcasts and often

Roger was the commentator. He worked a stint in Grand Prairie and also in Kelowna. In 1970 Janet and Stu were married; they quit their jobs, sold their cars and travelled in Europe. Three months and three thousand dollars later they came back to Alberta and work.

When Roger phoned Stu in 1971 and told him he should come to Fort McMurray where he was opening a station, Stu said, "Where is that again?" Stu and Janet came up for Thanksgiving, and stayed at the Peter Pond hotel. Franklin Avenue was full of snow piles as well as deep ruts. Stu saw the opportunities, liked the town and they moved. "Fort McMurray was a place where radio communications fit right into the community. The community was good to us; we were good for the community," says Stu in looking back over the years.

They hired an engineer from CHQT in Edmonton and the transmitter was installed at the top of the old Waterways-Airport road.

The Mortons did two stints in McMurray; one from '73 to '75 and then came back from 1983 to '89. Roger spent most of his time getting the new stations up and running, for some years he was at the St. Paul station and Stu at Westlock. Titles didn't mean much to the partners; they did whatever needed to be done whether it was managing, gathering and reading the news, selling ads, or fixing equipment. The radio station and its owners contributed to local charities and events.

When Roger and Stu sold their stations the Mortons moved to Canmore for ten years and now live in Kelowna. While in Canmore Stu built a studio and did recordings for the stations; now he has turned his hand to music production.

In 2006 Roger and Stu sold all their stations. The Alberta ones, including CJOK and KYK 98, were purchased by Rogers; the B.C. stations by Jim Pattison and Fairfield Broadcasting bought the Vancouver and Calgary stations. A love of radio, hard work and entrepreneurial smarts resulted in success for these two men. And it all started in Fort McMurray.

The Others

I guess really, we were the newcomers, but in 1967 when so many of us arrived in the already settled and close community it felt like we were "The Others".

We were all new, no grandparents to babysit, no close relatives, no friendly neighbour; they were new too. What it did was establish ties and bonds to others who also had newly come to the community that have never been broken.

And some of us were different too. We didn't belong to the established community, but also we didn't belong to community of new workers who had homes provided for them in a beautiful new subdivision, Block X.

Even so, I think most of we "others" fell in love with the community set in the midst of rivers, and brimming with excitement and activities. Together, with the established citizens and the plant workers, we endured the mud and the cold, relished the beauties of the northern lights, started clubs and sports groups and made a community. It wasn't long before all of us felt that this place was truly home.

Fort McMurray is an extraordinary community. Families come, generally intending to stay "two years", and then they remain while their children grow and finish high school. Or they leave to go "back home" and then find their true home and opportunities are in McMurray and they return.

Fort McMurray is a remarkable city where people from all over the world have come to make a living for their families. And a place where, when they come and settle into the community, they accept and work with all the others who have come from far-flung points of the globe. And when people do leave and retire elsewhere a part of their heart remains in this town where most everyone came from somewhere else and yet all worked together to make our city a very special place to live.

Doug Schmit,
Keyano's Founding President

Doug Schmit makes no apologies for choosing the vibrant colour of Keyano's Student Housing on the downtown campus. Not only does it stand out, Doug says, but also it is indicative of the colour of northern sunrises. The present buildings, the campus at Gregoire, broad advanced curriculum and the deep community involvement all owe much to the vision and work of its first president.

In the mid sixties the Alberta Government opened Alberta Vocational Centres in Calgary, Edmonton and Fort McMurray. The programs offered were primarily academic upgrading and pre-employment vocational level. In 1967 the Federal Government in cooperation with several provincial governments, funded a Newstart Program. The objective was to develop and research the type and delivery of programs in life skills and employment preparation that would be delivered to targeted communities in Northeastern Alberta. The communities of Kikino, Janvier and Fort Chipewyan focused on married couples that were interested in pursuing employment opportunities. Programs were also offered to preschoolers. A residential campus was established at Lac La Biche for single men and women. The next stage was to take the successful graduates from the four locations to the Fort McMurray AVC for more advanced training.

Doug and Inez Schmit, both from Saskatchewan, met on a blind date. In 1962 they moved to the Edmonton area and in '67 they and their four children moved to Lac La Biche. Doug joined Newstart head office staff of Jack

Shields, Jack Booth, Vince Burke and Lynn Knight. Doug's responsibility was to staff the residential campus then being built and develop training programs for the Lac La Biche Centre. In 1968 Doug was asked by the provincial government to take over the Fort McMurray AVC and develop transition programs for the graduates of the four Newstart Centres. The Cedar Lodge Motel was purchased for a female residence and men were housed at the AVC facility. As well the Newstart Program built a number of houses for families from the smaller centres.

In the early 1970s the Federal Government closed the Newstart program and turned all of the assets over to the Alberta Provincial Government. Jim Foster, the Minister of Advanced Education assigned Doug the responsibility of reviewing the results of the Newstart Program and making recommendations for follow-up. Lac La Biche became an AVC serving that area and Fort McMurray offered outreach programs to Fort Chipewyan and Janvier areas.

One of the major projects of Doug and the staff of AVC was to broaden the purpose of the AVC to not only serve the needs of the disadvantaged but to serve the broad community needs as well. At that time this goal was opposed by some Advanced Education officials who did not see the needs or potential of the local community. Many of the training programs incorporated local community projects such as roads, and major creek diversions not only in Fort McMurray but Fort MacKay, Janvier and even roads in the Kananaskis Park. The commercial cooking program run by John Nowalski and Elmer Nykiforuk attracted many community people to sampling the wares and also taking the specialized cooking courses offered in the evening. Heavy Equipment Programs cleared and levelled the land for the new Gregoire Campus that saved considerable development costs. In 1978 AVC was recognized as a public community college with an appointed Board of Governors and a President – Doug Schmit.

Roger Bernatski, CEO of the hospital was the first chair; other members were Ken Hill, Linda Costello, Dr. Allan Nicholson and Adam Germain.

In 1981-82 Doug took a sabbatical and along with Inez and their two youngest children moved to Bath, England. Doug's role was to give lectures on the Canadian post secondary system and advice and talks on post secondary management. Over the years when some of his British colleagues came to Fort McMurray they were amazed at the involvement of the community in our college.

Keyano's theatre brought people in the community close to the college as it became a focus for entertainment. Dick Mells, the first Keyano Theatre Director, utilized many community residents in the local productions.

A two-year nursing program, fully accredited with the University of Alberta, was initiated. University courses arranged through the Universities of Alberta and Athabasca leading to the four-year degree were offered by Keyano to save local residents the expense of relocating out of the city. If Keyano did not have the mandate or resources to offer a need, they would negotiate to broker the applicable course from another institution.

Some of the well remembered instructors and heads of departments included: Gerry Wills, Grant Eliason, Jack Golosky, Gerry Gregg, Bob Hayes and Claire Wadman who assisted Doug with the administration and the board. Meanwhile Inez Schmit was not idle. After the four children were all in school she was employed by the Public Health Service, led by Lynn Bryant.

Inez's work had her flying into Janvier to give immunizations, and driving the dusty road to Fort McKay to go to the schools. She also worked in the areas of TB, prenatal, baby clinic, STDs and HIV/AIDS. Inez continued her career in the field of community health when they moved from McMurray.

When the Schmits moved to Vermillion Doug took over as president of Lakeland College, a multi-campus college in northeastern Alberta. Doug Schmit, Keyano's first president, left behind an institution known as one of the best in Alberta.

Jack Shields, MP and Santa Claus

Whether he was dressed as Santa and flying his plane into the isolated hamlet of Janvier to distribute gifts to the children on Christmas morning, or sitting in the House of Commons, Jack Shields was at home.

An Alberta boy, Jack went to school in Grande Prairie, and at 17 joined the Canadian Armed Forces becoming the youngest sergeant to serve during the Korean War. He was wounded in action but returned to the front lines and then sent home with yellow fever.

At 27 Jack went back to complete his high school and teaching degree at the University of Alberta. He was sent into northern Alberta where he coordinated the construction and acted as the founding principal in newly built Alberta Vocational Training Centres in Grouard, Lac La Biche, Cold Lake, Janvier, Fort Chipewyan and Fort McMurray, The Vocational Centres were begun by the province primarily to train First Nation and unemployed people to take advantage of the upcoming oil sands plant (GCOS). The campus was a series of trailers at the end of Franklin Avenue on land that had held American army troops during World War II.

In 1967 a five-year program, Alberta Newstart, was headed by Jack Shields and headquartered in Lac La Biche. When the five years was up Jack returned to Fort McMurray and established a series of businesses, including Redwood Ready Mix. He opened, to the delight of McMurray residents, an A & W Drive Inn as well as five other restaurants.

Two memorable events were spearheaded by Jack when president of the Chamber of Commerce. The May Clean Up Weekend saw youngsters receive a coupon for an A & W hamburger and root beer for every bag of garbage they contributed to the clean up. Jack organized dump trucks, some his own, to convey many loads to the dump. So many kids turned up for their prize the A&W ran out of burgers and cost the restaurant thousands of dollars.

Midsummer Night Madness, another Chamber initiative, was held the weekend of the longest day. Without Town Hall permission, President Jack brought in carnival rides and situated them in the Franklin Avenue block between Hardin and Main Streets. Sidewalk sales and the rides drew hundreds of families. Sunday afternoon a sweep-off on Franklin Avenue between President Jack Shields and Town Board Chairman Chuck Knight sold tickets and raised money for charity. Citizens watched as the two raced down the street, brooms and dust flying. The Courier declared a tie win.

A former hockey player and avid fan, Jack had season tickets in Edmonton for more than 25 years. His Fort McMurray companies supported many of the junior sports teams in Fort McMurray.

Jack was fond of practical jokes and not above playing them on his close friends. He owned the ready mix company when his friend Dr. Des Dwyer went back to Ireland for a visit. And that was Northern Ireland, where some segments of the population are not fond of the English. So Jack, Tip Hlushak and some of their other cronies got a truck full of cement, a huge flag pole with a Union Jack at the top, and placed it all in Dr. Dwyer's driveway at the corner of Fraser and Father Mercredi. To add insult to injury when the Dwyers returned from their holiday, not only was there nowhere to park their car but also the Town of Fort McMurray presented them with a "Stop Work Order".

As well as being president of the Chamber of Commerce, Jack Shields served as Chairman of the Public School Board and was founding member of the Kinsmen Club, Rotary Club, Shriners and the United Way.

In 1980 J.W. Shields decided to run for parliament as a Conservative member and won the election handily. The Athabasca constituency was huge and he campaigned using his airplane. His great friend Tip Hlushak was campaign manager, and told of one time when flying south Jack asked him if he'd like a cup of coffee. Tip said yes expecting him to reach under the seat for a thermos. Instead Jack set the plane down on Highway 63 in front of the Wandering River café and proceeded into the restaurant for their coffee. Traffic just waited on the highway until they returned and the plane was in the air again.

Jack Shields represented his constituents well, and was appointed as Parliamentary Secretary of five different portfolios by Prime Minister Brian Mulroney. He delighted having his friends and constituents visit him in Ottawa, taking them to the Parliamentary Dining Room for lunch. At one such lunch he took an ashtray embossed with Canada's crest off the table and told a young visitor to put it in her purse. Now that there is no smoking in the Parliamentary Restaurant, the ashtray won't be missed.

The recession in Fort McMurray following the Liberal government's National Energy Program saw many established businesses close. The Shields family enterprises were not excluded. Although Jack and his sons and partners Clarence, John and Jim worked hard to avoid bankruptcy, it was inevitable. They lost all their McMurray businesses and some personal assets as well.

A second blow to Jack fell in 1993 when the Conservative party was wiped out in the election of 1993. He lost his seat to the Reform party.

It would take more than a total business loss and political defeat to keep Jack Shields down. Along with his wife Pat and son Clarence he opened a restaurant in the Nisku Truck Stop near the Edmonton International Airport. Here he followed his values of donating time and funds to many less fortunate. His charitable contributions were not just given to organizations but he took a personal interest in many young people with little or no opportunities. Each Christmas the truck stop sponsored a free Christmas dinner, and all donations went to the Leduc Food Bank.

For years in the latter half of the last century the Shields name was well known in every home in town. Jack's exuberance and colourful presence in our town enhanced the economic, political and educational life and he should not be soon forgotten.

Harry Aime,
RCMP To Judge

Harry Aime was one of McMurray's better-known residents for five decades. Whether you stood before Judge Aime in court, met him at the Rotary Club or the Chamber of Commerce, or saw him on Sunday at All Saints Anglican Church he would have made an impression.

Mr. Aime's earliest memories are of the family farm at Clandeboye, Manitoba; his dream from a young age was to join the RCMP. And this he did, reporting to the training depot in Regina in the fall of 1949 and after graduation serving in the province of Quebec.

In 1942 the young constable was told his next posting would be Fort Smith in the Northwest Territories. He travelled on the Northern Alberta Railway train to Waterways where he caught the *Radium Queen* on its last trip of the season. A three-day trip on the Athabasca River to Fort Fitzgerald was followed by a portage by taxi around the rapids to his new post in Fort Smith.

Constable Aime was stationed in Fort Rae for three years and then sent south to farm country in Peace River. In 1947 his posting took him north again, to the Eastern Arctic. Here he opened a new detachment at Resolute Bay. Canada, in cooperation with the United States, was opening up new weather stations across the north and this gave Cst. Aime the opportunity to go to Greenland and Goose Bay.

In the years Mr. Aime served in the Northwest Territories and the Arctic the RCMP played many roles in the communities in which they were posted. It was still a time of travel by dog team and canoes; sleeping in tents in sub-zero weather; administering medicines to locals when needed as well as settling disputes and keeping the peace. At this time virtually all supplies for the RCMP stations were shipped north by river via Waterways.

Mr. Aime's northern postings also included Fort Liard, Good Hope and Aklavik. He says, "…looking back, it was an adventure that most people would not have the opportunity of experiencing. It was in an era before extensive development and change began, a time when native people still maintained traditional values and ways. I had the opportunity of working with people who were pioneers in their fields, whether fur traders or government employees."

When he left the north Mr. Aime's postings took him to Vegreville and Lethbridge. After 25 years in the Force he retired and accepted an appointment as magistrate. In 1965 Harry Aime and his wife Joy, along with children Michael and Janet came to Fort McMurray. He was McMurray's first stipendiary resident magistrate, the first provincial court judge, and marriage commissioner. He was a warden of the Anglican Church and instrumental in starting St. Aidan's Society. He was secretary of the Chamber of Commerce for many years and the first person honoured with lifetime membership.

Joy Aime, who worked for some years for social services, was a long time diabetic and passed away in McMurray. Sometime later Harry Aime reconnected with and married Marjorie, a friend from his youth. One of my special memories of the Aimes is seeing them on their daily walk; the care and love they showed for each other was most evident.

Both Harry and Marjorie Aime wrote books after their retirement. Mr. Aime's first book was of his parents, entitled *Hazel Glen Farm*. His second book, *Overalls, Red Serge and Robes; Life and Adventures in the Canadian North* is just as the title describes it. Mrs. Aime's book *Northern Memories* depicts the life of a civilian posted with her husband in a northern outpost.

The Aimes left McMurray to retire in central Alberta. They added to our history and to our memories of the years of growth in McMurray.

Darlene Comfort, Recorder Of History

It didn't take long for Darlene Comfort to become involved in McMurray's history. Like so many families the Comforts moved to the Town of Fort McMurray in 1967 when Doug was working for Great Canadian Oil Sands. Almost immediately Darlene began researching and writing books about the area.

Doug Comfort, a native Albertan, was part of the design and construction team of Canadian Bechtel that built GCOS and the family moved north from Edmonton so he could continue in his role as part of the start-up team. Darlene had been working for the University of Alberta Hospital Laboratories doing medical research and writing papers on the results.

Population of the now booming town with its first oilsands plant was just over 2000. Subdivisions were being carved out of the wilderness, roads were dusty or muddy, schools were overcrowded and shopping was limited. Darlene's inquiring mind immediately delved into the history of the community. No better description of the town and its incoming residents can be found than in her first book, published in 1973, titled *Meeting Place of Many Waters*.

Darlene Comfort wrote: *Every small town has a history, a story to tell of its founding; some fully exploited, others exaggerated beyond recognition, some a more natural part of the setting. Rare are the towns which have failed to look back at the trail. In Fort McMurray we have lingered so long on the verge and promise of rapid growth that our sights appear fixed on the road ahead. On our first arrival we have been exhilarated by a vision of the true North, a road through tall, starving evergreens that disappointingly ends in a town where the houses are spaced no further apart and with no more variation than the cities and towns we have left behind...There exists for us an opportunity to witness and preserve the past first-hand...After hearing the Athabasca story and bearing witness to the town's past, we acknowledge at last that a history exists that extends beyond the trapped oils and that has roots in soil other than the fabled sands.*

With two young children and a third born in the next year, Darlene set out to research the community whose history intrigued her from her first weeks in town. She ordered rare journals through Library Extension services, and she and Doug paid *The Beaver,* official magazine of the Hudson's bay Company, to research anything and everything relating to their records of the fur-trading fort.

In the 1960s and '70s there were "old-timers" who had worked on the boats, laboured in the salt mines, and helped build the oil exploration plants. Darlene set out to interview these people, and transcribed the resulting tapes and donated the results to the University of Alberta Archives. She gave great credit to the town's librarian, Fern Brooks who helped her with library extension services and local resources.

Meeting Place of Many Waters chronicles the history of the area from the arrival of Peter Pond in 1778 to the establishment of Fort McMurray in 1870 by H.J Moberly and the looked for era of river boat transportation. Not only does she tell the story of the various explorers that passed this way but also there are detailed date lines of events, forts and reference books. Doug did illustrations and the 86-page book was typed, printed and stapled into a letter size format.

The very next year the Comforts published Darlene's second book, *Ribbons of Water and Steamboats North*. This book traces the history of river transportation from the founding by Moberly of the new fort throughout the heady days of "where steel meets keel" and northern river transport. A tremendous amount of research was done as evidenced by the footnotes and references; as well there are some remarkable photographs. The book itself, typed and printed by offset was then bound in hard cover by the family in the basement of their home on Bennett Crescent. Darlene was able to interview some of the riverboat captains adding interest to the history. She even touches on the adventurers who passed through McMurray on their way to seek their fortune in gold in the fabled Yukon. And then on their return empty handed and disillusioned.

Mrs. Comfort's next adventure into publishing was her research on the area's salt plants. Deposits of salt had been recognized early in the century and commercial operations at the mouth of the Horse River and in Waterways gave a boost to the local economy. *Pass the McMurray Salt*, Darlene's third book tells of the rise and fall of this industry, with the Waterways plant closing in 1950.

Not only was there a salt plant in Abasand at the Horse River but a town, school and oilsands plant. *The Abasand Fiasco,* subtitled "The rise and fall of a brave pioneer Oil Sands extraction plant" is a commercially bound large sized book with wonderful photographs and detailed stories of the early oilsands pioneers. Published in 1980, many details and characters of the community from the early part of the last century to the advent of Great Canadian Oil Sands are described. We get a picture of the hopes and dreams of these oilsands explorers and of their hard work and dashed hopes.

Doug left Suncor to work for a time at Syncrude; Darlene remained active in the community as well as serving on provincial boards that profited from her research and historical bent. Both retired now with a home in Edmonton, their days in McMurray will hold many special memories.

Those of us interested in McMurray's history owe a great debt to Darlene Comfort for the tedious, exacting research she did on our community's past.

Romance Of The Rumpels

When Yvette Owen left the Blood Reserve in southern Alberta to go with Indian Northern Health Services to the Arctic, she was looking for adventure and little knew she'd find a husband. Yvette was born in London, England and was a young schoolgirl during World War II. Along with her two sisters she was evacuated. The girls were not content to be away so sent their mum a telegram saying they were coming home, and come home they did to air raid shelters and bombs. Yvette's dad was a bricklayer and stone mason and worked for the Ministry of Works during the war; her mum also registered for war work. Yvette often queued with the family ration books for their food.

After nurse's training Yvette followed her two sisters to Canada, working for a time in Ontario and exploring eastern Canada and the United States by Greyhound bus. Soon her sense of adventure took her to the prairies where she was employed by Indian Northern Health Services in the Blood Indian Reserve at Cardston before transferring to northern Canada.

Her first posting was at Fort Norman and it was here she met the fair, handsome resident Mountie. Don Rumpel was the son of a Baptist minister and grew up in the depression days when money was scarce for everyone, particularly so for those of his father's calling. His father died when he was six and his mother later married another minister.

Don left home at 16 to make his own way. He worked at a variety of jobs, including the mine at Uranium City. He saved enough money to go back to school and complete his grade 12 and started apprenticing as an electrician. While in B.C. visiting his mother and stepfather he applied for the Royal Canadian Mounted Police and was sent to the RCMP training depot in Regina.

After graduation the young constable was posted to Saskatchewan for a year and then he was posted to the North West Territories. Single members were frequently transferred to posts at short notice. Don's postings included: Yellowknife, Cambridge Bay, Fort Smith, Fort Simpson, Fort Norman, Norman Wells, Aklavik and Arctic Red River. He often travelled along the mighty Mackenzie River. The Force, in those days, still used dog teams and a large amount of time was spent by his special constable catching fish to supply food for the huskies. While winter transportation on the patrols was by dog team, in summer a freighter canoe with a motor was easier going. The Mountie was called on for any emergency; Don was even asked to pull teeth on occasion.

The tiny young nurse, weighing about 110 pounds, was a contrast to the strapping tough-looking Mountie. After a few months Don proposed, but it wasn't that easy. He had to get permission from K Division to get married. At that time policemen had to be in the service for five years and had to have permission to marry.

Before the permission arrived Don was advised of a new posting. Just before he had to leave for his new posting, the waited for word arrived and the Pentecostal minister married the couple with all 12 local government officials turning out for the occasion. They went for a belated honeymoon to England and the continent and while there Don took a special course at the British Underwater Centre at Devon where he received his Master Certificate. In later years in Alberta he taught the RCMP small craft boating course for 10 years.

While in the north, all supplies for the nursing stations and police stations were shipped on barges in a large once-a-year order. At that time there were no roads in the north and their boxes were shipped from Edmonton by NAR to Waterways and then by barge to the various posts. We can just imagine the excitement as the whole community would rush to the riverbank as the first barge of the year appeared.

While stationed in Aklavik in the Northwest Territories the Rumpels first son was due. A plane took Yvette to the hospital in the newly built town of Inuvik. Eighteen months later Yvette went to stay with her mother-in-law in Vancouver while waiting for Gregory to join his brother Donald and complete the family. After eight years, with two small children, the couple decided it was time to "come out of the north."

Don was stationed in Edmonton for a time and then High Prairie. While in High Prairie Don was chosen, along with two other officers, to represent Canada at the International World Police Exhibition in Hanover, Germany.

When the orders came for his transfer to Fort McMurray in 1967, little did the couple know what waited for them at the end of the long unpaved road. As they did at each posting, the Rumpels fit right into the community volunteering for many groups. They explored the rivers and lakes with their canoe; one memorable summer catching many fish at Moose Point on Lake Athabasca and picking pail after pail of blueberries. In winter their skidoos got many workouts; Don Gibbon, Torchy Peden and Don Fleming along with Don Rumpel explored the entire area.

After a few months in low rentals at Willow Square, Corporal Don was put in charge of the outlying detachment and they moved to the old RCMP station at the corner of Main and Manning. Their spacious home was on the upper floor, the office on first floor and the cells in the basement. When new cells were built at the New Town Hall, Don converted the basement cells into a social area.

Don was known as a tough cop; often just the sight of him entering the Oilsands' tavern could quell a riot. And yet he was deeply compassionate too. Many a prisoner, released after an overnight stay in the cells, would have a bill passed to him for breakfast and cigarettes. Young people hero-worshipped him; his stories of life in the Arctic were intriguing.

Every Christmas season Yvette would prepare a huge dinner for all the young constables, many away from family for the first time. St. Gabriel Hospital was still standing at the corner of Hardin and MacDonald Avenue and

Yvette did some shifts there with head nurse Dorothy Berry. When the boys were both in school Yvette went to work at the local health unit that was on the main floor of the Professional Building on Franklin Avenue. Many former Father Turcotte students received their immunizations from her, and many mothers remember her pre-natal instructions and home visits.

In 1976 it was time to move on and the Rumpels moved to Red Deer, later to Wetaskiwin and then to a last posting at Jasper. They retired to Maple Ridge to be close to both mothers, and later moved to Kelowna. The couple loved to travel and were keenly interested in history as well as loving the outdoors. One memorable six-month trip took them on a circle tour of North America in their fifth wheel; my husband and I accompanied them in our unit.

In 2001 Don died of a heart attack. They had just returned from visiting son Gregory in New Zealand. That was the year Irwin Huberman wrote his book on Fort McMurray, it was when transcribing a taped interview with Don and Yvette that the book's title came to me. Irwin asked Don, "You lived in a lot of places in your career, what does Fort McMurray mean to you?" Don simply replied, "It is home." The book *The Place We Call Home* is a tribute to him and to the many others who passed this way.

Chuck Knight,
Champion Of Recreation

Chuck Knight will always be remembered in Fort McMurray as the man who kept MacDonald Island from a housing development to accomplish his dream of a recreational complex. Athabasca Realty Company, GCOS' housing arm, had proposed buying land and building executive houses beside the golf course on the island. A public hearing was held on June 7th, 1971 with 40 people crowded into the small town boardroom. People spoke for and against the housing development, but Chuck Knight spoke with passion and charisma. It was his eloquence that had ARC withdraw their application.

Chuck Knight had also triumphed in his personal life. He was an alcoholic who, through the help of Alcoholics Anonymous and the support of his wife Lue, conquered his addiction for 47 years and went on to become one of the north's most popular politicians.

In 1957 Chuck arrived in McMurray to work at the radar station at Stoney Mountain. He went on to work at Royalite, where he took supplies to their experimental plant at Bitumount. After a stint as timekeeper at Northern Transportation, Chuck worked at Cities Services and again for Royalite. When the Great Canadian Oil Sands plant was being constructed Canadian Bechtel hired him to act as purchaser. He later transferred to GCOS as purchasing agent.

After the rousing meeting in June, Chuck Knight decided to run for the town board in October of that year. This election saw a whole new board with members Claire Peden, Dave McNeilly, Ron Morgan, Walter Diener, Armand

Parent and Dr. Al Nicholson. At the first meeting of the new board Dave McNeilly nominated Chuck Knight as chairman of the New Town of Fort McMurray; he was elected by secret ballot.

These were busy construction and expansion years with the construction of the Syncrude plant. Chuck became full time board chair and in 1983 quit his job with Suncor to become full time mayor. He never lost an election, but did lose the position of chairman of the town board in 1977. Even though he led the polls, when it was time for the board to vote for chairman the majority voted for Ted Mason. For Mason's term the animosity could be felt between the two men who had very different governing styles. In 1983 Knight was elected as mayor and remained until he retired in 1989.

Chuck Knight liked people, and you could tell. He had a word for everyone he met. Politically, many disagreed with some of his decisions and he and the boards he chaired did not cooperate well with the provincial government. During his tenure the province appointed Vic Henning as Commissioner of Northeastern Alberta. The commissioner's role was to liaise between the town and the province, and he had direct access to the cabinet and Peter Lougheed. Thickwood Heights, Beacon Hill and Abasand were developed during these years.

Lue Knight worked for many years for the school district at the Dr. Clark School and the Clearwater School.

The Knights retired to the Okanagan and Chuck served as a councilor in Peachland for some years. Chuck died in 2001 at age 77.

Chuck Knight turned the sod for the original MacDonald Island complex that was named for him. The very same shovel Chuck used on the first project was used by his daughter Kim to turn the sod for the expansion of the complex.

In 2011 the huge expanded complex, including a swimming pool, exercise rooms and library, was opened. His daughter Kim, a former long time city employee, was present for the opening of the Leisure Centre. A wall fountain and plaque commemorate this former mayor. Also speaking at the opening festivities was former councilor Dave McNeilly, who recalled the exciting days when the realization of the dream of a recreational complex first began.

As with most politicians Chuck Knight was a controversial figure, but no one could deny that he was a huge supporter of Fort McMurray. We have to admire his personal victories, and his vision for the future of a central recreation area on the beautiful island at the end of the dyke.

The Hardins,
Business, Politics, and Service

The Hardins had a great influence on our town as it grew quickly in the late 1960s and '70s. Their move to Fort McMurray was a result of a conversation Sam overheard in a steam bath in Edmonton; things were happening in the north.

Sam and Selma met at a house party in Edmonton when they were both 16. Sam was not a dancer; Selma loved to dance and so turned Sam's advances down. However, said Selma, Sam was very persistent and they started dating.

Selma had grown up in Lac La Biche, and met Sam while attending Alberta College for high school. She was one of a family of five in a prominent Lac La Biche family. Selma's dad had come to Canada, not speaking a word of English, when he was just 12 years old.

One day early in the last century when young Ali was tending sheep with friends in Lebanon, his uncle came walking by. The 12-year old asked where he was going. "To Beirut, to catch a boat to go to Canada." Ali asked if he could walk with him. When they got to the ship Ali asked if he could go too. The uncle said yes, and sent someone back to tell Ali's parents that he had gone to Canada. Ali never saw his mother again, but did go back to the little town of Lala and helped to build a school there.

When young Ali Abouchadi landed in Halifax the man at immigration asked him to spell his name. Ali could not read or write and the official said, "I'll give you a good Scottish name." And so he became Alexander Hamilton. They first went to Montreal and eventually ended up in Edmonton where young Alex bought fans for five cents and sold them for ten. He became a peddler and soon settled in Lac La Biche. He never did learn to read or write, he said he could hire someone to do that for his business.

Mr. Hamilton was an enterprising pioneer and had many businesses including a mink farm, and a slaughterhouse; he built a pier and was a successful merchant. He used to follow the treaty boat, keeping ahead of the Hudson's Bay boat, as they both tried to take advantage of the annual payment to all the natives. He died at 96.

Sam's ancestors came from Russia; his parents met in Edmonton. Mr. Hardin, Sr. was a pharmacist as was Sam's brother.

Both Sam and Selma went to the University of Alberta. Sam started in engineering, but was non-conforming and was kicked out. He later went back and studied pharmacy. Selma took philosophy and psychiatry and then went on to UBC to take social work.

In 1964 Sam moved to Fort McMurray and started a small drug store in the Peter Pond Hotel. Soon he moved the store to a trailer and then into the store on the strip mall where the Peter Pond Shopping Centre is now. Then in September 1965 Selma and their five children moved to town, living in the hotel for two months. While their house was being built on Crescent Heights they lived on Fraser Ave.

Sam became interested in politics almost immediately. He served on Northland School Division board and then was elected to the board of the New Town of Fort McMurray in 1968 and was chosen as chairman. During his tenure the board hired its first town manager, Norm Crawford. Every Friday afternoon Sam and Norm would drive around town checking on progress of any works being done.

These were busy days with road works, natural gas installation to homes, construction of new housing and trailer parks. GCOS wanted to build houses on MacDonald Island. Athabasca Realty (GCOS' housing arm) offered to buy from the Town 58 acres for $2000 an acre, a fortune in those days. Sam Hardin told me some time later that GCOS had agreed to put a bridge across the Clearwater to Forest Heights to give access to a new area for expansion if they were allowed to build some executive homes near the golf course on the island. This application by ARC resulted in the now famous meeting of June 7, 1971 when citizens, led by Chuck Knight, opposed any development on the island.

In the fall election of 1971 Sam Hardin, along with Ron Wolff, lost his seat on the board. He ran again at the next election and sat on the board for another term. He also served on the Fort McMurray Public School Board during the years when new schools were being constructed.

Sam Hardin was a brilliant man, intelligent, witty and with a vision for the community. He was bored with the drug business but delighted to talk to all and sundry that came through the door. He was a prodigious reader, could add a column of figures as quickly as most could on an adding machine. He must have been an accountant's nightmare, as he'd turn up near tax time with a shoebox full of receipts.

Selma was asked to work temporarily for a town project called Preventive Social Services. Her first office was a table and chair in the library and services offered included homemaker advice, day care arrangements and counselling. She managed the program for 22 years and also served on the Provincial Social Services appeal committee for many years.

In 1986 just before the National Energy Program from Ottawa ensured the death of the Alsand's oil sand plant project, Sam sold his drug store to Shopper's Drugs and he and Selma moved to a condo in Vancouver. For many years they wintered in Scottsdale, Arizona, and daughters Nancy and Carol still live there. The two Hardin boys, Ali and Jimmy live in Calgary. Patsy worked in Vancouver and for the last years of Sam's life (he died in 2010) she was a wonderful support for her parents.

Up until the 1970s Fort McMurray had two King Streets, one by Keyano and the other downtown. Armand Parent, manager of Catalytic and a town counsellor instigated renaming the downtown street to Hardin Street. This influential family of the '60s and '70s will be forever recognized in our city.

Success Of The Sorges

Another family that arrived in McMurray in 1967 and went on to become a major success in the business community is that of the Sorges. Art and Rosalee Sorge, with their nine children, moved from Winfield, Alberta to work for Primrose Logging in Waterways. An equipment operator, Art then went to GCOS (Suncor) for a few years before he and Rosalee moved to Hinton.

When their parents moved, eldest sons Richard and Randy stayed in McMurray. It wasn't long before Tom, the youngest boy of the nine, came back. Always an avid outdoors person, while at school Richard had a dog team and trapped. He trapped with Katie Sanderson at Saline Creek and later in Fort Chipewyan.

Richard got his welding ticket, working for Tar Sands Machine & Welding and Fort McMurray Welding. He then went to work at BMC along with Doug Golosky and when Doug started Clearwater Welding Richard worked for him for seven years.

Then in 1988 it was time to branch out on his own and he started Sorge's Welding, a union shop, and Sorge's Pro Welding, non-union. They built a shop and normally employed 40 workers, including brother Tom. In his business endeavours his wife Janet was a strong partner. From Fort Chipewyan, Janet was tree planting on the Syncrude site when she met Richard. Janet managed the office and did the contracts, while Richard did the fieldwork.

Both love the outdoors, and part of the reason Richard wanted to be in business for himself was so they could spend most of the summers in their jet boat on the rivers and Lake Athabasca. Then after nearly 20 years in business the Sorges sold their business in 2007. Half of the company was purchased by the Athabasca Chip Band and half by a publicly traded company, Empire Iron Works.

It was time to sell and do other things, they said. And so now Richard and Janet enjoy their retirement in the great outdoors. They built a home at Buffalo Narrows in Saskatchewan and while Janet will drive the winter road, Richard goes by snowmobile at least four times a winter. The trip takes him across Gordon Lake, Gypsy Lake, and Garson Lake to La Loche and on to Buffalo Narrows. Sometimes if there is lots of ice he will go up the Clearwater and over the Meythe Portage. The trip takes seven to eleven hours through beautiful bush country.

They also love the mountains and Richard has a climbing snow machine as well as one for flat country. In the summer it is their jet boat for our rivers. A home in Vernon also has an attraction and they, like so many other McMurrayites like to travel. Richard says in the winter he'll go wherever there is snow, but they also have spent time in Mexico and the Dominican.

But Fort McMurray is home base. Two daughters and two grandchildren are one tie. The other is, as Richard says, where else can you live and be out of town into the bush in just ten minutes.

A success story of a McMurray youngster turned businessman, who relishes the wilderness our area offers.

John Wilson, Construction Magnate

When Howard Wilson and son John came to Fort McMurray in 1977 to do a summer contract, little would John have imagined this northern town would hold his future. From Dryden, in northern Ontario, the Wilsons knew all about cold, short construction seasons and shortage of skilled labour.

Their contract that summer was to provide grading and paving at the Syncrude towers being built by Bergman Construction. That summer they brought some of their crew with them, and housed them in Norm Simons' Heartbreak Hotel.

After completing university in 1980 John moved to McMurray permanently. His father came out to help in the summers for many years. Howard Wilson was a gentleman, his word was his bond; traits now seen in his son.

For many years the Wilson yard and office, with their many distinctive red trucks driving in and out, was located at the end of Franklin Avenue next to the Hangingstone River. When the city opened up industrial sites on Highway 63 north, the entire facility was moved to 30 acres north of the city.

While the company initially did paving it expanded, under John's leadership, to road building, sewer and water installations, oilfield construction and environmental clean up. The company spent five years cleaning up radioactive sites in the downtown area. In early days uranium was brought in by barge from Lake Athabasca sites and shipped out by rail. This former practice necessitated large chunks of the riverbank having to be cleaned up before any building could be done on the shore.

Most of Thickwood Heights streets were paved by Wilson and most recently their trucks and equipment have played a huge part in the reconstruction of utility lines and reconstructed roads and sidewalks in the downtown area.

John and his wife Leslie, with their four children, have maintained their home in McMurray. All the family are ski enthusiasts and enjoy winter ski holidays. It was the need for a skiing facility in McMurray that led John to spearhead the development of the Vista Ridge Ski hill. Complete with lifts, tube runs and a beautiful chalet, the facility located at Saprae Creek, is a favourite with residents.

The Wilsons have given back to the community they literally helped build. Leslie volunteers for the Keyano Foundation, and is much sought after to coordinate events such as "The Festival of Trees," for the Hospital Foundation.

There are very few projects in town that John Wilson has not had a part in. He served as chair of the Keyano Board of Governors, Regional Business Development Centre, United Way, the Construction Association and co-chaired the Arctic Winter Games. John Wilson is the most efficient board chairperson I have ever observed.

Because of the shortage of skilled workers in this northern area, John has been very active in apprenticeship programs. He also sat on the Alberta Chamber of Resources.

Recently H. Wilson Industries was sold to an international firm. For a time John will still be involved with the operations, and very involved in many community aspects. As long as we see those red Wilson trucks in town we will be reminded of the young man from Ontario who came west and literally helped construct our city.

A Tale Of Two Avery Families

Two families of the same name, albeit not related, have had an impact on our city. Those of us who have known the Averys can attest to their influence on the growth and stability of our town.

Art & Sylvia Avery: As Fort McMurray started to boom with construction workers building the Great Canadian Oil Sands plant and the new homes, the chartered banks from the east looked west and north at a new market.

Art Avery was transferred from Calgary to Fort McMurray in 1964 to manage the new Bank of Nova Scotia branch. It was in a trailer on Franklin Ave. just opposite the Haxton's Store. The bank was at one end of the trailer and Art and Sylvia lived in the other end. As business grew the bank purchased a lot on a key corner of the main street and Art supervised the building of a two-storey building on a full basement. The top floor was soon rented to accountant Jack Fowers, lawyer Norm Simons and a fabric shop.

Meanwhile the bank built a house on Crescent Heights and Averys lived there until 1967 when Art's three-year commitment to the bank was up. They decided to settle in the new community they had adapted to so well and where their son Gary was born. Art was a volunteer fire fighter from his first day in town. Sylvia worked at Haxton's General Store and in The Bay at Waterways. When Art left the bank they opened their own business of Top Mop Janitorial Service, and with employees, operated it for about 25 years.

Almost as soon as they came to town Art joined the Kinsmen and Sylvia the Kinette Club. Both served as president of their club. Both Art and Sylvia were valuable volunteers in town, particularly with seniors. Sylvia managed

Legion Manor and Araubasca House for 15 years and then at the Golden Years Society and as well delivered "meals on wheels" from the hospital to shut-in seniors. Art and Sylvia's kindness to many of the single seniors was exemplary.

Over the years Art worked at Beacon Hill Sports and then at McMurray Ford for Tip Hlushak. He also managed the Credit Union in Waterways and worked at the Federal Business Development Bank in McMurray. Art's final working years were at Jean's Office Supply as a sales representative. He has a keen interest in history and was a charter member of the Heritage Park Society and was on the board of the society that first published Irwin Huberman's book, *The Place We Call Home*.

The Averys bought the row housing units on Hardin Street that were built as rental units in the 1960s by Les Bodie of Fort McMurray Land Developments. They lived there for many years and had a beautiful flower garden in the last unit. In 2007 they sold and moved to Westlock, near the area where they both grew up.

Jack & Olga Avery were involved with the Public School District from almost their first day in town. The family moved from Medicine Hat to McMurray in 1967 and Jack worked in upgrading at GCOS, retiring from Suncor in 1991.

Olga began volunteering at the Dr. Clark School as soon as it opened in 1968. She soon worked full time as teacher's aid and in the office, and when she retired went back as a volunteer. Many of Dr. Clark's former students cherish the Ukranian Easter eggs that Mrs. Avery taught them how to make. She taught them map making, crafts and nature studies. She would accompany the students on their outdoor camping trips or the train rides to Anzac.

Mrs. Avery recalls the muddy schoolyard and the portable trailers that were set beside the school almost as soon as it opened. Dave McNeilly was principal and Ed Mitchell, vice principal. There was a constant influx of students whose parents came to town for jobs.

In 1969, one of the Avery's neighbours on Clark Crescent, Doris Deleff suggested Jack run for the new school board. Up until then our schools were governed by Northland School Division; a new Public Board was to be elected with local members. He served on the board for nine terms, a total of 26 years.

These were the boom years, with the average age in Fort McMurray at 19. New schools were needed and new schools were built. Jack Avery was on the board during construction of Clearwater School, Beacon Hill, Thickwood, Birchwood, Westview, Greely Road, Dickinsfield and Timberlea, as well as the Frank Spragins School in Abasand.

The divisive question of a joint high school haunted both public and separate school boards for some time. Location was also a sticking point with some residents favouring the school being built on MacDonald Island. Finally the decision was made to build a joint high school and Composite High was built in 1974, right next to the main campus of Keyano College. Ten years later the population in Thickwood Heights called for a high school there as well.

Mr. Avery served during World War II and is an active member of the Royal Canadian Legion.

Our schools have benefited from the Avery family involvement. When Jack retired from Suncor the Averys made the decision to retire in McMurray.

The Walsh Family,
First of the Newfoundlanders

The Walsh family name has been synonymous with real estate in this city since the 1970s. From the small office on Hardin Street in the old Hannigan's Burger Bar building to being the most productive Remax real estate office in the world is a big step.

It all started in Newfoundland, which was not a province of Canada when World War II broke out. Young Robert Walsh, like so many of his fellow colonists, sailed back to Britain at the start of the war. His family lived in Scotland. For seven years Bob Walsh served in the Royal Air Force as ground crew servicing the Spitfires and Lancasters as they came back from air raids and dog fights. While in England he met his wife Mary, who came from Swansea in Wales.

After the war Mr. Walsh worked for the Scandinavian Airlines and was posted in Gander, Stockholm and Providence, Rhode Island. When the family was in Stockholm one day a man approached him and said, "Mr. Walsh, you are a man without a country." It was 1949 and the Dominion of Newfoundland had just joined the Dominion of Canada. Mr. and Mrs. Walsh, along with one-year old Anne were taken to the Canadian embassy and sworn in as Canadian citizens. Tim says the family grew up on planes, and that hasn't changed in latter years. When they were children they would fly from Newfoundland to Prestwick, Scotland and their grandfather would meet them.

When he left the airline business Bob Walsh moved his family to Labrador City where he worked in the mines and also sold securities. There were tough times in Newfoundland and Labrador and in 1968 they moved to Edmonton. The company Mr. Walsh worked for went under and he came to McMurray to work for a few years for GCOS. It wasn't long before he got into the real estate and insurance business here.

Eldest son Tim had completed high school in Labrador, taken one year at Memorial University in St. John's and then finished his economics degree at the University of Alberta. He then joined his father in the real estate-insurance office in 1972. Sons Greg, Tony, David, Bernard, Michael and James all went to St. John's School in McMurray.

When their first office in the converted burger bar, shared with Gendreau's Hair Salon, became too small they purchased Grant's house on MacDonald Avenue, remodeled it and have maintained their office there ever since except for a few years when it was rented to the Chamber of Commerce and Business Development Centre.

Tim recalls that in the first years most of the real estate sold was commercial. The two oil sands companies supplied housing for their employees and there were few local houses in town to sell. They put the deals together for the Syncrude towers and for the city hall and the provincial building.

About this time Tim went into partnership with Frost Homes and they started building homes in Cold Lake as well as Beacon Hill and downtown. Then the National Energy Program and 23 per cent interest rates struck Alberta businesses at the same time. Frost Homes lost all their investments and went out of business. In the mid-eighties there were only 17 housing starts a year in this city.

Then Syncrude and Suncor decided to sell their houses. A move that resulted in every major apartment block owner, except Georges Brosseau, losing their buildings. Walsh Real Estate had a contract from Syncrude, through its housing arm Northward Developments, to sell approximately 4000 housing units. At the same time Athabasca Realty, Suncor's housing company, sold their units through the Fort McMurray real estate offices.

CMHC had foreclosed and repossessed many apartment buildings and then gave Walsh the apartments to sell. While these were tough times for property owners, the selling of the company homes turned the town into what Tim describes as "a mom and pop town," a regular community with committed home owners.

Walsh Real Estate had joined the international agency of Remax in 1988. In 2010 the firm was honoured with being the most productive real estate office in the world and their agents having the highest income. Certainly, the local firm has been the largest residential real estate developer in Fort McMurray. Like other developers Tim has found the province's control and slow release of the land for development very frustrating.

Looking to the future Tim says the spirit of Fort McMurray is still alive and well. We are a growing and mature wonderful city with great facilities, he claims. Our community has not changed in that it is a wonderful place to live with opportunities available here that are nowhere else in Canada.

Like all the Walsh boys Tim loves the outdoors, especially the riverboat trip to Lake Athabasca, to Fort Fitzgerald, Bustard Island and other beautiful points on the lake. He contributed to the community in many ways: chair of the Keyano Board of Governors, chair of the Hospital Foundation and active in the Kinsmen in the early days. On the national scene Tim was president of the Alberta Real Estate Board and then was president of the Canadian Real Estate Association.

Although still involved with Remax here in town, Tim lives part time near Parksville on Vancouver Island and he and his wife Marianne also have a home in Canmore. Tim says, "Alberta is best."

Bob and Mary Walsh retired to Vancouver Island in 1985, after Mary passed away Bob came back often; he always said the energy in the town was amazing. When he came back to visit his boys he would drop in to see the business people from the '70s and '80s. I remember him as always cheerful with a kind word for all and faith in our community.

The rivers and lakes of our area held charm for all the Walsh boys. Greg in particular has canoed the Clearwater River from Lloyd Lake in Saskatchewan, past Whitemud Falls, over the portages and down to McMurray. He has also canoed the Nahanni and lived in Yellowknife for some years. Tim says Greg is a dynamic realtor and he never regrets enticing him from his recreation administration job in Yellowknife to work in real estate here.

Mike is well known in the accounting field, and was the first chartered accounting student to article in Fort McMurray. He worked in New Zealand and Bermuda before returning home to the new firm of Roy, Solbak and Walsh, now merged with MNP. He served on the MacDonald Island Parks Board and was chairman of the Business Development Centre. His wife Roseann owned and ran for over 20 years a pharmacy and gift store in Thickwood Heights.

Like his brothers, our northern rivers have enticed Mike on many a trip, including one by sailboat from McMurray to Uranium City on Lake Athabasca.

When the downturn in the economy hit McMurray in the 1980s, Bernie moved to Toronto for a few years. He returned to McMurray in 1997 and has been part of development of the area since.

The Walsh family made their mark on the business community in Fort McMurray from the early 1970s on. Hard work, perseverance, and being in the right place at the right time paid off for the family, and they have made a lasting contribution to this city.

Bert MacKay, Ambassador And Promoter

Those two words aptly describe Bert MacKay and his relationship to our community. Even after leaving Fort McMurray, there is no one who actively promotes our town like he does. Irwin Huberman's book, *The Place We Call Home,* was first the brainchild of Bert.

Proud of their Scottish heritage, both Bert and wife Caroline were born and educated in the Inverness region. Belonging to a military family, Bert was well disciplined and became keenly interested in history from a very early age. Bert's musical talents shone when he formed part of a band that played all over Scotland, performing several times for Princess Margaret. Bert remembers meeting the Beatles in 1964. The surviving members of the band enjoyed an enthusiastic reunion in 2008. A book about their musical adventures is a best seller in the U.K.

In 1964 Bert and Caroline were married and moved to Canada in 1966. Bert was employed by Alberta Power and worked in Fairview and Valleyview. After noticing an advertisement that invited candidates to seek the "Athabasca Adventure", Bert applied to Great Canadian Oil Sands. Fort McMurray did not show on the map, but Waterways did.

When the MacKay family moved to McMurray in April 1967, there were 2600 people in the town, gas was 33 cents a gallon, and wages at the oil sands plant were $3.00 to $3.75 an hour. Houses were supplied by the company and sold to employees between $18,000 to $32,000.

Bert mentioned that the turnover at GCOS was 50 to 65 per cent in the first year. Extreme difficulties in plant startup, conditions of the town, lack of radio and television and the severe winter, prompted many to leave. Soon after he went to work Bert got involved with the union and helped write the first labour constitution and became secretary of the bargaining association. This first local union set the standard for wages and conditions in the oilsands and shortly thereafter met with the Alberta Government to change the eight-hour workday to 12-hour days, now the overall standard in the entire industry. Bert and others in the company had concerns about lack of aboriginal work and education and he was part of a Keyano College industry initiative to bring aboriginal workers directly into the workplace.

For 27 years Bert worked in operations and training and later was responsible for site safety and operations training. One of Suncor's senior managers wrote of Bert, "you didn't have to look over his shoulder, just point him in the right direction and don't get in his way......I had no hesitation in giving him tough assignments." When with Human Resources Bert took part in Suncor team projects on safety in Sarnia, Phoenix, Philadelphia and Puerto Rico. He was involved in the Suncor "Ten Year Club" organized to encourage workers to stay with the company. This club initiated the very first recognition of community volunteers in Fort McMurray and over 36 were recognized over the years.

When Bert took early retirement in 1995 he and others formed the Suncor Oil Sands Pioneer Club for retirees. The club has now grown to two major organizations in Fort McMurray and Edmonton and arranges social events with support from Suncor.

Bert received many accolades for his volunteer work over the years. These included: Alberta's centennial medal, Keyano's Distinguished Citizen award, Heritage Park Wall of Fame, International Volunteers' Guild of London, UK and royal recognition for co-hosting the Duke of Edinburgh's visit to the Oilsands in 2005.

Suncor's loss of Bert as an employee was definitely the community's gain. Bert headed up a fund raising initiative for the Interpretive (Discovery) Centre as Facility Supervisor. He and others raised about $2.5 million for the exhibit hall and Premier Klein cut the ribbon in 2003. The centre received the Alberta Premier's Award and the Alberta Petrochemical History Society Award.

Bert's energies were not all taken up with work at the centre, he spearheaded the research and writing of the book of Fort McMurray's history, raised money for Heritage Park, was a director of the United Way, Food Bank volunteer, helped to start the Big Brothers of Western Canada, and was a director of the local Robert Burns Society. It was Bert who always kept in touch with Mary Clark Shepherd, daughter of Dr. Karl A. Clark, and brought her to town for various events. No matter what the need, Bert was a volunteer extraordinaire.

Wife Caroline also played an important part in our community. She was administrative assistant to Doug Schmit at AVC (now Keyano), and while there started the college newsletter. She moved to the School District in 1979 and worked for four different superintendents, different school board trustees including the Joint High School Board. She played a key role in Fort McMurray's first United Way by acting as volunteer secretary in its founding meetings.

Caroline never stopped learning; she took various university courses most years and majored in English literature and women's history at the University of Alberta after the couple moved to St. Albert. She is an avid gardener.

The MacKays raised four children in Fort McMurray. It was families like them that gave our community the stability and strength through the last decades of the past century. We owe a great debt to Bert and Caroline MacKay for their continual promotion of our city, and his kindness and care of the people within it.

Norm Weiss,
MLA 1979 – 1993

Norm Weiss was the very first McMurray resident to represent this area in any level of government. The four term member of the Alberta government served as Minister of Recreation & Parks, Minister of Career Development & Employment, was Assistant Minister to Social Services & Community Health as well as serving as chair on the Northeastern Alberta Development Council and the Advisory Board of the Northeastern Commission. As well he served on the AOSTRA board and that of Syncrude Canada. And those were in the years when the town became a city, experienced an initial boom and then an economic downturn when the National Energy Policy hit the Alberta oil industry.

An Edmonton man, Norm married Carol from Camrose; they had one daughter, Jill. Norm worked for Shell Oil in Edmonton and his first contact with Fort McMurray was when, in the early 1960s, he was a member of the team that purchased land from the Golosky family for a Shell plant. He chose Jim Mutton to run the Shell business and Jim and Joan Mutton came to McMurray in 1966 when the bulk plant opened.

Norm was transferred to Vancouver for a few years and his next transfer was slated for Ontario. This was not to his and Carol's liking and so Norm quit corporate Shell, moved to Fort McMurray and went into partnership with Jim Mutton at the local Shell outlet.

Immediately active in the community, Norm served on the Chamber of Commerce board. And then in 1979 he ran in the March general election and was elected to the Legislative Assembly of Alberta. Norm quickly established a constituency office in Fort McMurray, staffed by Aris Coventry with furniture and equipment that he paid for. This was the very first constituency office in northern Alberta, but it wasn't long before Premier Lougheed endorsed the idea and every MLA had an office in their riding.

Norm said he always wanted what was best for this growing community full of young families who had opportunities and challenges, the like of which was not seen in other parts of Canada. Along with the opportunities were problems that come with rapid development. This was a young peoples' community and he wanted to ensure them of opportunities for a good family life. He said his role was to bring items and issues before the government to help the community and its people.

The Sapre Creek development owes its existence to MLA Weiss. Locals wanted acreages; the provincial bureaucrats were against releasing the land. Norm persuaded cabinet to do so and roads and services were installed. Then harder times hit and the people who'd bought lots couldn't pay their taxes and the government was going to repossess the development. Once again our MLA went to caucus and persuaded them to wait before taking the lots back. In the long negotiations Norm worked with the late Winnie Sommers, a city counsellor.

The Fort McMurray Golf Club sought the land overlooking the Athabasca for a golf course; the land price was $750,000. Norm arranged for the city to have the land for $1 on a 99-year lease. This ensured the public, as well as club members, had access to the beautiful course.

The Oil Sands Discovery Centre, opened as the Interpretive Centre, was another project Norm ensured got built as promised. The official opening of the Centre in 1985 was the last time Peter Lougheed was in Fort McMurray as premier.

Norm was instrumental in obtaining funding for the Golden Years Society, the Snye Park and extended care at the hospital. Funding of the YMCA, which enabled it to become a reality, was also on his plate.

Actually, all the projects, and there were many, undertaken during these growth years had Norm Weiss' stamp on them. He said he was proud to represent our community and made sure Fort McMurray got its share.

Our MLA served with three premiers and commented on each. Peter Lougheed, he said, was a genius; he shone in a crowd; he was able to guide caucus in right decisions. Don Getty was a very caring and compassionate Premier; unfortunately his term of office was plagued with the severe downturn in the energy sector. Ralph Klein, the latest Premier he worked with, was his own man, a people person and not afraid to make tough decisions.

In 1993 Norm had served four terms and decided to retire. After a few years he and Carol moved to Courtney, B.C. to a home they'd purchased while on holidays there in 1974. For some years they wintered in Arizona. Norm still enjoys golf and is active in the Conservative Party on Vancouver Island.

In June 2004 very early in the morning after the federal election I received a call from Norm Weiss. He said, "I'm sitting at my kitchen table, with tears in my eyes, reading about your son being elected to parliament. I'm so glad a young man who grew up in McMurray will represent the city." Kind words.

Fort McMurray was fortunate to have Norm travel the unpaved (mostly) Highway 63 to Edmonton for 20 years. His integrity, hard work, and caring nature were just what we needed.

Al Burry,
Manager And Developer

The influx of employees to Great Canadian Oil Sands in 1967 included Edmonton born Al Burry, already a CGA, computer savvy, and having run and sold a couple of successful businesses. At GCOS Al was part of the audit team, and later took on the role of manager of Athabasca Realty Company, the housing arm of GCOS.

While working for ARC Al successfully negotiated with the province and town to build residential lots in Thickwood Heights. When ARC bought Dim Silin's property it was the largest real estate deal ever in town. Roads and services were installed and in 1974 the first residents moved into the Thickwood area. It was at this time too that ARC built Ptarmigan Park, then the largest mobile home park in Canada.

And then it was time to strike out on his own. Always an entrepreneur Al bought rental properties and soon progressed to industrial development, being among the first to build in Area 6 (Gregoire Industrial Park). Along with partners he built the Morrison Centre, more than 20 developments in Gregoire and office buildings on the Prairie and downtown.

The National Energy Program of the 1980s hit all McMurray businesses hard and the Alcor companies were no exception. Rather than closing their doors, Al and wife Yvette met all their obligations and looked around for opportunities. They managed company bankruptcies, of which there were many in town. They also started more property management and storage of electronic information for the oil companies. Whatever the need, the Burrys sought to fill it.

When the Alberta economy stabilized the Burrys once again bought property but also managed facilities for many companies, employing tradesmen of every type to ensure their clients would have all their needs met with one call. Not only did Alcor handle rentals for companies coming to town but also they would furnish and equip the units for the company's employees.

Both Al and Yvette gave back to the community. Yvette was active in the Girl Guides and they sponsored the Ringette Club in town. Al was a director of the Alberta Summer Games in 1985, chairman of the fundraising board for the Salvation Army homeless shelter, and founding chair of the Hospital Foundation.

Retail and publishing were new challenges for the Burrys. They bought Irwin Huberman's weekly newspaper *The Express,* with Irwin remaining as editor. They sold to the Sun Newspapers but kept up ties to Irwin, and along with Ken and Diane Hill, myself and my son Brian Jean, attended Irwin's ordination as a rabbi in New York in 2009. Along with partner, Randy Koroluk, the Burrys started Fort McMurray Stationery on the corner of Franklin and Morrison. It was later sold to giant Grand & Toy.

With their two sons and two daughters grown and away, Al and Yvette built a beautiful home in Edmonton. They travel often, and still keep their pulse on the McMurray businesses. Al had contacted polio at 19 and was left with acute arthritis of the spine. He was told he would not be walking when he was thirty. That time is long past, and although both Al and Yvette have some health problems it hasn't slowed them down or hindered their enjoyment of life. Nor is the word retire in their vocabulary.

The Burry story is another success story of those who looked for and seized the opportunities in this vibrant community, who worked hard, took risks and ultimately were able to contribute to the place they called home for many years.

The Wolff Family

"It was a great move," said Evie Wolff of the family's time in Fort McMurray, "everyone was a pioneer, we helped the town grow and we and our kids grew up with it." Ron Wolff echoed the sentiments, speaking about the camaraderie of the newcomers, the projects undertaken and accomplished and how everyone worked together.

Ron and Evelyn Wolff both grew up in Evansburg; Ron's dad owned a creamery that year after year took the blue ribbon for the best butter at the Toronto fair. Ron worked in the creamery and then when it was sold helped his dad in their grocery store and dry goods store. Then in the spring of 1965 one of their salesmen told them they should have a look at Fort McMurray.

Ron and his father came up to look the town over and a few months later Ron came back with Evie, children Kim and Trudy, and opened a men's wear store in a new building beside Hill Drugs. They had a trailer sent in on the train for the family to live in and located it in the Park Plaza trailer park.

In the late 1960s there was no underground gas service. Huge propane tanks were located around the town and serviced the new residential areas. In October 1968 the filling hose broke on the tank at Plaza trailer court. The propane ran under a trailer and the hot water tank ignited the fuel and the trailer caught fire. Right next door was the Wolff's trailer and it was so badly damaged that they had to move. Accommodation was almost nil in the town so they moved to the Cedar Lodge Motel until they were able to relocate, first to a trailer at the GCOS camp, and then Siggi Lucas' apartment at the corner of Alberta Drive and Franklin. And then they found one house for sale. Phil Poulin sold his Solo store in Park Plaza, sold his Franklin Avenue lot to the Jean family and the Wolffs bought his house on Alberta Drive.

These were busy times in the clothing store. That is evenings were busy. The store was open from nine a.m. to nine p.m., and literally 98 per cent of their business was done in the evenings. GCOS provided a bus to come in to town each night; the men shopped, picked up their liquor at the government store opposite the town hall, and got back on the bus at nine-thirty in front of Wolff's store. For the store stocked parkas and work boots, socks and shirts; everything a worker needed. As the town grew so did the variety of stock with quality men's dress clothes.

With the nine to nine hours that both Ron and Evie worked one would think there was no time for play. Not so, they both curled and on Sundays there was family curling. And then there were the Kinsmen and Kinette Clubs.

Ron was first president of the Kinsmen Club, Vince Burke, the Royal Bank manager, was the secretary. Other charter members included Art Avery, Tip Hlushak, and Sam Hardin. Not to be bypassed, the wives started the Kinette Club and worked with the Kinsmen in every project they took on. Gwen Burke was the first president and Evie followed as president the next term. Other early Kinette members included Selma Hardin, Sylvia Avery, Joyce Hansen, Sally Pauls, and Bettyanne Hlushak.

The Kinsmen's most exciting project was to build a swimming pool. They raised money in a variety of ways; there were raffles, residents bought "bricks" and there were fund raising dances. But the most ambitious fund raising idea was the car raffle. They had a vehicle shipped in from Edmonton by rail, drove it to the GCOS plant and parked it between the recreation centre and the cafeteria and sold tickets. The first car lasted just a week. The Centennial Swimming Pool on Franklin Avenue opened in 1970, one hundred years after Moberly established the fort here.

The Blueberry Festival on Labour Day weekend was sponsored by the Kinsmen. This was a huge community event with baseball tournaments, carnival rides and of course the Kinettes had a hot dog stand. In February it was Winter Carnival time and the Kinsmen sponsored "The longest dog team race in the world", from Fort Chipewyan down to McMurray. Crowds gathered on the ice under the bridge to watch the teams, which had stopped down river to be decked out in their finery, complete with bells, come into town.

Ron was asked to run for town council and was elected in 1968, serving three years on the New Town of Fort McMurray board. Three board members, Bill Isbister, John Polonuk and Len Gurel, were from the Alberta Municipal Affairs department. It was a frustrating time, with construction in rainy, muddy summers and new areas being developed.

In the 1971 election Ron lost his seat on the town board. He was appointed to the hospital board in 1972 and then ran for election every term and was on the board for 22 years, 12 of them as chair. He also chaired the building committee that turned the small hospital on the hill into the many-storied facility we have today.

Wolff's Men's Wear had three different locations in town. When the Hills wanted to expand their drug store the Wolffs moved to the Peter Pond Shopping Centre and later to Park Plaza. In 1989 they closed their store, stayed in McMurray but wintered in Arizona. Then in 1995 they moved to Fairmont and now divide their time between Fairmont and Calgary. Their son Kim returned to McMurray after university and practices law just a door away from his parent's original store.

The Wolffs did more than supply clothing for the oil sands workers. During their time in our town they were influential in the political and social life and helped build a great community spirit.

Men Of Baseball

I wrote this story for FOCUS magazine in 2003. The MacDonald Island fields were built in 1984 and replaced the old field next to the Community Centre on King Street (now Composite High School). On Sept. 6, 1987 City Council with Mayor Chuck Knight officially dedicated the four fields on the island to four people greatly responsible for fastball in Fort McMurray. Each field had a plaque bearing their name. These are their stories.

Tip Hlushak sponsor and back catcher for the McMurray Hardware Lynx team was one of the prime movers in the early ball scene. He started the team in 1967, naming it after a northern animal, as his hardware store was part of the Link buying group.

Tip and Betty Anne, with their two children, came south to McMurray from Uranium City to open a hardware store. Until the new strip mall was built the store occupied space in the Peter Pond Hotel. There was no road and supplies came in twice a week by the NAR train. Tip recalled he and Sam Hardin, of Fort Drugs, would go to the train station in Waterways and check with Dave Brooks to see if their freight had come in. Dave would tell them what car their freight was in; they'd back their truck up to the open boxcar and load it on. Not once did they have anything missing from their shipments.

Ball games were held on the field beside the town arena, now the site of Composite High School. In the spring, Tip related that all the teams got together with rakes and shovels to get the field in order. They put up bleachers, painted fences and prepared for the season. There were five or six teams in the league.

The Kinsmen had organized Blueberry Festival to be held on Labour Day weekend and they decided to host tournaments with teams coming from Edmonton, Uranium City, Yellowknife and other points in Alberta. Up to 25 teams competed during most of the '70s. Tip Hlushak and Jim Mutton were co-chairs and Fern Brooks was the official statistician. During the Kinsmen tournaments the locals found they had to literally "pull up their socks" and respond to the challenge of the out of town near-professionals by becoming great players themselves.

By 1975 the Hlushaks bought a plane and Tip would fly his team to compete in other towns. It would take two to three trips to get all the players to the destination.

Team members of the Lynx included: David Brooks (NAR and hospital) as pitcher; Ernie Otway (RCMP), first base; Ernie Buziak and Paul Stanke, shortstop, Ernie Yurkiw (PWA) and Bob Hayes. The latter, a Keyano employee, was, according to Tip an incomparable back catcher and stole Tip's position so he was content to coach. The team disbanded in the '80s, having played what Tip described as "incredible ball" – and all for the love of the game. These were the glory days of fastball in Fort McMurray, started by dedicated, hard-working players.

Jim Mutton, was second base player on the McMurray Hardware Lynx team and helped organize the renowned Blueberry Festival Tournaments.

Jim and Joan Mutton, with their one-year old son, drove to Fort McMurray over the brand new bumpy, dusty Highway 63 in September 1966. Jim drove a two-ton truck and pulled the family house trailer, while Joan followed with a pick-up and smaller trailer. Jim helped finish building the Shell Bulk plant behind the Riviera Hotel. It opened in December of that year and Jim operated it until the Muttons left McMurray in 1984.

Jim had been involved in ball all his life and immediately joined the new Lynx team. He was still playing ball, but slow pitch, and competed in the Senior Games in McMurray in July 2003, playing on the Jim Mutton field.

In 1971 the Fort McMurray Men's Fastball League gave Jim the All-Star designation for best second base player in the league.

The Muttons retired to San Gudo, Alberta, the town where Jim grew up and developed his love of ball. In speaking of his McMurray days Jim says the opportunities for involvement in the town were unique. Because so many were new it was easy to get involved and be an influence on events. Jim was president of the Kinsmen Club, president of the Chamber of Commerce, a member of the Police Commission and with Don Rumpel formed the Sno Trakkers Ski-doo Club.

Like his co-chair Tip Hlushak, Jim says they played for fun, but he qualifies, "It is more fun when you win!"

John Lambert came to Fort McMurray in 1966 as recreation director for Great Canadian Oil Sands. He organized social events for GCOS, including the famous summer barbecues on Peden's Point, children's Christmas parties and the Christmas dance.

As well as GCOS events, John's mandate was to help set up recreational activities in the community. When the Miskanaw nine hole golf course was built on MacDonald Island, GCOS provided much of the machinery and manpower to build it and John coordinated this.

He was instrumental in the setup of the Noralta Figure Skating Club, the Fort McMurray Tennis Courts, the Drama Club and the Ski Club on the Simons-Lukas property in Abasand.

The GCOS Tigers baseball team had John Lambert as coach. Some of the players included Wayne Jones, Cliff Skeats, Sylver Kushniuk, and Garth Phillips. He later coached the Riviera Wildcats, the team Ron Morgan played on.

Originally from Montréal, John came to McMurray via Edmonton and Yellowknife. In Montreal he played professional hockey and with his team competed in England. He was also an avid ball player and turned down an invitation to join the Boston Red Sox so he could concentrate on hockey.

As head of GCOS recreation John soon met Pat who worked with the purchasing department. They both quit their jobs in 1971 to travel to Australia. This was part of Pat's dream to see the world. She had come from England in 1968, worked her way across Canada and lived in Clearwater Terrace. The lure of the north brought the couple back to McMurray, and John with Richard Pliska started Norex Expediting.

The Lamberts moved to Vernon in 1980, but returned to Edmonton in 1981 when John was diagnosed with terminal cancer. Pat returned to McMurray for a time and worked as executive director of the Keyano Foundation.

Paul MacPherson: Just three weeks after Paul and Gail MacPherson and their three children arrived in McMurray, Paul was practicing for his first season's play. Syncrude recruited Paul from New Brunswick where he'd always played.

Gail said they made their friends through ball, their first friends in McMurray and the longest lasting. Paul was head of the McMurray Men's Fastball League for three years. He played for the McMurray Colour Centre team in third base position. He also coached a men's team as well as his daughter's team for several years.

Some of the players on the Colour Centre team included Guy Boutilier, Ron "Tiny" Turner, Doug Wiebe, Doug Lovegrove, Rolly and Darcey Rustad, Hugh Marchesi and the pitcher Brian Henstridge.

Paul died in 1986 of a heart attack. For a few years ball players in McMurray competed in the Paul MacPherson Memorial Tournament with all proceeds going to the United Way. Gail said she and Paul loved McMurray and were honoured by the dedication of the field that carries his name.

A great story about early ball games is in Irwin Huberman's book "The Place We Call Home."

The Jeans Take Root In McMurray

When my very good friend Mrs. Jean (yes - even after almost 30 years, I cannot make myself call her Frances) told me she was settling in to write her book, I thought what better ending to **More than Oil: Trappers, Traders and Settlers of Northern Alberta,** *than with the arrival of the Jean family in our Centennial year.*

This book's author was reluctant to write of herself, her family or the impact that a 1967 event has had on Fort McMurray. It is my pleasure to write the Jean family story on her behalf.

– Anne M. Young

In 1967 Bernard and Frances arrived with five strapping boys: Larry, Blair, Mark, Philip and Brian, their daughter Evelyn, a love of land and a strong sense of community. Many that came to Fort McMurray in the formative years of the oil sands took up residency with thoughts in terms of a couple of years. The Jeans could not have imagined that they would become one of the longest standing business identities in the community; that they would help develop and forward no end of community-based organizations; that one son would enter politics and be elected to public office not once, but as of this printing, a convincing four times, representing Fort McMurray/Athabasca in Stephen Harpers' Conservative Government. They could not have imagined that their love of land would see their sons own traplines and all their children, including daughter Evelyn successfully shoot the rapids below Whitemud Falls.

When Bernard Jean was discharged from the army, the Ontario resident relocated to Westbank, B.C. ranching and farming. The move to McMurray saw the Jean family quickly adapt their agriculture roots from the Okanagan Valley to the more rugged landscape of McMurray and area mastering river travel, as well as land. Hunting became a family passion, as did discovering trails on land and water routes throughout Northern Alberta and into the Territories.

While Bernard took on employment with Catalytic as supervisor of contracts at the Great Canadian Oil Sands (Suncor), his life partner Frances, became his business partner, as they met the first of many community needs they would address through the years and launched Jean's Gifts and Stationery on Franklin Ave. It would become a downtown landmark for the next 34 years. They met the retail demands of the growing population and its ever-changing needs and wants. Toys, gifts, office supplies, books and magazines evolved from early days of supplying seeds, plants and canoes to fine china and crystal including a four-year stint as publishers of a weekly newspaper, *The McMurray Courier*, from 1970 through 1974. The weekly led the way to a daily newspaper when it was sold to Bowes Publishing in 1974 and became *The Fort McMurray Today*.

Not having experience in running a press or publishing did not deter the Jeans. Bernard approached it like everything he did in life, with determination and hard work. This same determination and his strong faith enabled him to fight back from a stroke in 1994 to regain speech and mobility.

The Courier publication was resurrected in 2001, in FOCUS magazine, re-running stories that often mirrored many of McMurray's present issues as once again Fort McMurray was experiencing a rapid growth period with oil sands expansion. Issues like accommodation, enough classroom space and difficulty in retaining a workforce were echoes of the 70s in McMurray. While the main street commercial property remains under Jean ownership, today it houses other entrepreneurs and business services.

While Bernard balanced full time employment with Catalytic, running a press and assisting in the running of the store, he always managed time for his core values of family, faith and community. He joined efforts with Frances full time in 1970 and one of his early accomplishments was to draw the first composite map of the town site.

Active in the Fellowship Baptist Church, Bernard designed the original building that stood at the corner of Franklin Avenue and Alberta Drive. He was a director of the church's summer camp at Gregoire Lake for a number of years, taught Sunday school and led Bible studies in his home. His large home library of books and tapes reflected his studies of the Bible.

The Jeans may have been well-rooted in McMurray but enjoyed years of travel including a trip around North America in their fifth wheel.

In his retirement years from business, Bernard channeled his energies back to his early roots of tending and enjoying a garden. Through the years, there was a large garden on the family trapline up the Clearwater River. This family site is proudly maintained by son Philip who spent a season in 2001 hewing logs and building a new one-bedroom cabin all by hand. It remains a popular family retreat and many visitors have enjoyed the river trip and spent a day or two as guests.

While Bernard coped with diabetes since he was a young man, he succumbed to congestive heart failure Feb. 29, 2004. One of his many legacies to his children was his love of the land. All remain committed to the outdoors and when time permits Mark, Philip and Brian enjoy the brotherly competition of who is first that season to get a moose. Evelyn drew on her father's same determination to overcome illness, conquering life-threatening cancer in 2010.

Family matriarch, Frances was first to claim Fort McMurray as "home." She believes everything has "it's time," and in 1967 it was time to establish the Jean family in the community. Her attraction to McMurray with all its nature was instantaneous she recalls. And 45 years later that love of Fort McMurray endures.

The family had hardly settled into the new town when the idea of opening a business was formulated. While raising a young family, the self-described shy person, buoyed through the support and encouragement of Bernard, launched herself into the business community. She emerged as a strong business leader with an out-going personality. She attributes this personality trait in part to her years as reporter and editor of their weekly newspaper. She had to overcome shyness and talk to people and ask questions. Assuming the role of reporter of the McMurray Courier was however, not her first reporting gig. News of World War II aired at 6 p.m. on the BBC. As that coincided with the farming routine of milking the cows, the task fell to the then eight-year old Frances to listen and record the news and carry it to the barn and report it to her father. It was a role she relished.

It was this developing trait that enabled her to step up with a voice of confidence and champion for women's rights. She shrugs off the notion that she was fighting for women's rights. She simply wanted a place in the Chamber of Commerce. She was after all a business person in the community. In a Courier editorial she said if the Chamber was exclusive to businessmen then it should be called a "men's club," and not run under the banner of a Chamber of Commerce, but call it what it was - a club for men. Her editorial brought the hoped for response and shortly thereafter Frances, along with Grace Dafoe and Alice Haxton were voted in as Chamber members. In short order she was asked to be secretary/treasurer, a role which kept her busy for the next few years.

The decision to sell the weekly newspaper in 1974 was made in favour of family. The nights to produce and publish the paper took a toll on family time. "It's time," Frances recalls thinking and then sharing her thoughts with Bernard who agreed.

The Chamber of Commerce would not be the only volunteer position she would accept in the community. Through her 45 years in McMurray she has supported more community groups and events than could be listed in a mere chapter. There have been stints on municipal tax reviews, downtown parking studies; Keyano College Solicitation Committee work; several terms serving on the Downtown Business Revitalization Zone Association board of directors; and the Alberta Summer Games board of directors. In 1997 Frances was recognized by Keyano College as Distinguished Citizen of the Year.

Her love of history joined with like-minded residents and in 2001 published *The Place We Call Home*, authored by Irwin Huberman. Frances also compiled, wrote and published her own cook book *Cooking with Memories* now in its 3rd printing. Known and recognized for her cooking, baking and preserves by a large circle of family and friends, Frances still makes bread every Sunday - white and brown - a selection of buns and often cinnamon rolls. Tuesdays and Fridays scones are baked and served for breakfast. For years, Frances took the extra scones to the store where employees as well as the occasional customer or delivery person enjoyed the treat.

"It's time," echoed in 2002 when Frances determined the Gifts and Stationery portion of the Jean family enterprise should close. Following 34 retail years, the changing needs of the community prompted the closure. In its 34 years of operation, Jean's was named Retail Business of the Year by the Chamber of Commerce in 1983 and Frances Jean was named Business Owner of the Year. The following year the business was recognized as Provincial Business Owner of the Year. The printing side of the business then owned and operated by Brian, who also practiced law locally, was sold in 2008. In 2001 City Centre Auto Wash and Dog Wash, owned and operated by Brian and Frances, was opened on the property of the former home of Mr. and Mrs. Walter Hill.

In recognition of the Jean family's love and respect of nature, the City named the boat launch area on the Snye the Jean Family Boat Launch.

After alluding to writing a book over the years, she finally said "it's time," and in 2011 Frances began her research and writing, celebrating her 80th birthday February 2012 with the release of *More than Oil: Trappers, Traders and Settlers of Northern Alberta*, by Frances K. Jean

Postscript

This book is missing many interesting McMurrayites; people who left their mark on this town, and people on whom the town left its influence. Just to randomly mention a few:

Maureen Billings, who along with Ron Morgan and I did a live television program on ABC Cable every Friday night. Ron Morgan who did the sports cast on ABC but also was heavily involved in little league baseball and a town councilor of many years. Danny and Sheila Law, part of the U.K. recruitment for GCOS and great volunteers. Lew Babcock, head of the Forestry department, who reported on fires to *The Courier*, and planted a small forest around his house on Biggs Ave. Jack and Lee Fowers, Jack had an accounting office in the upstairs of the Bank of Nova Scotia building.

Ches Dicks, sportsman, instrumental in starting the Oil Barons and was on the first Mac Island board. Armand Parent, head of Catalytic at GCOS, town councilor and community booster. Rev. Dawson Beaver, All Saints' Anglican minister who also conducted services for the United Church. His wife Norma worked with Dot Berry at St. Gabriel Hospital. Jim Pauls who owned the town's first electronic shop, sent out "canned" CBC TV for four hours each night, one week late. Sally Pauls worked in the OR at the hospital for many years. Phoebe Spice, volunteer and Hospital Board chair during major expansion.

Dr. Allan Nicholson, McMurray's longest serving doctor, a member of the town board, head of the Health Unit, and Chief of Staff at the hospital. Bob Campbell and Adam Germain, partners in McMurray's oldest law firm, huge supporters of community sports. Ernie Wittke and Walter Diener who started the most profitable store of the prairie-wide MacLeod franchise. Walter was town board member in 1971.

Dave McNeilly, well respected, long time principal of Dr. Clark School and town board member, who after retirement became a real estate salesman and trapper. Frank Peters, principal of Turcotte School who came to McMurray from Ireland. Bob and Trudy Crow, who came with a wave of early immigrant teachers. Les Stalke, the Lutheran minister responsible with Hank and Ruthild Offeriens for starting the Fort McMurray Overture Concert Assn.

Don and Mary Fleming. Don was head of social services in town, went on to be deputy minister in Edmonton. Mary was assistant to dentist Dr. Florence and then to Dr. Joel Clark, who was a part time canoeist and trapper. Allan Askeland and wife Carol came to manage Diversified Transportation. Al was president of the Chamber of Commerce. Another Chamber president in the busy years was Kit Leitch, a builder of many of the Thickwood Heights homes.

Bank managers of note: Bill Bannister of the Royal, who in boom day line-ups would man the counters with his staff, and authorize loans over the phone. (He knew his customers). Vic Neufeld of the ATB, Chamber of Commerce director and McMurray Dollar promoter. Bruce Otterdahl, Bank of Montreal, went on to work for the city, and serve on the Federal Parole Board. Dave Elaschuk, of the Bank of Nova Scotia, who cleaned up litter on Hardin Street and Franklin Ave. every morning on his way to work.

These and so many more interesting people could have occupied space in the pages of this book but time is fleeting and all things must end.

A WORD ABOUT THE ARTIST. Roger Witmer, now retired, is an artist of renown from Ontario. He first started painting at 14, and after high school gave art lessons and did weekend art shows. Then for many years he and his wife Anne had a successful studio and business in St. Jacobs, near Kitchener.

In the 1980s Roger first came to McMurray to take part in one of the earliest trade shows. Jean's Gifts had a booth and Roger displayed and sold paintings and collector plates.

Roger, with Bernard Jean, flew into Whitemud Falls and canoed down the beautiful Clearwater River. He took rolls and rolls of film and painted many scenes of our area. Two years later he and Anne came back, and with Bernard and Frances Jean, Evelyn Jean and Bernie Ulrich, did another canoe trip from Whitemud Falls.

Our family was so pleased when Roger agreed to do sketches for this book. His exceptional talent, his interest in the history of our area as well as his love of the beautiful scenery has added immeasurably to *More than Oil*.